Contents

Part 1: What can children do? Sociocultural factors in development

Part 2: Working with children: extending opportunities for participation

Part 3: Multi-professional practice: developing empowering communities

Part 4: Comparing children's worlds: making the familar strange

Part 5: Researching practice: developing critical engagement

vi

Contributors

Dr Verity Campbell-Barr is a lecturer in early childhood studies at the University of Plymouth. Prior to joining the University of Plymouth she worked as a researcher where she gained experience of conducting both national and local level policy evaluations. Her subject specific research interests include the mixed economy of early childhood education and care provision, family decision-making on work-life balance and multiple perspectives on the quality of early childhood education and care.

Rebecca Carter Dillon is a lecturer in early childhood studies at the University of Plymouth, with a background in community development work with disadvantaged children and families in Manchester, London and sub-Saharan Africa. She wrote her MA thesis on the educational experiences of refugee and asylum seeker children in the UK, and her teaching and research interests focus on poverty and well-being, social inequalities and service provision.

Dr Norman Gabriel is a sociologist with over ten years' experience of teaching on Early Childhood Studies degree programmes. His research interests are in the sociology of early childhood and the relation between sociology and developmental psychology. Inspired by the work of Norbert Elias, he is co-editing a book with Professor Stephen Mennell on *Norbert Elias and Figurational Sociology*, part of the *Sociology Review: Monograph Series*. He is currently researching historical changes in parent-child relationships and the role of affective bonding in young children's development.

Dr Ulrike Hohmann is senior lecturer in early childhood studies. She worked as a research associate at the University of Newcastle on a number of social policy projects before she joined the University of Plymouth. She holds a German childcare qualificiation and has worked in a wide range of childcare settings in Germany. Her research interests include children and social policy, childcare settings and the relationships that develop between children and their adult carers. She is also interested in comparative, cross-national research. She is a member of the editoral board of the journal *Social Policy and Society*.

Valerie Huggins is subject leader for the ECS (Early Childhood Studies) specialism on the BEd programme as well as the PGCE early years pathway. She is an experienced early years teacher and worked for several years as a consultant for a local authority. Before taking up her current post she spent some time with VSO training teacher educators in Ethiopia. Her research interests centre on different approaches to effective Early Education, including the use of the outdoor environment, the use of digital media to share children's interests and early years provision in the developing world. She is currently studying for an EdD with a focus on the professionalisation of the early years workforce.

Dr Caroline Leeson is a senior lecturer and joint programme leader on the BA (Hons) Early Childhood Studies degree at the University of Plymouth. She has particular interests in the welfare of looked after children, children's centre leadership and reflective practice. Her PhD looked at the involvement of looked after children in decision making processes. Before working in higher education she worked as a social worker in child protection, fostering and adoption.

Dr Julia Morgan originally trained as a health professional and has worked in various NHS hospitals around the country. More recently she has worked as a researcher on a child development study, for The Children's Society, for Sure Start and for the family support charity Home-Start. Her research interests include Social Policy; Social Justice; Child Development; Children's Health and Well-being; Children's Perspectives; and Cross-Cultural Studies of Childhood.

Rod Parker-Rees is co-ordinator of Early Childhood Studies and joint programme leader for the BA (Hons) Early Childhood Studies degree at the University of Plymouth. He taught 3 to 5 year old children in Bristol and conducted research with the National Primary Centre (South West) before joining the University of Plymouth. His research interests centre on very early communication, playfulness and the role of young children as active social agents. He is a co-editor of *Early Years: an International Journal of Research and Development*.

Philip Selbie is a lecturer in Early Childhood Studies at the University of Plymouth. He taught KS1 and Reception children in Southampton before moving overseas to teach 3 to 5 year old children and lead the early years in two international schools in Prague, Czech Republic. Philip is currently researching for a PhD on the contribution of John Amos Comenius (1595–1670) to early childhood care and education.

Karen Wickett trained as a nursery nurse and her first appointment was as a nanny in London. In 1991 she established and developed a day nursery in Cornwall. She was the day care manager for nine years. Then she decided to train as a teacher. Her first teaching post was in a SureStart Local Programme in Somerset (now a Children's Centre). Throughout she developed her vision of establishing a learning community. To develop this vision she made links with the University of Plymouth and in 2009 became a part time children's centre teacher and a part time lecturer in early childhood studies. She is interested in exploring environments where children and adults lead their learning together, working with parents/carers and documenting learning.

Jenny Willan is currently teaching undergraduates on a University of Plymouth BA (Hons) programme in ECS (Early Childhood Studies). She previously worked in educational research at the University of Cambridge and the National Foundation for Educational Research. She has written on children's writing, gender studies, teacher action research and Sure Start programmes in rural areas. Her most recent publications have been on the legacy of Susan Isaacs for early years provision.

The Early Childhood Studies team at the University of Plymouth dedicate this volume to our families and to all our students.

Preface

For any book to go into a third edition is a welcome event, not least because it testifies to the fact that it has established a substantial and sustained readership, thereby securing an important place in the market. The demands of markets change, however, as do the demands on those working with children. With the changes resulting from the progressive development of the *Every Child Matters* agenda and the implementation of the Early Years Foundation Stage, an up-to-date understanding of early childhood has never been more important. Along with the shift of emphasis from the narrow focus on child protection to the much broader concerns embodied in the notion of safeguarding, and the consequent growing awareness of and emphasis on the neglect of children, an understanding of children's development in their early years and the significance of this for their future is now of greater relevance than ever to those working with children.

A further significant shift in the landscape that provides the current context for early childhood studies is the emergence of a children's workforce, comprising not just those traditionally concerned with early childhood, such as teachers, but all of those who provide services for children and who are therefore required to assume responsibility for both their achievements and their safety. Such developments across traditional professional boundaries make a multi-professional and multi-disciplinary approach to early childhood not only desirable but essential. This, then, is the challenge faced by the editors of and contributors to this third edition, a challenge to which they have risen enthusiastically and successfully by building on the strengths of previous editions.

Apart from the revisions that the preparation of the new edition has made possible, particularly welcome are the new chapters that have been included. These will encourage readers to reflect not only on some of the main theoretical perspectives on childhood that are predominant in the Minority North, but also on some of the very different contexts in which children experience their childhoods in the Majority South and the implications of such differences for our understanding of childhood and discourses on children's development. Also welcome, at a time when there is an increasing demand for practice that is evidence-based and evidence-led, are new chapters on policy and research, which outline some of the political parameters to practice and research in the field of early childhood, as well as providing valuable guidance to those wishing to build research into their own practice. Taken in conjunction with the new chapter on the provision of environments that enable children's learning, and chapters from previous editions such as that on adults' concepts of childhood, the book provides a comprehensive, thought-provoking, contextualised and reader-friendly analysis of the field.

At a time when children are increasingly being recognised as social actors and bearers of rights, but when childhood is being increasingly problematised by many politicians and adults, this book will provide a valuable foundation for all students and practitioners in the children's workforce who have the responsibility for working with our children and shaping their childhoods.

Adrian L James
Professor of Applied Social Sciences
University of Sheffield

Introduction

Rod Parker-Rees

The first edition of this book was published in 2004, with the intention of introducing readers to the multi-professional and multi-disciplinary range and scope of Early Childhood Studies (ECS) and to a variety of ways of studying the richness and complexity of children's lives and children's worlds. Writing this book together as a teaching team proved invaluable as a way of sharing what we felt was most important about our work on the University of Plymouth's BA Early Childhood Studies degree and on the ECS specialism in our primary BEd programme. In 2007 we revised the book for the second edition, allowing new members of the teaching team to contribute and now again we have had the opportunity to review the overall shape and contents both of the book as a whole and of individual chapters. While it is gratifying that the book, like our programmes, has met with very positive responses, we are always looking for ways to adapt what we offer, both to meet the changing demands faced by students and to reflect the developing interests of our team. For this third edition we have added new chapters on frameworks for understanding development (Chapter 1), on providing enabling environments (Chapter 6), on the experience of childhood in the developing world (Chapter 12), on the complex interplay between research, policy and practice (Chapter 13) and on action research (Chapter 16).

We are passionately committed to enabling students to develop their skills as advocates for young children and we are convinced that ECS provides unique opportunities for personal growth and the development of sensitivity to the needs and interests of other people; adults as well as children. Studying issues which shape children's lives and worlds offers powerful opportunities to develop personal qualities which will enable ECS graduates to make a significant contribution to improving children's lives and worlds. Developing a critical perspective involves more than just challenging everything (though this is a good start!); it requires a willingness to subject other people's ideas to careful scrutiny, matching them against one's own developing values, beliefs and principles and investigating any interesting discrepancies. Being critical means being willing to question and adapt one's own views, as well as other people's. Developing a personal understanding of complex issues also requires much more than just accumulating knowledge (though, again, this is a good start). Knowledge can only be woven into understanding when the shared frameworks of what everyone knows are 'coloured in' with personal significance and the unique richness of personal experience. Understanding requires an ability to move between the cool clarity of generalised theoretical models and the fuzzy, messy detail of particular cases. For example, 'failure' to meet developmental milestones for speech development at the 'normal' age may be indicative of articulatory difficulties but it may also reflect a family context in which other forms of communication make clarity of speech less important.

The study of early childhood presents us with frequent opportunities to stand back and reflect on how our own position relates to that of young children. How would I feel if someone treated me like that? Would I talk like that to another adult? What would it be like if we, as adults, could only study alongside others of the same age or if we had no say in what we had to study? How do I feel when I enter a situation in which I don't know anyone and I don't know how I'm supposed to behave?

This introduction cannot hope to represent the full range of ideas which this book will address but I hope to give you a feel for what you will find in each chapter by showing how the different themes and topics which make up the rich mix of Early Childhood Studies can provide opportunities to learn about yourself as well as about the lives and worlds of young children.

Part 1 – What can children do? Sociocultural factors in development

The Early Years Foundation Stage (DCSF, 2007a, 2008a-c) and the standards for Early Years Professional Status (EYPS) (CWDC, 2006) have emphasised the need for early years practitioners to extend their understanding of development in the first three years of life and Part 1 has a particular focus on encouraging the reader to reassess the accomplishments of very young children. Because in our first years we learned fast and effortlessly, we can easily assume that what we learned must have been 'child's play', simple and trivial, but think for a moment about how your world would be turned upside down if you were to forget how to control the movements of your body, how to make sense of speech sounds, how to read other people's moods and emotions or even how to adjust your behaviour to different expectations in different contexts. When you imagine the effects of losing what you learned in your first three years in comparison with losing what you have learned in the last ten years, you may begin to appreciate the scale of what infants manage to learn.

The title of this section – *What can children do?* addresses the question of what children are *able* to do, recognising the need to acknowledge their capabilities, but it also touches on what children are *allowed* to do. Whenever we talk about children's developing abilities we must recognise that what they can do is influenced by the tools, opportunities and support which we provide for them. While it has always been tempting to look for ways to accelerate children's development, to hurry them along, we must also recognise that more rapid development in one area may come at the cost of limited opportunities to develop in other ways.

In Chapter 1, *Frameworks for understanding development*, Julia Morgan begins by outlining the main features of three rather different ways of understanding children's development, from the behaviourist approach, developed by Skinner and Watson from the work of Pavlov, to the constructivist approach developed by Jean Piaget and the social constructivist model which was initially proposed by Lev Vygotsky and later developed by others including Jerome Bruner and Barbara Rogoff. While the differences between these models of learning and development may tempt students to identify which is the 'right' way to understand the changes we can see in children's abilities and interests, it is more helpful if we can recognise the distinct contributions which each has to offer. To this end, the chapter concludes with a review of the ways in which each model has contributed to the development of the documentation for the Early Years Foundation Stage (DCSF 2007a, 2008a-c). For students on ECS degrees it is important to get beyond just knowing what Piaget and Vygotsky wrote. Thinking carefully about the ways in which individual interests and motivations engage with cultural opportunities and constraints can help students to see how they can help to support young children's development but it can also help them to understand aspects of their own learning.

In Chapter 2, *Active playing and learning*, Rod Parker-Rees explores the relationships between children's developing ability to bring their motor activity under deliberate control, their active, inquisitive and playful exploration of how their actions affect their environment (including other people) and their ability to discover patterns and consistencies in the effects they are able to produce. This is one of the first modules on our BA degree and we encourage students to make their own connections between what they find out about infants' learning and how they think about themselves as learners. As adults we don't tend to find out about the world of ideas by mouthing things, banging them against the floor or throwing them but we can still recognise the importance of active engagement in learning – our equivalents may be active participation in discussions, purposefully looking for connections between new ideas and our own experiences and playful exploration of other ways of thinking about things. The language of ideas is riddled with metaphors drawn from motor activity and it is not difficult to discover the value of poking and prodding at other people's theories, wiggling them loose, taking them apart, rearranging them, noticing anything interesting that happens and then showing other people and seeing how they react. Students also discover that doing things with other people, especially things that involve movement and touch, generates an energy within the group which is less common when the main activity is talking and listening. Feelings of awkwardness and embarrassment quickly give way to exhilaration, laughter and a strong sense of community which can make other, more sedentary, group activities feel more comfortable and convivial.

In Chapter 3, *Developing communication: enjoying the company of other people*, Rod Parker-Rees argues that careful examination of the earliest stages of infants' communication with other people can help us to recognise that the shared enjoyment of joint attention may be more important than we realise. The 'workaday' model of communication, which focuses on the transfer of information from one brain to another, fails to acknowledge the social importance of the playfulness of conversation. While gossip and idle chat may appear 'unprofessional', this kind of unstructured interaction can be a valuable way of getting to know other people as individuals, with their own interests, perspectives and priorities. Students are likely to have experienced the difference in 'feel' between tutors who deliver lectures *at* them and those who try to engage *with* them in conversations. They will also be aware of the very different *feel* of settings where staff talk *with* parents and children rather than *to* them or even *at* them.

In Chapter 4, *Children's health and well-being: investing in the health of the nation*, Norman Gabriel and Philip Selbie chart some of the changes in our understanding of the meaning of health and well-being, showing how, like development and learning, these concepts can only really be understood when they are considered in wider sociocultural and historical contexts. Attempts to separate the health of the body from the health of the mind or to see health as a biological property of individual bodies fail to recognise the relational core of well-being. If we focus only on diagnosing and treating illness we may fail to recognise the importance of human relationships in determining how well we feel. In this chapter historical examples, particularly associated with the Boer War and the two World Wars of the twentieth century, are used to show how concepts of children's health have also been shaped by the bigger picture of national struggles for survival. Ironically, it was concerns about the poor health of conscripts that led to the development of the National Health Service and to wider recognition of the need for society as a whole to accept responsibility for providing the conditions in which children can thrive. The first weeks and months of life as a student can be particularly stressful and students will be able to recognise the degree to which their own well-being depends on the strength of relationships, both with family and with new friends and tutors.

Part 2 – Working with children: extending opportunities for participation

Any study of early childhood must include substantial experience of spending time with children, both working with them in a professional capacity and just enjoying their company. Direct, experiential learning offers special opportunities and challenges, not least because learners must always acknowledge their responsibility for the effects of their actions on the children and they must tiptoe among the eggshells of professional sensitivities – mistakes here have real consequences. But ECS students can be rewarded by the energy, vitality and openness of young children which can help them to refresh and nurture 'an inner life invigorated by a connection to the taproot' (Plotz, 2001, pxvi).

In Chapter 5, *Observing children*, Jenny Willan shows how important it is to acknowledge the environmental factors and the contexts which influence children's behaviour and their experiences. While it is sometimes important to take children out of familiar contexts to examine details of their behaviour and development it is always necessary to remember that what children do, and especially what they *don't* do, in these odd situations may not accurately reflect what they may be able to do in situations where they feel more at ease. You can probably identify with this through your own experience of what happens when you are subjected to questioning in stressful conditions. Because it is so easy for adults to take aspects of their contexts for granted we do need to adopt a purposeful, investigative stance when we attempt to understand what it might be like to be a particular child in a particular situation – we need to observe carefully, to study rather than simply notice. We can also learn from new approaches to studying children which show that, when they are encouraged and given the time, space and tools to explore and represent what matters to them, they can participate effectively in conversations about improving the quality of their lives and worlds. In Reggio Emilia preschools the practice of documentation involving children, staff and families in recording, representing and revisiting children's developing understanding of an area of interest, offers an excellent model of how the study of children can leak into the fabric of a setting, becoming part of the way of life, for the children as well as for the adults.

In Chapter 6, *Providing an enabling environment*, Philip Selbie and Karen Wickett remind us that there is much more to the environment than just the physical provision of space and resources. If we aim to create the conditions in which children will be enabled, not merely allowed, to explore, learn and develop then our understanding of the environment must extend to the people, ethos and principles which frame the opportunities available to them. We can learn from other countries and other traditions, recognising some of the ways in which very different environments can enable children in different ways but it is important that our 'borrowing' from other traditions should go beyond just collecting 'features', like souvenirs from our travels. Every environment extends into time as well as space. Like a story, an environment has meaning which is built on what has happened in the past; practitioners draw from traditions which have been shaped and refined by the experience of many others and children are able to draw on experiences shared with their peers. A community of shared history can be enabling because it allows people to feel comfortable and supported enough to take on challenges which would otherwise appear too daunting. For students the new environment of lectures and seminars may be disabling at first but as friendships and relationships develop, participation may begin to feel less scary. This experience can play a valuable part in helping students to *feel* the importance of an enabling environment.

Chapter 7, *Tackling inequality in the early years*, by Ulrike Hohmann, focuses on a particularly important aspect of any learning environment. Much as health cannot be understood simply as the absence of illness, so equality of opportunities implies much more than just avoiding discriminatory practices. Where 'integration' has sometimes been interpreted as helping 'different' children to fit in unobtrusively among their 'normal' peers, 'inclusive' approaches acknowledge the need for settings to make such changes as are necessary to provide an environment in which *all* children can thrive together. The focus on inclusion is driven by changes in provision for children with special educational needs but it fits comfortably within an early years philosophy which insists that every child must be respected as an individual, with different needs, interests and concerns. Teachers of older children will often throw their hands up in horror at the idea of preparing individual lesson plans for every child in their class but there is no need for this if all children are offered open, flexibly resourced provision and allowed space and time to choose for themselves what will best fit their needs at any time. Providing equal opportunities then means ensuring that the resources on offer do meet the needs of all children, not just those who happen to share the tastes and values of the adults who hold the purse strings. The real value of the concept of inclusion is that it can help us to move beyond tokenistic provision of 'exotic' costumes, cookware and play props towards a genuine celebration of our differences.

Part 3 – Multi-professional practice: developing empowering communities

Anyone who considers a career working with children because they get on better with children than with other adults will soon discover that virtually every possible kind of work will necessarily involve working with parents and families as well as colleagues and professionals from other agencies. Learning how to get on with other adults and how to help them to achieve their full potential is an essential part of any professional training and fortunately we all have plenty of experience of working with others in different kinds of groups and teams, collaborating, submitting to leadership and also, perhaps, leading. We each have a considerable stockpile of both positive and negative examples of factors which affect how people get on, both with each other and with the task in hand. In the early stages of any career our main priority will be to survive being led by others (drawing on our creative ability to interpret what we are expected to do) but sooner or later (and this is alarmingly soon for most early years professionals), we will find ourselves leading other adults as well as children. The experiences we can gain while studying alongside a range of other adults of different ages, with different backgrounds and, possibly with different career interests, as well as our experiences of working in real early years settings, on placements, in a voluntary capacity or in part-time work, can also help us to deepen our understanding of what makes people tick and how to oil the wheels when friction between individuals prevents a team from working together smoothly.

Chapter 8, *Working with colleagues*, by Caroline Leeson and Valerie Huggins has been substantially revised to reflect the increasing emphasis on 'joined-up' planning and delivery of services for children following enquiries into several well publicised cases where young children have died following failures in communication between different agencies involved in their care. While the authors welcome wider recognition of the importance of strengthening relationships between early years practitioners, specialists from different professional backgrounds, parents and children, they recognise that pressure for increased partnership may also be motivated by a need to reduce the costs of service provision. Partnerships are complex, social relationships which must be forged between individual practitioners, not between 'services', and this requires adequate levels of resourcing. For example, an infant needs to be able to build familiarity with a particular key-worker rather than with whoever happens to be allocated the relevant slot on the staffing rota. In working relationships between adults there will always be a mix of person-to-person and role-to-role forms of interaction but an emphasis on the latter at the expense of the former can lead to fragile and insincere forms of partnership. Martin Buber (2004) has written powerfully about this difference between '*I-thou*' relationships and '*I-it*' relationships and students will be well aware of the difference between tutors or placement staff who take the trouble to engage with them as a person and those for whom they remain 'a student'.

In Chapter 9, *Leadership in early childhood settings*, Caroline Leeson points out that much of the existing research on effective leadership draws on models derived from studies of businesses or big organisations which have tended to be led by men. In early years settings, on the other hand, the majority of leaders, whether in room, setting or area teams, will be women, whose preferred leadership style may tend to be more collaborative than competitive. This style may prove particularly appropriate for leaders of complex, multi-professional children's centres, where practitioners from a wide range of backgrounds must be encouraged to support and learn from each other if they are to develop and improve the quality of provision. It can be learnt and practised in any early years context, where children from a wide range of backgrounds must be encouraged to support and learn from each other. This chapter also makes the important point that studies of the role of the leader can only go so far. All leaders are individuals, with unique personal histories and cultures, which cannot fail to influence their style, their decisions and their priorities. Effective early years practitioners and leaders cannot refer to an instruction manual to decide how to respond in a particular situation; they have to acknowledge the individuality of each of the children, parents and colleagues with whom they work.

Chapter 10, *The benefits of comparison: recent developments in the German early years workforce*, Ulrike Hohmann shows how debates in Germany about proposed changes to training for early years practitioners can help to provide a bit of perspective on arguments in the UK about the education, training and accreditation of early years professionals. It may be particularly difficult for students on an ECS course to stand back from their own motives, experiences and aspirations enough to be able to consider what kind of preparation would be best for people who intend to work with young children. Do we need relatively short, low-cost, competence focused training to equip students with the skills they will need to work safely and effectively with young children, or should we focus on more extensive, and more expensive, degree level education programmes which support the development of students' abilities to evaluate policy initiatives and interpret them creatively in different contexts? Awareness of some of the cultural, social and policy factors which complicate decisions about how to improve the training of the early years workforce in Germany should help students to notice similar, but different, factors closer to home.

Part 4 – Comparing children's worlds: making the familiar strange

The fact that we have all been children may, at first, appear to give us a good foundation for studying childhood but this familiarity can also make it more difficult for us to notice what is right under our noses. Like the proverbial fish which remains totally unaware of the existence of water until taken out of it, we can easily assume that children do what they do because that's just what children do. However, as soon as we begin to introduce some distance between our own experience and the children and childhoods we study, we can realise that what children do is heavily shaped and constrained by what adults in a particular culture at a particular time want, expect, allow and even need children to do. What we see children doing, in other words, should not be taken as evidence of what they could do, given different circumstances.

Chapter 11, *Adults' concepts of childhood*, Norman Gabriel explores the ways in which our understanding of childhood is intricately bound up in social practices and relationships. Examining attitudes to poor children, children within families and children in schools reveals some of the ways in which 'taken for granted' practices have been challenged and contested, leading to changes in adults' 'take' on childhood. Adults have an interest in childhood which extends well beyond consideration of how best to care for children and, once a contrast is recognised between childhood and adulthood, childhood acquires an important status as a way of defining adulthood. If adults value social polish and civilised manners then childhood is a time of wildness, associated with all that is uncontrolled, passionate, dangerous and exciting. If adults are jaded by the restrictions and artificiality of social conventions then childhood is seen as a time of freedom, innocence and naturalness. The shifts and changes in our attitudes to nature are particularly interesting and remind us of the need to step outside our familiar mindsets when we read accounts of childhood which were written long ago. This chapter traces some of the ways in which changing concepts of childhood have reflected wider changes in the organisation and structure of societies, reminding us that careful reflection on these changes can lead students of early childhood into far-reaching reappraisal of values and assumptions which might otherwise pass unchallenged.

In Chapter 12, *Children's well-being in the developing world* Rebecca Carter Dillon and Valerie Huggins also invite readers to adopt a wider perspective. Recognising the very different kinds of challenges which face policymakers, practitioners and families in countries which do not share our relative wealth and stability can help us to recalibrate our assumptions about what is really important in children's lives. This chapter explores some of the consequences of the very uneven distribution of natural, physical, human, financial and social capital both between and within countries and identifies some of the consequences for children's economic well-being, their access to health care, education and adequate nutrition and their exposure to exploitation, armed conflict and other destabilising social and cultural situations. The efforts of non-governmental organisations to offer aid and support in areas where local governments are unable to meet people's needs raise some very difficult questions about how 'better off' nations can support the 'developing world' without imposing inappropriate cultural, social and political frameworks. The inhabitants of 'poor' countries certainly do not appreciate being treated like children by paternalistic or proselytising 'do-gooders' but by investigating these issues students of early childhood can develop a heightened critical sensitivity to the workings of power relations in settings and in families.

In Chapter 13, *The research, policy and practice triangle in early childhood education and care*, Verity Campbell-Barr examines how policies are developed, how they are sometimes informed and often challenged by research and how they are interpreted and adapted, often in a variety of different ways, in practice. While studying the history of concepts of childhood or exploring the ways in which childhood is experienced in other parts of the world can help us to reassess our assumptions about what matters for children, research can also help to stir the waters and reveal aspects of policy and practice which merit closer critical scrutiny. Policies which are presented as being in the interests of children may also have other effects, on families for example, and on the wider economy. On the other hand, policies which may not appear to have anything to do with young children may turn out to have dramatic effects on children's lives. Practitioners may be excused for sometimes feeling that the intricacies of relationships within the research, policy and practice triangle make it difficult to be sure about anything but the upside of this necessary uncertainty is that there will always be some 'play' in any policy, some room for creative interpretation and fine adjustment to the particular needs of individual settings, families and children. In the early stages of any career we may crave some clear guidelines and fixed points of reference but we should also appreciate the opportunities and responsibilities which come with a professional role. Simply following instructions and 'delivering' policies is not an option but this means that there is always scope for playfulness in our critical, research informed interpretation of policy frameworks.

Part 5 – Researching practice: developing critical engagement

One of the aims of any programme of study should be to leave students with a greater awareness of how much more there is still to learn. We have to be careful not to allow such programmes to be reduced to training exercises, aimed at enabling students to collect competences until, when they have enough, they can be considered 'done' and safe to enter a particular area of work. The risk of this training model is that it can leave students feeling that no further study is needed once they have achieved the necessary levels of competence unless, perhaps, they wish to proceed to the next rung on their career ladder. It is particularly important that people who will be working with young children and their families should actively promote a positive attitude to continuing learning and personal development because their example can shape children's learning dispositions at a time when these are especially sensitive to social influences.

In Chapter 14, *In praise of reflective practice*, Caroline Leeson shows how an inquisitive, investigative attitude to all aspects of your own practice can help you to make the continuing development of your professional skills, knowledge and understanding an integral part of your working life. Reflection must always have a strongly personal component, drawing on soft intuitions as well as hard facts, but it can be supported by interaction with other people. Talking with colleagues about an issue may be a particularly effective way of clarifying your own ideas. Collaborative action research, when a group of practitioners agree to meet up to explore an aspect of their practice in a systematic way, has been shown to be one of the most powerful forms of professional development (Edwards, 1999). Most importantly, by modelling enthusiasm for questioning, challenging and probing aspects of what you do, you will be providing a powerful example of positive learning dispositions, not just for the children you work with but for parents and colleagues as well.

In Chapter 15, *Research projects in early childhood studies: students' active explorations of children's words*, Jenny Willan offers a helpful framework for planning, conducting and writing up a small scale research project. The research project or dissertation can provide opportunities for you to explore an area of personal interest at a depth which will often result in you knowing more about it than most of your peers and, in many cases, more than some of your tutors too. Developing an area of personal expertise can enable you to make the transition from seeing yourself as a knowledge consumer, dependent on work done by others, to thinking of yourself as a knowledge producer, able to make your own personal contribution to the sum of what is known about the lives and worlds of young children. The process of devising, developing, analysing and presenting your own empirical study can also give you valuable experience of a range of strategies for exploring, testing and refining aspects of your own understanding of how things work in early years settings. While you may not regularly conduct similar studies in your working life, you may well find that these strategies prove useful when you need to cope with difficult or unfamiliar situations or when you want to make sense of something that interests or puzzles you.

Finally, in Chapter 16, *Action research*, Ulrike Hohmann and Karen Wickett show how practitioners in settings can establish enquiry and learning as central features of everyone's involvement in a setting's own learning community. While undergraduate students have to work around the ethical and practical issues of negotiating access to settings, families and children as part of their research projects, practitioners enjoy daily access to rich opportunities to examine and reflect on how they go about supporting young children and their families. The chapter includes an account of Karen's work in the children's centre where she works part time as a teacher. Her work with her colleagues to explore and develop their use of documentation provides a real-life example of how shared enquiry can contribute to the development of a 'buzz' within a setting as everyone is swept along by enthusiasm and interest in a common focus.

The first chapters in this book explain how young babies' active, physical exploration of their environments enables them to extract much more information than would be available from a passive observation of what just happens to pass before them. The last chapters bring us full circle, showing how you too can benefit from adopting an active, probing, challenging and playful approach. One of the great advantages of studying early childhood is that you will frequently have opportunities to discover connections between what you know about the lives and worlds of young children and what you know about your own life and world. Adopting an active, critical approach to your own learning will enable you to breathe life into what might otherwise feel like dry, dusty theoretical models and also to find some meaningful structure in what might otherwise feel like chaotically complicated real world experiences.

Part 1

What can children do? Sociocultural factors in development

1 Frameworks for understanding development

Julia Morgan

Introduction

What does the term development mean to you? Do you think of development in terms of children, of norms of development, of development as holistic or of development as a process? In psychological terms, for example, 'development refers to the process by which an organism (human, animal or plant) grows and changes through its life-span' (Smith et al. 2005, p5). Human development therefore, according to this definition, is about change and is viewed as a dynamic process which occurs both in childhood and continues into and throughout adulthood – a process that starts from conception and ends in death. Now think about whether you view human development as a property of the individual person or do you think that development occurs through a process of interaction with other people? Think about what would happen if we didn't interact with other people – would we develop? What about factors such as the environment, history or culture; how are they implicated in human development?

Examining these types of questions and focusing on how we, as humans, develop is the focus of much academic endeavour which has produced a vast amount of research findings and a number of 'grand theories' which aim to explain human development. Some of these theories see development as an individual process while others see development as a social cultural-historical process which occurs in collaboration with other people from the same community. In this chapter I will examine three theories in more detail and then briefly examine how these theories have influenced a policy document – the Early Years Foundation Stage (EYFS). By doing this I hope to highlight how knowledge of theory enables and empowers practitioners to interpret policy documents such as the EYFS.

Behaviourist theories of development: the conditioned child

Behaviourism is an early attempt at explaining human development and is an approach which focuses attention on how animals learn new behaviour. The results were then extrapolated to humans and it is argued that children develop because they are 'conditioned' to learn new behaviour. Emphasis is placed, therefore, in behaviourist theories on the important role that the environment and direct experience have in children's development. There are two main approaches to conditioning: classical and operant conditioning.

Classical conditioning: learning by association

Pavlov is probably most famous, at least among undergraduates, for his research on digestion and dogs which led to the theory of classical conditioning (Mook, 2004). Pavlov theorised that dogs who were hungry could be conditioned into associating a biological reflex (i.e. salivating when presented with food) with an external environmental stimulus (i.e. the ringing of a bell). This external stimulus (the bell) had no prior association with either food or salivating. Pavlov rang the bell at the same time that food was presented to the dogs and after many repetitions the dogs were 'conditioned' to salivate at the sound of the bell even when food was not presented. The dogs had learnt to associate the sound of the bell with food. Pavlov's work was replicated most famously by Watson (1924) who conditioned an 11 month old baby called 'Little Albert' into fearing rats by associating a loud noise, which Little Albert was scared of, with a rat, which Little Albert had previously not been afraid of. After the conditioning episode Little Albert became scared of rats and anything that looked like a rat even in the absence of a loud noise. Classical conditioning, therefore, offers a very basic explanation of how children could possibly develop through learning by association. However, as a grand theory of development it does leave a lot to be desired and it is open to debate how much a child who has been conditioned, through the use of association, to respond in a particular way to a stimulus can be said to have truly 'developed'.

Operant conditioning: learning by reinforcement

Thorndike (Mook, 2004) laid the foundations for the theory of operant conditioning by carrying out a number of experiments with cats. Thorndike found that hungry cats placed in a 'puzzle box' learnt to operate the levers to get out because their behaviour (i.e. their response) was reinforced and rewarded both through the use of food and through the act of escaping itself. Skinner (Mook, 2004) expanded on Thorndike's original work using rats in puzzle boxes and developed the theory of operant conditioning. He proposed that human behaviour could be 'shaped' by reinforcing desired behaviours or responses through the use of rewards and decreasing undesired behaviours or responses through the use of punishments. For rewards and punishments to be successful, however, they needed to be immediate, consistently applied, of a suitable size (i.e. is the cost of doing the behaviour worth the benefit of the reward) and of relevance to the child (if the child was bored of stickers, for example, they would be of little use as a reward). Operant conditioning, therefore, 'proposes that all behaviour is learned and maintained by its consequences' (Oates et al., 2005, p59). However, this is problematic in itself and if we only learnt behaviour through having it rewarded or punished the process would be very slow and difficult indeed and would not truly reflect how quickly humans learn.

Classical and operant behaviourist models of development were once very influential in child psychology, and we can see that many of the strategies which are currently used in behavioural management (for example stickers, praise, golden time, time-out, and response cost/removal of stickers) and with children with special educational needs (for example applied behavioural analysis where tasks are broken down into small steps and each step and the associated appropriate behaviour is positively reinforced) are still informed by these theories (see Oates et al., 2005). However, behaviourist theories of development are no longer seen by most academics as offering a full and coherent explanation of how children develop and they can be criticised for viewing the child as having a passive role in their own development. There is little explicit acknowledgement, in behaviourist theories, that children bring to their experiences their past learning, their emotions, their ability to solve problems, their motivations, their culture, their social world, their biology and their own interpretations and beliefs. Instead, children are seen to develop in a stimulus/response/reward bubble devoid of any cognitive input from the child. What goes on inside the child's head, because it cannot be directly measured or observed (the technology at the time precluded this), is of little consequence and development is seen to occur only through a child's direct experience of the environment which brings about a corresponding change in the child's behaviour.

Piaget's theory of development: the active thinking child

Piaget, however, viewed development differently and one of his many contributions to understanding human development was his focus on the active role of thinking children in their own development.

> *To express the same idea in still another way, I think that human knowledge is essentially active…..By virtue of this point of view, I find myself opposed to the view of knowledge as a copy, a passive copy, of reality…..To my way of thinking, knowing an object does not mean copying it – it means acting upon it.*

(Piaget, 1970, p15)

Piaget's child, unlike the child in behaviourist theory, is an active child who individually constructs personal knowledge through direct engagement with the environment. Through actively engaging with their environment children, according to Piaget, internalise their actions by constructing schemas or cognitive frameworks for making sense of their experiences of the world.

Piaget believed that schemas are dynamic and undergo change according to the child's stage of biological development or maturation but also because children actively assimilate and accommodate new information from the environment into existing schemas. Children assimilate and accommodate new information because they are intrinsically motivated to learn and hence actively solve problems in situations which challenge their existing schemas/knowledge and lead to disequilibrium. For Piaget, trying to reach equilibrium was a 'fundamental… factor' in children's development (Piaget, 1977, p23), and as a result children develop in part because they are 'driven' to understand their environment by actively solving problems by using what they already know.

Some key Piagetian terms

Schemas – mental frameworks or representations built up by the child through their action on the environment.

Assimilation – a process by which new experiences are fitted to existing schemas. So for example a child's experience of animals may be limited to cats. When they encounter other small four-legged furry animals for the first time, e.g. small dogs, they may try to adapt or fit this new information about dogs into their existing schema of cat and hence for a while call small dogs – 'cat'. Furthermore, by assimilating this new information about small dogs into their existing schema of cat children may, for a time, ignore information about small dogs which does not fit into their schema of cat. They are, therefore, actively trying to make sense of the world in light of what they already know.

Accommodation – the process of changing a schema to fit in with the environment. After assimilating information about small dogs into their cat schema children begin to actively focus on the differences between cats and small dogs and as a result their cat schema is modified to include dogs. This may result in new schemas being developed to incorporate this new insight/information or their cat schema being expanded to include the notion of dogs being different to cats. The information, therefore, about small dogs being different to cats is no longer ignored and their schema undergoes change to incorporate this new insight.

Adaptation – a process where children actively strive to understand their environment by assimilating and accommodating new information from the environment into their schemas. Development occurs when children adapt to their environment.

Intrinsic motivation – the biological need to learn and reach equilibrium.

Equilibrium – the balance or fit between a child's schemas and their environment.

Disequilibrium – a state of cognitive conflict. When new experiences challenge or do not easily fit into existing schemas.

However, development for Piaget is not all about the environment but is also in part biological or genetic. This can be seen in the idea of children being intrinsically motivated to learn and to adapt to their environment but it can also be seen in Piaget's detailed discussion of his stage theory of development (for a fuller discussion of Piaget's stages of development see Smith et al., 2003 and Piaget, 1977). In brief, Piaget argues that all children pass through four stages of development which are qualitatively different from one another with thinking becoming less egocentric/concrete and more decentred/abstract as the child develops. Piaget suggests that children pass from one stage to another not only by assimilating/accommodating new experiences from the environment into their developing set of schemas but also because they reach a level of biological maturation which enables information to be processed, understood and manipulated more efficiently. There is, therefore, in Piaget's work an emphasis on children being biologically or innately 'ready' for learning and for Piaget children do not benefit from being taught something they are not developmentally ready to learn.

Piaget's work has had a massive impact on Western understandings of child development and these influences can still be seen today (DCSF, 2008a). However, there have also been numerous critiques of his work (see Oates et al., 2005; Smith et al., 2003; Sutherland, 1992). Donaldson (1978), for example, has critiqued many of the experiments which Piaget used to underpin key aspects of his stage theory. Donaldson and her colleagues replicated Piaget's research and found that younger children in her experiments were more able to perform at a higher developmental level if they understood the 'human sense' of the experiment. Experiments which had little social or cultural relevance were likely, it was argued, to have little meaning for the children and hence the younger children were not able to succeed – they didn't understand what was being asked of them. As a result, it has been argued that Piaget not only underestimated what children could actually do but also underestimated the importance of the social and cultural context in which development occurs (Donaldson, 1978). However Piaget's work, though often misunderstood, is of great importance and has provided the 'most comprehensive account of cognitive growth ever put forward' (Smith et al., 2003 p412).

Vygotsky's theory of development: the sociocultural child

Vygotsky provides an alternative theory of development to Piaget and places emphasis on the social and cultural context in which children develop. For Vygotsky children are born with what he termed lower mental functions which appear biological in nature and include such things as reflexes (Bodrova & Leong, 2006). However, children are also born into a cultural and social world in which objects and events have particular meanings and it is by interacting socially with more experienced members of that cultural world that children learn and develop 'higher mental functions' (Bodrova & Leong, 2006). Higher mental functions, therefore, build on lower mental functions but are social and cultural in origin as opposed to 'natural' and include such things as memory strategies, logic, self regulation, focused attention and introspection.

Social interaction and the cultural context are, therefore, critical in Vygotskian theories of human development; 'human learning presupposes a specific social nature and a process by which children grow into the intellectual life of those around them' (Vygotsky 1978a, p88). It is by observing and interacting with others that children are able to see and understand how more experienced members of their cultural group interpret situations, solve problems and use the 'cultural tools' of their society. Cultural tools include such things as language, ways of thinking, signs and symbols, music, art, ways of behaving and physical objects such as pens, hammers, chairs, books, maps – knowledge of which is passed on from one generation to another. As a result the cultural tools that we use today have their roots in yesterday and for Vygotsky history has a major influence on human development.

Development for Vygotsky, therefore, occurs first on a social level or interpersonal plane which is external to the child and then second 'within the child' on an intra-psychological plane (Vygotsky, 1978a, p163). Children's development is thus a process by which the social, the cultural and the historical are gradually internalised in the mind of the child and made individual. Vygotsky argued that:

> *we become ourselves through others and that this rule applies not only to the personality as a whole, but also to the history of every individual function.'*

(Vygotsky, 1966, p43)

Understanding of cultural tools and culture is, therefore, passed from more experienced members of the culture to children as well as being actively sought and acquired by the children themselves. As a result, through social interaction and individual internalisation culture is actively taken from one generation by another. What is also evident from Vygotsky's work is that culture influences *what* children think through their use of cultural tools such as books, maps and counting systems for example but also *how* they think by influencing internal cognitive structures (i.e. through the child's active internalisation of culture and the tools of culture). Human development, therefore, is both social and cultural as the sociocultural 'context molds cognitive processes and is part of the development process' (Bodrova & Leong, 2006, p10).

What do we mean by the term 'culture'?

'that complex whole which includes knowledge, belief, art, morals, law, custom, and any other capabilities and habits acquired by man as a member of society' (Tylor, 1871/1924, p1)

'an historically transmitted pattern of meanings embodied in symbols, a system of inherited conceptions expressed in symbolic forms by means of which men communicate, perpetuate, and develop their knowledge about and attitudes toward life' (Geertz, 1973, p89)

Many theorists have been influenced by Vygotsky's work on culture. Rogoff (2003, p3) is one such theorist and she sees human development as a cultural process whereby children actively appropriate 'the intellectual tools and skills of the surrounding cultural community' (1990, p11). For Rogoff, therefore, culture 'matters in human development' (2003, p7) and without culture children would not develop as development occurs through participating in cultural processes. However, different cultures provide different experiences for children, due to specific cultural beliefs about what it is to be a child and what it is to be human and this means that human development is dynamic and varied. Development, therefore, is dependent on what particular cultural communities expect from members of that community at any given time in history.

An important factor, for Vygotsky, in the child's internalisation of cultural tools and hence their development is the concept of the Zone of Proximal Development (ZPD). The ZPD is:

> *the distance between the actual developmental level as determined by individual problem solving and the level of potential development as determined through problem solving under adult guidance or in collaboration with more capable peers.*

The zone of proximal development defines those functions that have not yet matured but are in the process of maturation, functions that will mature tomorrow but are currently in an embryonic state.

(Vygotsky, 1978a, p86)

Vygotsky's concept of the ZPD, therefore, appears to be concerned with those psychological functions which are not yet fully matured but which are in the process of maturation. By focusing on these maturing functions, an adult or more experienced peer is able to extend a child's learning and thus extend their development. The ZPD, therefore, can be seen as a property of the shared thinking which exists between the child and the more experienced member of their culture at any given time as well as a property of a child's engagement with culture, including their use of cultural tools (see Chaiklin, 2003 for more detailed discussion of the ZPD). As Bodrova & Leong (2001, p9) state:

Higher mental functions exist for some time in a distributed or 'shared' form, when learners and their mentors use new cultural tools jointly in the context of solving some task. After acquiring (in Vygotsky's terminology 'appropriating') a variety of cultural tools, children become capable of using higher mental functions independently.

As a result activity within the ZPD can be seen as a joint endeavour whereby a more experienced member of the same culture engages with the child and through a process of co-construction, using the cultural tools of that society, extends psychological functions which are not yet fully mature in the child. The child will eventually be able to carry out these problem solving tasks independently after internalising the thinking strategies that are needed and making them their own. For example, external memory aids such as a parent helping a child remember where they had put their pen by asking 'where did you last use it' are internalised by the child and used as their own method of memory recall. Vygotsky's concept of the ZPD lays emphasis, therefore, on the importance of social interaction, the importance of culture, the use of cultural tools and instruction. Play has also been identified as essential to the ZPD and Vygotsky states that:

Play also creates the zone of proximal development of the child. In play, the child is always behaving beyond his age, above his usual everyday behaviour; in play he is, as it were, a head above himself. Play contains in a concentrated form, as in the focus of a magnifying glass, all developmental tendencies; it is as if the child tries to jump above his usual level. The relationship of play to development should be compared to the relationship between instruction and development.

(Vygotsky, 1978a, p102)

The zone of proximal development and its role in extending children's development has attracted much attention from practitioners, theorists and researchers. Wood et al. (1976), for example, introduced the idea of scaffolding to explain how adults could support children's development within the ZPD. Scaffolding is the process by which a more expert adult or peer offers sensitive support and assistance to a child in order to help them achieve goals which they would be unable to achieve by themselves. As the child becomes more proficient, the assistance or scaffolding is reduced so that eventually the child will be able to complete the task independently. However, it is important not to see scaffolding and the zone of proximal development as things which an expert does to a non-expert. Instead, both scaffolding and the zone of proximal development are best viewed as forms of co-construction where the child or non-expert is as active in the process as the more experienced person. Furthermore, through a process of intersubjectivity, whereby each of the participants takes on board the other's perspective, both of the co-constructors come to a shared understanding of the problem at hand.

Some sociocultural terms

Co-construction – because children develop in a social environment; their development is not seen as an individual process but instead is viewed as a process which is jointly co-constructed by the child and members of their cultural community.

Intersubjectivity – communicating with other people to arrive at a shared understanding. Meaning is shared between people through exchanges with other people. These exchanges could take the form of discussion, negotiation, collaboration, and awareness of other people's emotions, feeling and thoughts. Harris (1989), for example, showed how young babies look to others for social referencing cues on how to act in particular situations. This intersubjectivity, i.e. awareness of the emotions and facial cues of others, may lead to babies changing their own understanding of a situation.

Rogoff was also influenced by Vygotsky's work on the ZPD and introduced the idea of guided participation. Rogoff states that children develop by appropriating the cultural tools and norms of their own culture. They do this by participating as apprentices in their everyday cultural surroundings, for example, in families, in friendship groups, in schools or in preschools (Rogoff, 1990). Rogoff uses the term guided participation to explain how being an apprentice is a two-way process – children learn about their culture and what it is to be a member of that culture by actively participating in their culture but at the same time they are guided in their participation and development by more experienced members of their community. However, when Rogoff refers to guided participation she is not simply talking about children being instructed rather she is talking about everyday activities in which children participate with others in cultural processes; this could include a child helping their parent or caregiver in the garden or a child cooking with their parent. Rogoff gives the lovely example of one of her graduate students who wrote to her about his childhood in El Salvador and how he learnt to build an oven to bake bread with his mother (his mother had built an oven herself to bake bread as a child). He wrote:

Out of this experience what strikes me the most is that through this process [of building the oven and baking bread] I learned who my mom was and how her life had been as a child. I also learned about parental expectations. Every step of the way in the process of building the oven, there was a story. Language was the tool my mother used to assist me in the task, as well as the tool to teach me the meaning and the importance of what we were doing together. Her stories were filled with values, beliefs and meanings that reflected our social reality.

(Rivera, 1995, cited in Rogoff, 2003, p282)

As can be seen from the above example, human development is not just about acquiring new skills and knowledge but

consists of individuals changing their ways of understanding, perceiving, noticing, thinking, remembering, classifying, reflecting, problem setting and solving, planning and so on – in shared endeavours with other people building on the cultural practices and traditions of communities.

(Rogoff, 2003, p237)

Vygotsky's work has influenced many theorists and researchers from many different disciplines. In early childhood education Anning et al. (2009 p1) state that 'early childhood education has been challenged by a theoretical sea change that has seen individualistic developmental explanations of learning and development replaced by theories that foreground the cultural and socially constructed nature of learning' – this theoretical change is a direct result of Vygotsky's theories of development. However, although Vygotsky's work is highly influential there are some difficulties with his body of work due to his early death which resulted in many of his ideas not being fully elaborated and in some cases being rather vague (Cohen, 2002). The Zone of Proximal Development, for example, is a case in point where more clarification from Vygotsky was needed (see Daniel, 2005 for more discussion of the numerous interpretations of the ZPD). However, notwithstanding this Vygotsky's emphasis on the social and cultural nature of human development is not only highly original but is also extraordinarily insightful.

Piaget versus Vygotksy: poles apart?

The theories of Piaget and Vygotsky are very often presented as being poles apart – at opposite ends of a spectrum. This, however, is not entirely the case and there are as many similarities between the work of Piaget and Vygotsky as there are differences (for discussion of the similarities see Kozulin, 2001). One of the most cited differences between the theories of Piaget and Vygotsky is that Piaget focused only on individual development and ignored the social context whilst Vygotsky focused on the social nature of development and ignored the individual. However, examining Piaget's work, for example, shows that he identified *four* factors which, he thinks, shape human development: maturation, environment, social transmission and equilibration (Piaget, 1977). He states:

Social life is a necessary condition for the development of logic. We thus believe that social life transforms the individual's very nature.

(Piaget, 1928/1977, p239 cited in Rogoff, 1990, p33)

Vygotsky, on the other hand, also identifies the importance of the active individual child adapting to the environment and he states that each new stage arises:

not from the unfolding of potentials contained in the preceding stage, but from actual collision of the organism and the environment and from active adaptation to the environment.

(Vygotsky, 1981, cited in Richardson & Sheldon, 1988, p65)

However, whilst both the social and the individual are evident to some degree in both theories, it is the case that Piaget laid more emphasis on individual development and individual construction of knowledge whilst Vygotsky laid more emphasis on the role of social factors in human development seeing 'development as participation in communities of practice' (Burman, 2008 cited in Anning et al. 2009, p55).

There are, however, at least three major differences between the theories of Vygotsky and Piaget. The first difference is in how Piaget and Vygotsky viewed the relationship between development and learning. Piaget's stage theory very much put emphasis on the importance of development leading learning so that it would be counter-productive to teach a child something if they were not developmentally ready. Vygotsky, on the other hand, thought the opposite and suggested that learning within the ZPD can extend psychological functions and as a result can take the child on to the next developmental stage. Instruction, therefore, within the ZPD was paramount for Vygotsky whilst for Piaget instruction could only lead to a superficial understanding as children had not solved the problems themselves.

The second major difference is how each theorist approached the relationship between language and thought. For Piaget, the development of cognition and language occur separately and cognitive development must precede the development of language. Very young children's language is, according to Piaget, egocentric and represents their stage of cognition. By this he means that very young children are more likely to see the world from their own viewpoint and struggle to take on board the views of other people because of their level of cognition. This cognitive egocentrism is reflected in young children's language and can be seen when young children talk to themselves oblivious of anyone around them. The child's egocentric language, according to Piaget, only becomes 'socialised' when children reach a particular level of cognitive development – in this case the concrete operational stage where they are cognitively able to see other people's point of view. Vygotsky, however, saw the development of language and cognition as being initially separate but gradually becoming merged. For Vygotksy language plays two critical roles in cognitive development. First, language is social and is the main means by which adults transmit or communicate culture to children. Second, external language becomes gradually internalised by the child and becomes a tool for thinking, that is, it becomes inner speech or thought (language and cognition become merged). Egocentric speech, therefore, for Vygotsky is not a reflection of cognitive ability but is a reflection of young children using, and beginning to internalize, speech for thought.

A third major difference between the theories of Vygotsky and Piaget is the emphasis that they place on the role of culture in human development. Rogoff (1990, p4) suggests that Piaget's 'primary efforts were devoted to how the individual made sense of an unexamined "generic" world common to the species as a whole' and as a result his work showed little recognition of the historical, political and cultural influences on both the environment and especially on children's development itself. Vygotsky, on the other hand, saw culture and cultural tools as catalysts for development and argued that without culture, development would be impossible (Cole and Wertsch, 1996).

The EYFS and the influences of Piaget and Vygotsky

The Early Years Foundation Stage (EYFS) is a play based curriculum which became statutory in England from September 2008 and 'requires providers to ensure a balance of child-initiated and adult-led play-based activities' (DCSF, 2008b, p7). Even though the EYFS document does not explicitly refer to theories of development, the EYFS can be seen to draw on the theories of Piaget and Vygotsky. The Piagetian influences can be identified in the emphasis in the EYFS on child initiated activities, the idea that children learn by doing or acting as opposed to being told, the emphasis on the unique child whose development is seen as primarily individual and the focus on the child as an active learner who solves problems. Furthermore, these influences can also be seen in the focus on the crucial role of the practitioner in planning and developing 'a challenging environment' which can be used to 'support and extend specific areas of children's learning' so that children can reach their own 'learning goals' (DCSF, 2008b, p7). This would sit very much within a Piagetian framework where the child's direct engagement with the environment is seen as crucial to their development and where the role of the practitioner is to provide an 'enabling' environment which will challenge 'individual' children in their 'spontaneous' activities (DCSF, 2008b, p7).

Piaget's idea of children passing through stages of development can also be seen to influence the EYFS's six broad phases of children's development, which although they overlap, still represent a linear development trajectory based on age which is individual to the child. Children pass from one broad phase (for example birth–11 months) to another (8–20 months) and so on. At each phase of development the guidance states that 'there are some important steps for each child to take along their own developmental pathway ' (DCSF, 2007a, Child Development Overview) and that these 'steps' ensure that 'most' children will reach their early learning goals by the end of the EYFS (DCSF, 2008a, p12). For example, if we examine the Personal, Social and Emotional Development Area of Learning (DCSF, 2008b, pp24–40) we can see that at 16–26 months old most children should 'take pleasure in learning new skills' whilst at 22–36 months most children should 'begin to develop self-confidence and a belief in themselves' (p26). Chronological age or overlapping chronological age ranges are the basis for understanding children's development in the EYFS and this influences assessment and the planning of children's activities. The idea, however, of age or age ranges being a reliable indicator of development has been challenged and it is suggested that a child's age 'cannot serve as a reliable criterion for establishing the actual level' of their development (Vygotsky, 1998, cited in Anning et al. 2009, p5).

The influence of Vygotsky can also be identified in the EYFS and the practitioner is seen as not only providing challenging environments for children but also providing scaffolding and guidance to enhance learning.

The adult may introduce a particular material, skill or idea. Often when an adult initiates an activity, for example demonstrates the skill of weaving, the child's need for adult involvement will decrease over time as they master the skill.

(DCSF, 2008b, p7)

This indirect reference to the ZPD and Wood et al. (1976) notion of scaffolding continues and the guidance states that 'children learn better by doing, and by doing things with other people who are more competent, rather than just by being told' (DCSF, 2007a, card 1.1). Vygotskian ideas about the importance of social interaction in development are also evident in the EYFS and practitioners are urged, for example, to 'engage in conversations with babies' because 'babies and children are sociable and curious, and they explore the world through relationships with others and through all their senses' (DCSF, 2007a, card 1.1). This indirect reference to the co-constructed nature of children's development and the importance of intersubjectivity is continued:

In the most effective settings practitioners support and challenge children's thinking by getting involved in the thinking process with them. Sustained shared thinking involves the adult being aware of the children's interests and understandings and the adult and children working together to develop an idea or skill. Sustained shared thinking can only happen when there are responsive trusting relationships between adults and children. The adult shows genuine interest, offers encouragement, clarifies ideas and asks open questions. This supports and extends the children's thinking and helps children to make connections in learning.

(DCSF, 2007a, card 4.3)

There is also some reference in the EYFS to the importance of engaging with children in 'contexts that they understand' and that 'babies …are especially tuned to learn from other people and the cultural and material environment' (DCSF 2007a, card 1.1). However, although culture is mentioned there is very little engagement with the cultural nature of development. When the term culture is used in the EYFS it is very often used to refer to 'cultural differences' (DCSF, 2008b, p27) as opposed to the idea of culture in its widest sense (see definition of culture above). This lack of reference to the cultural nature of development could be seen as problematic, if as Anning et al. (2009, p1) suggest there is a 'sea change' in how children's development is being viewed in the early years, that is a move away from individualist accounts of development to a move towards taking account of the social and cultural context of development.

In conclusion, although the influences of both Piaget and Vygotsky are evident in the EYFS the guidance is rather vague on why children develop by engaging with more experienced people, how practitioners can effectively scaffold development, and why social interaction is important for children's development. It is only by having knowledge of the theories themselves that we can understand the relevance of the environment and of social interaction, the importance of intersubjectivity, why child-initiated activities are important, the important role of the child in co-construction and the relevance of culture for children's development. Theory and practice are, I would suggest, inseparable and practice cannot be removed from its theoretical roots and contexts. It is, therefore, important for practitioners to be aware of different ways of thinking about children's development so as to enable them to effectively interpret and implement policy documents such as the Early Years Foundation Stage. Furthermore, it is also important as influential studies such as the Effective Provision of Preschool Education (EPPE) project (Sylva et al., 2003) have indicated that effective provision is characterised by both adult-initiated and child-initiated activities (Siraj-Blatchford and Sylva, 2004). As a result, practitioners may need to draw on and understand a number of different theories to enable them to support children's development effectively.

ACTIVITY *1*

Carry out some ethical observations of young children undertaking an activity, for example children playing in the home corner, and assess the contribution made to their play by the child, other people (including peers), cultural tools (for example equipment and language) and context.

ACTIVITY *2*

Critically examine the environment in your own home, a nursery setting, a childcare setting or a foundation stage unit and reflect on how culture is mediated through that environment. For example, this could include an examination of the materials provided and why they are provided, how time and materials are organised, who makes decisions and why, who undertakes particular tasks and what is expected of children in that environment.

ACTIVITY *3*

Examine an area of learning from the Early Years Foundation Stage, for example, problem solving, reasoning and numeracy and reflect on what you think is implied about the nature of development by the differences between the 'stages' of development as mapped out in that particular area of learning.

FURTHER READING

Anning, A, Cullen, J & Fleer, M (2009) *Early Childhood Education: Society and Culture*. London: Sage.

This book offers an in-depth examination of how sociocultural and historical approaches to development can be applied in the early childhood context.

Oates, J, Wood, C & Grayson, A (2005) *Psychological Development and Early Childhood*. Milton Keynes: The Open University.

An introduction to theories of development ranging from behaviourist theories to Vygotsky as well as other theories such as information processing and social learning theory.

Rogoff, B (2003) *The Cultural Nature of Human Development*. Oxford: Oxford University Press.

Rogoff focuses, in depth, on how human development is a cultural process and examines subjects such as child-rearing, gender roles and learning from a cultural perspective.

Smith, PK, Cowie, H, and Blades, M (2003) *Understanding Children's Development* (4th edn.) Oxford: Blackwell Publishing.

An introduction to children's development in general as well as the work of Piaget and Vygotsky in particular.

WEBSITES

See also the following websites/web pages for more on Watson, Piaget and Vygotsky:

www.marxists.org/archive/vygotsky

www.marxists.org/archive/vygotsky/works/comment/piaget.htm

www.piaget.org

www.thepsychfiles.com/2008/02/episode-47-the-little-albert-study-what-you-know-ismostly-wrong) – website has an interesting link to Watson's experiment on YouTube.

2 Active playing and learning

Rod Parker-Rees

Introduction

One of the tasks of Early Childhood Studies is to challenge the common assumption that later stages of development are necessarily more important and more interesting than what happens earlier in life. By paying careful attention to early accomplishments, which may be taken for granted because they are usually achieved so easily, we can show how these 'simple' first steps establish core patterns and habits which continue to inform our behaviour throughout our lives.

One of the commitments listed under the 'Learning and Development' theme in the Practice Guidance for the Early Years Foundation Stage (EYFS) (DCSF, 2008b) is 'Active Learning' and the aim of this chapter is to show why active, physical and imaginative engagement is essential for both play and learning. It is widely acknowledged that play provides an important mechanism for children's learning (Bruce, 1996; Moyles, 2005; Smith, 2010) but the motor activity of babies and young children is still often seen merely as preparation for the more serious, more cerebral, learning which will come later. We may acknowledge the need for young children to spend some time in the verdant but muddy foothills of 'Mount Piaget' but our ambition is always to move them on up towards the snow-capped summit and the cold, clear light of formal operational processes.

Movement, the controlled activity of our bodies, is at the core of what we are and what we do. Even a process as seemingly straightforward as perception requires co-ordinated motor activity. We do not passively receive sensory information, we take it in, actively steering our attention towards whatever attracts our interest. Our activity also extends beyond the immediate requirements of our situation into anticipatory exploration of our environment:

> *movement is the mechanism whereby an organism acquires information about its present and past environment*

> (Cotterill, 1998, p339)

We bustle about, poking our fingers into things, leaving no stone unturned and generally gathering up bits and pieces of information which might come in handy later. This active, exploratory probing of the environment is particularly visible in young children's play, down in the valleys around Mount Piaget, but it is also at the heart of all 'higher level' research activity.

In this chapter, I aim to examine the relationships between movement, play and learning, with a particular focus on the importance of self-initiated activity in learning at all levels. Beginning with a brief account of the place of movement and play in the 'wiring' and tuning of the brain, I will go on to explore ways in which the exuberant motor activity of infants allows them to develop patterned and increasingly purposeful movement schemes. I will consider how pretend play can help children to generalise and represent their experiences and enable them to make sense of the patterns, roles and rules which shape their social lives and constitute their culture. Finally, I will argue that thinking about how activity and play contribute to young children's learning may help us to understand more about how we learn as adults.

Your brain is just one part of your body

Given the widespread assumption that our identity is somehow located within our brain, it is surprising how little most of us know about how this part of our body works. Recent work in Artificial Intelligence (AI) (Clark, 2001; Pfeifer and Bongard, 2007) has begun to acknowledge the fact that intelligence cannot be understood simply in terms of how a central processing unit 'crunches' data from sensors in order to decide what motor responses are appropriate. Trying to understand how brains work without acknowledging their interactions with bodies is as futile as trying to understand how 'individuals' function without acknowledging that they are situated in families and communities. The following brief introduction will focus on the centrality, both in position and function, of those areas of the brain which are particularly involved in movement, touch and proprioception (awareness of the position and condition of all parts of the body).

The brain grows, a bit like the head of a cauliflower, up and out from its central stem at the top of the spinal cord. It is not surprising, then, that the oldest parts, both in evolutionary terms and in the development of an individual, will be found nearer to the base, with the latest innovations near the surface.

First, the brain stem, right at the top of the spinal cord, is involved in the control of autonomous body functions, such as breathing, heart-rate and temperature regulation, of which we are seldom consciously aware. The brain stem and the cerebellum, or 'little brain', which plays a very important part in co-ordinating movement, together make up what is often described as the 'reptilian' or 'acting' brain.

Above the reptilian brain comes the limbic system, a complex cluster of bits and pieces, described as the 'mammalian' or 'feeling' brain, which processes emotion states, 'drives', and survival functions, including the famous 'four Fs': fighting; feeding; fleeing and reproducing.

Finally we arrive at the brain's surface, the wrinkled, walnut-like, cerebral cortex, which co-ordinates and organises information from the body and the limbic system, enabling us to make sense, learn, represent, predict, and plan. The central strip of the cortex, the parietal lobe, is associated with movement, sense of position in space, proprioception and touch – the most primaeval and most obviously *embodied* forms of awareness. Behind this motor core are areas associated with the processing of other forms of sensory information, first taste and smell, then hearing, and, at the very back of the brain, occupying nearly half of the cortex (in terms of number of neurons), vision (Cotterill, 1998). The relative positioning of sensory areas reflects the progressive expansion of our perceptual world from the within-body world of proprioception to the body space defined by how far we can reach, then the larger space from which tastes and smells can reach us, then the limits of our hearing, the wider expanses opened up to us by vision and now, perhaps, the even greater realm of information available to us through books, the internet and other media.

Moving *forward* from the motor core also takes us from the realm of immediate, bodily experience, through areas which prepare and co-ordinate future motor activity (including specialised areas for directing our eyes and for controlling speech movements), to an area which is associated with more intangible, abstract kinds of activity – such as thought, anticipated action, speculation and planning. This foremost part of the brain, the frontal lobe, seems to have developed most recently in our evolution and is last to develop in the individual, with some areas not fully active until early adulthood (Carter, 2009).

In the cerebral cortex, then, the motor control area lies in the middle, between the areas which process information about the world beyond our body space (where we are) and the frontal areas which process information about our possible futures (where we want to be).

The cortex is also divided into two hemispheres, each of which plays a slightly different part in the processing of information. Much that is written about brain lateralisation and differences between 'left brain' and 'right brain' activities is grossly oversimplied because the two hemispheres are joined by a huge number of connections (the corpus callosum) and most brain processes involve simultaneous activity across a wide range of brain regions. Nevertheless there are real differences between the hemispheres (McGilchrist, 2009). The left hemisphere contains proportionally more grey matter, the dense network of branches, or dendrites, which connect neurons with their close neighbours, while the right has relatively more white matter, made up of myelinated axons, the neurons' 'output connections' which carry signals over longer distances. This physiological difference may explain why the left hemisphere is more involved in the processing of systems and discrimination of fine details while the right hemisphere is more specialised for processing multiple forms of information in a more holistic way. Guy Claxton (1994, p45) explains a possible benefit of brain lateralisation (the division into distinct hemispheres) by comparing the right hemisphere to a candle and the left to a torch with a tightly focused beam. Used together, a candle and a torch may be particularly effective since areas of possible interest picked out dimly by the candle can then be examined more closely with the torch. Lateralisation maximises the amount of information processing which can be achieved with given resources by teaming up general, intuitive awareness of what is significant or promising, with active, systematic exploration. The same strategy can be seen in the combination of fuzzy but extensive peripheral vision with a small, central area of the retina which is more densely packed with light sensitive cells; peripheral vision allows us to pick out what is worth looking at and to move our eyes so that we can bring it into this foveal area where we can see it much more clearly.

Tuning, pruning and plasticity

Although everyone's brain has many common structural features each is also, like other parts of our bodies, unique in the finer details of its organisation. Starting from a broadly similar set of specifications, our brains must tune themselves to the unique demands of a particular body living in a particular environment. From before birth and well into childhood, neurons grow a mass of branches, or dendrites, which allow each to connect with tens of thousands of others in a network of mind-boggling complexity. Young children's brains are much more densely interconnected than adults' brains because the tuning of this network is accomplished by selective reinforcement of some connections and pruning of others. For example, of many possible networks processing control of a particular muscle, some are quicker or more reliable so get used more frequently and are then reinforced while less effective alternatives fall into disuse and die off or are pruned out. This process can be compared with the development of paths and road networks across a landscape; the tracks which come to be used most often are developed into roads, or even motorways and railways, while unused paths become overgrown and eventually disappear. By actively exploring and adapting to feedback as connections are used, each person can develop a much more efficient network than could be produced by any genetic blueprint. This combination of generating a vast number of possible connections and then selecting what works best also ensures that the brain is highly adaptable or 'plastic'; if a pathway is damaged or obstructed, 'traffic' can be diverted to alternative routes.

Activity, play and brain development

There is a striking correlation between the size of an animal's brain, relative to its body size, and the extent to which it will engage in play activities – animals with bigger brains play more (Iwaniuk et al., 2001). Animals with proportionally bigger brains are generally better able to adapt their behaviour to changes in their environment. Simpler animals, like insects and reptiles, have to rely on hard-wired or instinctive responses, which may serve them very well (cockroaches may have better survival prospects than we have), but animals with more elaborate brains can learn how to move, act and react, and play seems to be a particularly effective strategy for this kind of learning.

Play involves exuberant movements (think of gambolling lambs, puppies or kittens) which combine elements of different kinds of mammalian brain activities (feeding, aggression, reproduction) and which allow animals to experiment with what they are able to do with their bodies. The fact that animals expend high levels of energy in play suggests that it must have significant survival value. The levels of energy devoted to the repetitive, exploratory and adventurous movements seen in play may be justified by the training this provides in patterns of correspondence between muscle activity and the resulting effects on how the body moves. How far do I jump if I put this much effort in? What happens if one leg pushes harder than the other? The motor 'cause and effect' patterns learned and reinforced in this play activity are gradually built into a 'virtual body' in the cerebellum, the 'little brain' which, across a wide range of species, reaches a peak of synapse formation (making connections between neurons) just as this play activity begins (Bekoff and Byers, 1998; Lewis and Barton, 2004).

As the range of possible movements is explored in play, it is mapped in the neural networks of the cerebellum and, like an explorer's charts, this map can then be used to plan the fine details of muscle activity required to achieve future actions, even those which have never been tried before.

Try poking your left index finger into your right ear, passing your arm behind your head. You are unlikely to have had prior experience of this set of movements but your cerebellum's internal model can still work out exactly what each muscle must do to produce a smooth, precise movement.

Unlike an explorer's maps, however, the cerebellum's virtual movement model can also make allowance for different starting positions, levels of muscle tiredness, stiffness, balance, uneven ground and a whole host of other complicating factors (Noë, 2004).

Every time the movement model is used it is also updated, refined and, if necessary, corrected as information from the motor cortex about the results of movement is compared with what was intended or expected. The mental model, map or theory stored in the cerebellum is thus able to work in tandem with the exploratory processes in the cortex; the cerebellum can deal with the fine details of *how* movements will be executed, freeing up the cortex to focus on *what* movements are needed.

The cerebellum also plays a crucial role in allowing us to tell the difference between changes in our perceptual world which result from our own activity, for example changes in our visual field when we move our eyes, and changes which have nothing to do with what we are doing, such as changes in our visual field when something moves in front of us (Prinz, 2005 in Parker-Rees, 2007a). It can be very important to tell the difference between what we are doing and what is being done *to* us. Consider the difference between how it feels if a) you run your fingers lightly along your leg or b) you receive exactly the same sensory information from your leg but without having touched your leg yourself! This is why you cannot tickle yourself; your cerebellum knows exactly what your fingers are up to, so the sensation they produce is boringly predictable (Blakemore et al., 2000).

The ability to co-ordinate awareness of what you are doing with awareness of how this affects your perceptual world is much more important than these rather frivolous examples may suggest. By mapping our own activity and feeding awareness of this into our processing of sensory information we are able to construct a highly sophisticated mental model of our environment which is infinitely more useful than the information which would be available to a passive receiver of environmental inputs (see Activity 1 at the end of this chapter) (Blakeslee and Blakeslee, 2007).

The playful exploration of patterns in the relationships between what we do and what we perceive is fundamental to what Piaget (1952; 1954; 1962) described as the sensorimotor stage of development. Largely through careful observation of his own children, Laurent and Jacqueline, Piaget identified a sequence of stages through which babies passed as they learn to control their active engagement with the world around them. Each 'stage' allows infants to construct elements, or schemes, which are combined and co-ordinated in the next stage. This 'stage model' of development offers a useful, simplified framework for understanding how activity can become increasingly co-ordinated, skilful and purposeful but it is important to remember that the clarity of any theory or model can only be achieved by systematically smoothing out, or choosing not to be distracted by, the tangles of individual variation which complicate the picture whenever one moves in for a closer look.

Thelen and Smith (1994) have shown, for example, how the task of developing control over reaching may be quite different for different babies. Gabriel, a very active, flappy, baby, had to learn how to damp down his arm movements if he was to exercise sufficient control to bring his hand into contact with a desired object. Hannah, on the other hand, though alert and socially responsive, was much less physically active and her task was to rouse her arm to life. Thelen and Smith make the very important point that the appearance of patterns in development, such as Piaget's sub-stages, may have more to do with the level of detail at which we observe than with the existence of organising structures at work in individual babies:

> *Hannah's problem was different from Gabriel's, but it was also the same. She, like Gabriel, had to adjust the energy or forces moving her arm – in her case to make her arm sufficiently stiff or forceful to lift it off her lap. … Their solutions were discovered in relation to their own situations, carved out of their individual landscapes, and not prefigured by a synergy known ahead by the brain or the genes.*

> (Thelen and Smith, 1994, p260)

The tidying-up inherent in any 'ages and stages' model of development can be criticised, but this sort of simplification is an essential part of all theory building or mapping of experience. The selective reinforcement of certain patterns of neural connection resulting from repeated experience is perhaps the most primitive form of this mapping. The precise details of each experience are 'smoothed out' as a more generalised, and more generally useful, pattern or scheme emerges. A brief review of Piaget's account of the sub-stages of sensorimotor development may help to show how babies learn to discover and explore patterns in their own activity (for more detailed accounts see Keenan, 2002, pp121–25, Smith et al., 2003, pp393–8 or Doherty and Hughes, 2009, pp261–3).

1. Reflexive schemes: 0–1 month

Piaget used the word 'scheme' to refer to a pattern of physical or mental action which could be repeated in different contexts. The first schemes, Piaget argued, are reflexive – automatic responses to stimuli (e.g. 'rooting' or turning to suck an object when touched with it on the cheek, or grasping when touched on the palm). As babies suck and grasp different objects, their sucking and grasping schemes are extended and differentiated and their world is organised into distinct kinds of experience; grasping a handful of hair is both like and unlike grasping a finger or a handful of cloth.

2. Primary circular reactions: 1–4 months

Circular reactions are patterns of movement which the baby is able to control and reproduce. After accidentally bringing a hand up to her face and sucking her fingers, a discovery which may well have been made in the womb, she eventually learns how to *make* her fingers move to her mouth. The combination of motor commands needed to move her arm, hand and mouth is developed into a motor scheme which is consolidated and generalised by frequent repetition, enjoyment and playfulness. Babies really appear to delight in the 'joy of being a cause' (Cooley, 1902, p196) as they find that they are able to affect their sensory experience in predictable ways by controlling their movement. Babies can now respond differently to different stimuli (e.g. to a nipple, a teat or a finger) because different stimuli 'trigger' different motor schemes.

3. Secondary circular reactions: 4–9 months

When babies learn to sit up, their attention moves out beyond the bounds of their own bodies to objects within reach of their new means of exploration; their hands. A chance discovery that an object can be made to do something interesting (rattle, squeak, roll etc.) leads to deliberate attempts to repeat the action. Movements are now performed not just for their own sake but also in order to make things happen. Actions can also be combined, producing more co-ordinated activity (the rattle is grasped *and* shaken). The special activity prompted by different objects may provide the first form of non-verbal categorisation (*this* is the thing I rattle, *that* is the thing I cuddle). Elinor Goldschmied's work with 'treasure baskets' (Goldschmied and Hughes, 1986), offering sitting infants baskets of varied and attractive objects to manipulate and explore, recognises the developmental importance of this interaction between the infant's body and a wide range of different kinds of object.

4. Co-ordination of secondary circular reactions: 9–12 months

From about eight or nine months of age, as most babies are beginning to crawl, they are also learning to combine earlier action patterns in novel ways (e.g. combining a scheme for moving an object with a scheme for grasping another which the baby wants). Action now looks much more purposeful as the cerebellum's virtual body map is well developed and movement is smoother and more automatic, allowing the now mobile infant to focus more on the goals generated in her cortex than on what she must *do* to achieve them (as an experienced driver changes gear without needing to think about the separate movements involved). The organisation of fluid, multi-dimensional activity into a linear sequence of planned steps, the action equivalent of combining words into sentences, greatly expands the baby's movement repertoire and may also provide foundations for the development of language which soon follows (Bridgeman, 1992).

5. Tertiary circular reactions: 12–18 months

As babies take to their legs and become toddlers their worlds continue to expand in many different ways. This is when infants really become 'little scientists' or little explorers, deliberately and playfully varying their actions in order to find out what will happen. Where secondary circular reactions were rather serious, goal-directed, affairs, which occupied all of the infant's attention, tertiary circular reactions are more experimental and exploratory, as toddlers are free to pay more attention to the effects of their activity both on the physical world and on other people.

6. Invention of new means through mental combinations: from about 18 months

By the time they reach the age of about 18 months, children are increasingly able to escape from the limitations of the immediate 'here and now'. The use of words or signs to label objects, events and intentions marks the beginning of an ability to represent ideas internally, and the ability to pretend shows that toddlers can hold in mind both what they are *really* doing and what they are *pretending* to do (Perner, 1991). They can now imitate not only what is happening in front of them but also something that happened earlier and elsewhere. Mental models enable toddlers to envisage or imagine what they *might* do, to explore possible courses of action without actually having to move, and they expand their perceived world back into the past and forward into the future, just as learning to walk and learning to talk expand their spatial and cultural worlds.

Working things out and playing things in

It is important to remember that babies do not have to work their way through sensori-motor development unaided and alone; even before they are born, babies are surrounded by culturally mediated information emerging from the social activity of people around them. By separating out aspects of their world for special attention in pretend play, children are able to develop their understanding of what objects and events *mean*, not only to themselves but also to other people. When children pretend, and especially when they engage with others in social pretend play, their attention is focused less on the mechanics of their actions than on the *significance* of what they are doing.

Pretend play enables children to loosen the ties between the specific motor details of their own activity and their increasingly sophisticated awareness of concepts which can be shared with others. When a child first pretends, for example, to drink from an empty cup, her movements may be very similar to those she would use if she were really drinking. By *pretending* to drink, she loosens these movements from their previous functional scheme and at the same time begins to loosen the concept of 'drinking' from the movements normally associated with it. Once 'drinking' has been freed from its motor scheme it can be used more playfully, offering a cup to a doll or teddy and eventually having a doll bring a cup to her own lips. What was once a specific set of motor instructions for *my* body now becomes a generalised 'type' of movement which *any* body can perform.

Early imitation and pretend play is highly dependent on contextual details. Two and three year old children seem to need the prompt provided by familiar sensory stimuli to fire up patterns of behaviour. So a two or three year old will pretend to talk on a real phone, or on a realistic toy telephone but the external sensory input offered by these play props becomes less necessary as the child's internal representation of 'talking on the telephone' is strengthened – a four year old will chat happily to anything remotely resembling a telephone, a wooden brick, perhaps, or a banana, or even to a phone which is present only in imagination.

The ability to conjure up mental representations of objects, events and ideas in the absence of any of the sensory stimuli formerly or normally associated with them is clearly an essential requirement for the development of imagination. It is also both a fundamental requirement for the symbolic forms of representation on which language depends and a product of language use; the word 'cup' does not make us think of cups because it resembles cups we have known and used but rather because we have learned that this is the noise people around us use when they are talking about cups.

Lev Vygotsky (1968, p6) observed that 'The world of experience must be greatly simplified and generalised before it can be translated into symbols' and common features of children's play (repetition, fragmentation, exaggeration, rearrangement) seem to help children to take their experiences apart and reduce the bits to core concepts which are free from the contextual complexities of specific instances, as a map is free from the distracting complexities which are present in an aerial photograph. This allows children to 'go beyond the information given' (Bruner, 1966), to experiment with recombinations of bits of what they know and thereby to escape from the world of 'here and now' (direct sensory information) into a world of imagination in which anything can happen 'beyond the map'.

In Piaget's account of the stages of children's play (Piaget, 1962), sensorimotor play is followed by symbolic play, in which language is increasingly important and, much later, when children reach the age of six or seven, by games with rules. For Piaget 'games with rules' are games with a pre-specified and finite set of rules, such as might be printed in a set of instructions, but for Vygotsky (1978b) children's play is controlled by rather different rules. For Vygotsky, rules are much more like the patterns children notice in their active exploration of their world, particularly the habitual patterns of behaviour which can be found in what people tend to do 'as a rule'. Vygotsky noted that although children's pretend play may appear free and unconstrained, it is in fact even more bound by rules than is their ordinary activity. When a child decides to 'be a doctor', for example, she chooses to constrain her activity within the rules (the role) of what doctors can and can't do. Playful 'dressing up in rules' enables children to work out the significance of the conventions which shape people's behaviour. When groups of children play together there are additional opportunities for each to notice how the others perform their roles and to challenge and question interpretations which differ from their own. A personal concept of 'mum', for example, can be enriched by a wider awareness that 'mum' may mean something slightly different 'as a rule'; comparing our own mum with the general stereotype can help us to observe features which would otherwise be too familiar to be noticeable.

By voluntarily submitting their activity to the constraints imposed by social roles, children are able to explore aspects of their culture, much as adults are able to use the constraints of, for example, a musical score. A skilled musician can use the protected space defined by the score to explore personal meanings which can be expressed (and discovered) through nuances of interpretation (Parker-Rees, 1999).

Playfulness and interpretation of rules

Like maps and symbols, all forms of cultural rules are necessarily simplified and tidied up so that they can apply across a wide range of different contexts. A playful approach allows us to find our own ways to relate these public structures to the private, more complex networks of understanding which we have abstracted from our own experiences. Stig Broström (1997) has argued that teachers must be careful to prevent play from becoming 'a mechanical and narrow reproduction of reality', instead encouraging children to see it as:

a creative activity through which the child changes his or her surroundings, transforms knowledge and understanding, invents and creates new insights through experience.

(Broström, p20)

Adam Phillips (1998) has suggested that the way we experience our relationship with all forms of authority can be transformed by a playful willingness to 'dress up' in rules, to accept them as Vygotskian patterns of convention rather than as uniforms which deny the individuality of their wearers:

To treat an order, or any kind of rule or instruction, as merely suggestive – to turn it into something a little more to one's taste – is radically to revise the nature of authority (obedience would be merely fear of interpretation).

(Phillips, 1998, p87)

Although older children and adults may no longer need to explore their world by physically manipulating objects, they still need to take an active part in their engagement with new experiences, changing and transforming them in their words and in their thoughts until they turn them into something a little more to their own particular taste.

Borrowing and interpreting an existing framework

Tina Bruce (1996, p8) offers a useful four part framework for understanding the central, co-ordinating role of play in children's lives. With only very minor transformation, this framework can also be used to map the issues addressed in this chapter. Bruce's 'First-hand experience' acknowledges the importance of self-initiated activity and sensorimotor learning in the tuning of brain and body. Activity 1 (below) demonstrates the extent to which awareness of what we are doing increases our ability to extract information from our sensory input. Bruce's 'Representations' is focused on 'making products' but if it is expanded to also include internal representations (from co-ordinated networks of neurons to motor schemes, concepts, symbols, maps and words) it can represent the many ways in which the complexity of experience has to be simplified, generalised and 'diagrammed' if it is to inform future action. The repetition and variation of behaviour provided by play seem to be particularly effective devices for allowing children to discover (and represent) patterns in their experience. Bruce's 'Games: understanding rules' acknowledges the range of rule systems that children can explore in their play but I would prefer to retitle this section 'Rules and conventions' to focus more on the ways in which play enables children to explore the significance of social patterns and habits as they dress up in these rules and roles in their social pretend play. At the core of Bruce's framework lies play, the co-ordinating activity which brings together first hand experience, representations and rules. I am not sure that I would differentiate so clearly between activity, experience and play but playfulness does provide a powerful mechanism for establishing personally satisfying relationships between one's own direct actions on the world, one's ability to map or represent aspects of experience and one's awareness of the rules and structures which frame one's own and other people's behaviour.

If you have ever tried to find your way along a route which you have only previously travelled as a passenger, you will know how much more information your brain takes in, largely without your awareness, when you are in the driving seat. The active sensorimotor exploration of babies and the social exploration of older children show us how important activity is in early learning, but active engagement remains essential in learning at any age. To know about Bruce's mapping of the relationships between play, exploration, representation and rules is one thing but to understand it requires an active process of interpretation, of playing with it until one finds a way to fit it to one's own first-hand experiences. As Adam Phillips (1998, p6) has observed, 'the given is inert until it becomes the made'.

Issues for debate

Is there a role for playfulness in professional activity? See Parker-Rees (1999), Maclure (2006) and Manning-Morton (2006).

ACTIVITY 1

Working with a partner you should each prepare a 'touch puzzle' by cutting a simple shape (e.g. a capital letter or a geometric form such as a square or triangle) out of card (a cereal box is fine) and sticking this onto a larger square of card. Don't let your partner see the shape you have chosen! Now shut your eyes and hold out one hand, palm down, keeping your fingertips absolutely still while your partner moves his/her shape puzzle to and fro under them. You will probably find it very difficult to 'read' the shape using only the passive touch sensations this provides. If, however, your partner now holds the touch puzzle still and allows you (eyes still shut, of course) to run your fingers over the shape for yourself, you should find that an 'image' of the shape will quickly pop into your head as information from your cerebellum about the position and movement of your fingers is combined with information from nerve endings at your fingertips. Now do the decent thing and allow your partner to experience the difference too.

ACTIVITY 2

Begin to collect phrases and idioms which include the word 'play' and which are used to describe aspects of adults' behaviour, for example, 'playing the markets', 'he made a play for her', 'playing the fool' etc. Organising the phrases into categories according to different dichotomies (play/work, playful/planned, playful/serious etc.) may help you to unpick the range of meanings we ascribe to play.

ACTIVITY 3

Watch out for hidden movement metaphors in the language we use to talk about abstract ideas, for example, 'hold a belief', 'understand', 'follow the steps of an argument' etc. You may be surprised by how dependent we are on movement concepts when we try to explain intangible ideas. Many of the words we use to talk about ideas are borrowed from Latin or Greek and this makes it even easier to miss the movement metaphors they contain. To abstract was originally to pull out, complicated once meant 'with folds' and 'explain' meant 'flatten' or 'smooth out'.

FURTHER READING

Engel, SL (2005) *Real Kids: creating meaning in everyday life*. Cambridge, MA: Harvard University Press.

Engel argues that conventional approaches to studying children's development have tended to neglect the active part which children play in making sense of real social situations. She makes a strong case for more naturalistic studies of what children do in everyday contexts as well as laboratory studies to test researchers' hypotheses.

Fogel, A (2001) (4th ed) *Infancy: Infant, Family and Society*. Belmont, CA: Wadsworth/Thompson Learning.

A comprehensive introduction to research on very young children, with a series of linked movement activities to help readers to experience what it feels like to be a child at different stages of motor development.

3 Developing communication: enjoying the company of other people

Rod Parker-Rees

Introduction

The *Early Years Foundation Stage* (EYFS) (DCSF, 2008b) illustrates the potential for confusion when considering the role of communication in work with young children. The preamble to the Practice Guidance seems to adopt a 'postal' model of communication when it refers to 'successful *delivery*' of the EYFS (DCSF, 2008b, 1.6, p6) and urges practitioners to '*deliver* personalised learning, development and care' (DCSF, 2008b, 1.7, p6). According to this model, when someone decides to communicate an idea, they package it into words and deliver it, either in speech or writing, to someone else who unwraps the parcel of words to receive the message. This 'discrete state' model of communication (Fogel, 1997) can lead to the idea that we communicate information *to* other people, or even *at* them and it is particularly evident in the Area of Learning entitled 'Communication, Language and Literacy', which focuses almost exclusively on the development of language and literacy. But the EYFS also goes much further than any previous documentation in emphasising the importance of a much more inclusive, 'warm' model of communication. The Area of Learning entitled 'Personal, Social and Emotional Development' includes sections on 'Making Relationships' and 'Sense of Community' and one of the four overarching themes, Positive Relationships, reminds practitioners that 'children learn to be strong and independent from a base of loving and secure relationships with parents and/or a key person' (DCSF, 2008b, 1.5, p5). In this chapter I hope to show how, as is so often the case in Early Childhood Studies, examining how infants acquire and develop particular skills can help us to re-examine how *we* use these skills ourselves.

Any form of work with young children and their families requires highly developed communication skills: engaging with children who have only recently learned to speak, who cannot speak or who choose not to speak but also encouraging effective dialogue between colleagues, families and children. We need to be able to 'deliver clear messages' but one of the five key outcomes of the Children Act 2004 is that every child should have the support they need to 'Enjoy and Achieve' and we should also acknowledge the importance of enjoying the more playful, unpredictable flow of social conversation *with* children, parents and other adults.

Mapping communication

We all regularly engage in a huge range of different ways of communicating. Try going through a typical day in your mind, noting all the different forms of communication which you might experience, from touch, gesture and movement through various forms of speech to writing, texting, reading, responding to signs and labels and reacting to web pages or programmes on TV. When you have built up and developed this list, adding other, less everyday forms as they occur to you, you can try arranging these different kinds of communication in a spatial array, with the most intuitive, natural forms (like touch, facial expressions and body language) at the bottom and the most formally structured, rule-bound forms (like mathematical formulae, musical notation and other symbol systems which have to be learned) at the top. Working on this with one or two friends should generate some useful arguments about where particular forms should be placed and you will probably find that you need to unpick some of your categories; drawing, for example, could include doodling, plans and blueprints, diagrams and countless other forms of graphic communication. Where would you put dancing, choice of clothes or how you smell? We do, after all, choose our clothes, hairstyles and toiletries to give other people messages about who we are and how we are feeling.

When communication is mapped in this way it may be tempting to see development in terms of a progression from innate abilities to those which require formal and extensive training. You may also notice shifts in the qualities or 'feel' of communication as you work up the list: from intimate to public; from warm passion to cool reason; from involuntary and uncontrollable to deliberate and purposeful. You may also notice that the lower part of your map of communication is more crowded and that more of your communication is represented here than in the higher reaches, although we are so used to thinking only about the visible tip of this iceberg that you may not have captured everything that is going on beneath the surface. Touch, for example, is one of the most primitive forms of communication, appearing early both in phylogeny (development of the species) and ontogeny (development of the individual) but it is also one of the most powerful. Its influence is never displaced by later developing, more systematic languages, so even the coolest of formal operational thinkers will still respond strongly to a pat on the back, a hug or a shove.

Communication and concepts of development

Each person's understanding of child development is closely bound up with their concepts of childhood (see Chapter 11). If we think of development in terms of raising ourselves above our baser animal origins we will tend to value the civilised orderliness of formal, invented systems such as reading and writing, logic and mathematics. If, on the other hand, like many who choose to work with young children, we share Rousseau's romantic view of childhood, we are more likely to value the passion and intensity of more 'primary' forms of communication (Parker-Rees, 2007b), such as touch, eye contact and gesture, and to resist what we see as overzealous attempts to 'move children on'.

Development has often been compared with acquiring and assembling building blocks, an image which informs arguments about the need to provide firm foundations (QCA/

DfES, 2000; Fisher, 2002; DCSF, 2008b) to provide a secure base for later learning. But the 'foundations' analogy can imply that what children learn when they are very young is destined to be buried beneath the more visible 'above ground' parts of the building. I hope to show that early, social interactions are much more than just underpinnings for the construction of later, more civilised and educated forms of communication. These first ways of engaging with other people are primary not just because they are easiest to acquire but also because they continue to shape and influence all aspects of our adult lives. In all kinds of communication we need to acknowledge all levels of our engagement, so that we do not, for example, simply expect our colleagues to switch off their emotional concerns and 'leave their personal problems at the door' when they come to work.

Communication plays a central role in our development well before we are born. From conception we are immersed in an intimate, but by no means simple or straightforward, relationship with our mother. Foetal development involves social processes from the outset, including chemical and immunological conflicts as well as opportunities for the foetus to tune in to the mother's eating and sleeping patterns, to the structure of her speech and even to her favourite music and the signature tunes of TV programmes which she watches regularly (Hepper, 2003). As we grew inside our mother's womb, we had plenty of time to become accustomed to some of the patterns that shaped her life, so that we were born already attuned to her and able to 'sing along' in early forms of communication (Trevarthen, 2003).

At birth, our motor development lags considerably behind our sensory capabilities, ensuring that we enjoy the ideal context for refining and tuning our early awareness of patterns in the structure of our social world. Imagine how different the relationship between mother and child would be if the baby's development was fully precocial, like a foal or a lamb. If, within hours of birth, babies were already on their feet, gambolling and frisking around the house, there would be much less opportunity for mother and baby to study the details of each others' movements, expressions, sounds and rhythms.

Imitation

When Meltzoff and Moore (1977) recorded evidence of very young babies imitating facial expressions they were intrigued by this evidence of an innate ability to connect perceptual information with patterns of motor control. How can the newborn baby relate the still very blurry and indistinct visual image of a protruding tongue to the combinations of muscle actions required to make its own tongue stick out? And, no less puzzlingly, how might a baby benefit from this precocious ability to imitate facial expressions?

Later research has suggested that babies' brains are equipped, from birth, with 'mirror neurons' (Rizzolati et al., 1996), particular links in the fantastically complex web of neural connections which perform precisely this function, linking motor control with sensory perception so that simply observing someone else performing an action will stimulate the equivalent premotor activity in our own brain. You may have noticed that your hands get twitchy as you watch someone struggling with a tricky manipulation, such as a child trying to fit a piece into an inset puzzle or someone having difficulty opening a packet or container.

Imitation is much more than a simple, automatic process of 'monkey see, monkey do' (Hurley and Chater, 2005; Parker-Rees, 2007a). Other studies have shown that when we observe another person's facial expressions, our premotor response, triggered by our own mirror neurons, produces in us the emotional state that we have learned to associate with these expressions (Kugiumutzakis et al., 2005). When you see someone frown, the neurons associated with the earliest stages of producing a frown are stimulated in your own brain and this mirror response triggers a feeling of puzzlement or distress. On the other hand, seeing someone else smile or hearing other people laughing may be enough to lift your spirits – smile and the world smiles with you!

This built-in ability to empathise, to respond to other people's mental states by responding to their physical expressions, combined with plentiful opportunities to pay close attention to a caregiver's actions, expressions, and interactions, means that the human baby is well placed to develop intersubjectivity – the ability to make one's own intentions known and to recognise the interests and concerns of other people (Trevarthen, 1979).

After a couple of months of 'peripheral participation' (Lave and Wenger, 1991), observing others from the outside while recovering from the trauma of delivery (and allowing their mothers to recover), babies show the first clear signs of primary intersubjectivity (Trevarthen, 1979) when they begin to participate actively and intentionally in communicative exchanges. This is a very special time, not only in the development of the baby but also in the development of the bond between baby and a primary caregiver (usually, but not necessarily, the mother).

Communication and socialisation

On the spectrum of communication mentioned earlier, this primary intersubjectivity is clearly well down in the intuitive depths where communication is not so much about exchanging specific items of information as a form of communing which serves to establish and maintain relationships and which is enjoyed for its own sake. Robin Dunbar (1998) has argued that language developed out of the social grooming used by other apes to allow members of groups, literally, to 'keep in touch' with each other. As group sizes increased, possibly to provide greater protection from large predators, providing social strokes through physical contact would have become increasingly impractical and speech may have emerged as a more efficient alternative, allowing us to commune with up to three others at the same time. Gossip or 'idle chat' preserves this social function and most people would agree that the pleasure to be derived from this kind of interaction has very little to do with the topic of conversation. As in the intimate exchanges characteristic of primary intersubjectivity, the interaction is enjoyed for its own sake, as a way of maintaining and celebrating social contact and trust among a group of friends.

From very early on, babies are aware of a difference between people, who generally adjust their own behaviour in response to the baby's actions, and objects, which generally do not respond in this contingent way. In a study of babies' memory, Carolyn Rovee-Collier (Rovee-Collier and Hayne, 1987) tied a ribbon to babies' ankles, connecting them to a mobile suspended above their cots so that their kicking would cause the mobile to move. The babies were quick to notice the relationship between their movements and the movements of the mobile and appeared to be delighted by their ability to exercise control at a distance. What I find particularly interesting, however, is that the babies would often smile and coo at the mobile as they played, responding to its contingent response to their movements as they would respond to an interested human playmate.

This sensitivity to contingency has also been demonstrated in a series of studies by Cohn and Tronick (1987) in which babies' reactions to 'live' feedback from their mothers was compared with their response when their mothers adopted a 'still face', deliberately avoiding giving their babies any facial feedback. Three-month-old babies would often turn away from their mother's still face or show signs of distress. Murray and Trevarthen (1985) built on Cohn and Tronick's earlier studies, observing two-month-old babies' reactions to a live video link with their mothers, which meant that babies could see their mothers on a TV screen as their mothers responded to a closed-circuit TV image of them, preserving the real-time contingency of the interaction. Murray and Trevarthen then repeated the observations but this time with a delay which meant that the babies saw their mothers' reacting to what they had been doing 30 seconds previously. Even this short delay was enough to disrupt the babies' ability to sustain interaction and again some babies were clearly disturbed by their mothers' failure to respond properly to their efforts at communication. Further evidence of babies' sensitivity to the contingency of their communication partner's responses comes from studies of mothers who suffer from post-natal depression (Field, 2005). Depressed mothers are less likely to engage fully with their babies and, as a result, their babies may be less interested in initiating interaction with their mothers.

We may not be consciously aware of the ways in which we respond to other people when we engage in communication with them, indeed we may feel slightly uncomfortable about talking with people who seem to manage their responses to us a bit too deliberately – we don't like to feel we are being manipulated. Nevertheless, even when we communicate with young babies, our interactions are co-regulated (Fogel, 1997) or jointly and simultaneously 'steered' by *everyone* involved. In the early stages this co-regulation is not symmetrical, adults work quite hard to give babies what they want and babies have limited scope for returning the favour. Babies are, however, armed with a very effective tool for rewarding adults who take the trouble to engage with them in co-regulated, contingent interaction. The intentional smile, when skilfully deployed along with its partner, the furrowed brow and quivering lip, can entrap adults into devoting huge amounts of time to entertaining a baby.

The emotionally intense, highly empathetic gooiness of these early exchanges provides the ideal environment for advancing the baby's awareness of the social rules which shape interactions within a particular culture. The mirror neurons which provided a point of entry into other people's interests and concerns are now supplemented by what Rochat (2004, p267) has described as the *social mirror*:

> *Metaphorically speaking, the adult caretaker orients a mirror that is **magnifying** back to the infant an image of emotional expressions that are greatly exaggerated.*

Rochat argues that this exaggeration of the baby's expressions in the adult's responses helps to differentiate between the adult's 'ordinary' actions and those which intentionally reflect the baby's, much as 'motherese' or Infant Directed Speech (IDS) serves to differentiate between speech directed specifically towards the baby and (less interesting) speech for others. But what the adult offers is much more than a mirror, even a magnifying one. By tidying up the baby's actions, gestures, expressions and sounds and returning them in a form which follows the rules of social and cultural conventions, the adult is acting as the baby's *social editor*. A baby's first draft of a smile comes back in the form of a fluent (and exaggerated) social smile. Accidental sounds of early babbling are returned in the form of a sequence of phonemes, the common, public sounds of a particular language. Parents are keen to impute meaning to the sounds produced by their babies and it is no accident that the baby's first 'words', mama, papa, dada, have been adopted in almost every language as labels for their eager parents.

The process of social editing combines affirmation of the baby's contribution with a gentle induction into the patterns, rules and structures of conventional systems of communication. Babies are extraordinarily good at discovering patterns and distinctions in the relationships between their own actions and the changes in perceptual information which result from these actions (e.g. I shake *this* and I hear *that – see Chapter 2*). This intuitive gift for learning from experience allows the baby to extract information not only from what adults do and say but also from how they edit the baby's own actions – what is kept, what is left out and what is changed. As adults we do the same when we get to know others by unconsciously noting the ways in which they transform stories, anecdotes, and, most tellingly, accounts of other people's behaviour.

In a fascinating study of jazz, improvisational theatre, conversation and children's play, Sawyer (2001) has argued that one of the fundamental rules of improvisation, the 'yes, and …' rule, informs effective social interaction in each of these kinds of cultural activity. The 'yes, and …' rule requires that any contribution should be both acknowledged and built on, so that each participant contributes to the emergence of both a shared performance and a satisfying feeling of community. In interactions between babies and their parents, social editing operates in just this way, showing the baby that his contribution has been acknowledged but also adding something to it by returning it in a more culturally regulated form.

First-hand exploration

After several months of wallowing in this pure form of communication, at about the age of four months, babies tend to turn away from their adult partners, seeming to prefer active exploration of the physical world of manipulable objects to the indolent, lotus-eating luxury of primary intersubjectivity. By this age, babies are developing the muscle control and strength that will allow them to sit up, freeing their hands for exploration of the stuff around them. This development heralds a shift of focus, from a Vygotskian participation in social exchanges to a more Piagetian dedication to exploration and investigation. While social editing may be hugely beneficial for learning about cultural practices, it is less welcome when the focus is on empirical examination of one's physical environment, where what is needed is, quite literally, first-hand experience. In some cultures this transition is marked by turning the baby around to face out towards the world from its mother's lap, where before it had faced in towards her (Martini and Kirkpatrick, 1981). In

Western cultures, however, parents may experience a slight sense of loss as their cooing, gurgling partner starts to push them aside in favour of single-handed voyages of discovery. But if children are to take their place in the social processes of conversation they must acquire their own experiences so that they too can contribute (yes, and …) as well as listen and observe.

In the course of this exploratory period, infants begin to realise that they can influence other people's behaviour by indicating their own intentions. To begin with, gestures such as reaching and pointing may be features of the child's relationship with an object but, as the child notices that her actions can influence the behaviour of other people, the focus of her attention shifts to the person whose behaviour she is trying to control. Reaching for an object, especially if accompanied by appropriately plaintive noises to attract attention, may be enough to cause someone else to bring the object within one's reach and holding up one's arms may let someone else know that one wants to be picked up. Garcia (2002) and Acredolo et al. (2002) have explored ways of extending this natural vocabulary of gestural communication by using a form of hand-signing. When parents use 'baby sign' to support their interaction, babies as young as six months old can begin to develop a vocabulary of signs which they can use to let other people know what they want and to understand what people want from them. Many of the gestures used in baby signing resemble the actions they represent so, in Bruner's (1966) terms, they bridge the gap between enactive and iconic modes of representation and prepare the ground for the emergence of the symbolic representation required for language, where the connection between sounds and the ideas they represent is almost entirely arbitrary. Merlin Donald (1991) has argued that the evolution of the human mind involved a transition period, which he calls 'mimetic culture', when people were able to communicate deliberately through action, signing or mime. Donald argues that mimesis would have allowed early people to develop a shared culture of rituals, formalised patterns of movement, which would enable communities to share knowledge and, most importantly, to pass knowledge from one generation to the next. What seems to be important, both in baby signing and in this concept of a mimetic culture, is that certain kinds of action, signs, are given a special status, lifted out from the ordinary processes of dealing with the physical world of objects.

Noticing what others notice

From about the age of nine months, infants show signs of what Trevarthen and Hubley (1978) describe as secondary intersubjectivity. Where primary intersubjectivity was entirely contained within the interaction between the people involved (usually the baby and a parent) secondary intersubjectivity involves three-way relationships between the child, another person and an object or event to which *both* are paying attention. What seems to be particularly important about this 'relatedness triangle' (Hobson, 2002) is that the child can now pay attention to the *meanings* which adults attach to objects and events, including intentional communicative gestures such as signs and speech.

When children under the age of nine months are confronted by a surprising situation they will usually stare intently at whatever caused this surprise but children over nine months are more likely to look at a familiar adult, to read their reaction for clues about how this situation should be understood (Gauvain, 2001). This 'social referencing' provides immensely valuable access to the cultural worlds of other people. By communicating with others about objects and events, infants can not only learn about their environment, they can also learn about the meaning other people attach to aspects of their world; what is considered important, dangerous, disgusting, funny, rude, kind or cute. Towards the end of their first year, children are particularly interested in how adults react to what they do, actively exploring ways of using this knowledge. Once a child knows, for example, that approaching something dangerous or disgusting will provoke a strong response, this knowledge can be used very effectively to control an adult's attention. If your mum is pre-occupied, talking on the phone perhaps, and not offering as much attention as you need, all you have to do is toddle over to the bin and begin to rummage. The attention you get may not be exactly what you would like but it may be much better than no attention at all. What this example highlights is that what you *do* (rummaging in the bin) may be pretty insignificant in comparison to your communicative intentions – fiddling with a plug socket or pulling the cat's tail would probably do just as well. When children begin to use words and later phrases, sentences and stories, to communicate, it is as well to remember that what they are saying may be much less important than the levels of communication which lie beneath the surface of their words. When a parent cuddles up with a child to share a book the communication which they both enjoy is much richer than words and pictures could ever convey. The book provides a useful tool for sharing attention but what it contains is not as important as the communicative experiences with are associated with it.

Enjoying the company of other people

As you read the following account of what is involved in joint attention, try to relate it to your own experience of the kinds of social interaction which you most enjoy – chatting with friends over a drink or two, having a laugh or perhaps debating an issue about which you feel strongly:

> First, the social partners know that they are attending to something in common. Second, they monitor each other's attention to the target of mutual interest. And, third, they co-ordinate their individual efforts during the interaction using mutual attention as a guide. Interactions involving joint attention help children to learn much about the world around them, including things that are important to pay attention to and how these things are valued by others in their community. Because these interactions are set in the context of interpersonal relationships they are a rich and motivating setting for learning.

(Gauvain, 2001, pp86–87)

What do you learn, about yourself as well as about your friends, from these interactions and how does the emotional 'feel' of this kind of communication compare with situations which have been deliberately organised to support your learning?

How should an understanding of the social core of the early stages of communication affect the way we think about how we communicate as adults? After years of formal education, where communication often centres on a trade in information, we may have set up artificial distinctions between 'work communication' and 'play communication', between talking and writing to get things done quickly and efficiently and talking simply for the pleasure of other people's company. Nell Noddings has challenged this dissociation between work and play orientations in the context of school settings, arguing that we should be more concerned about children's social environments and less preoccupied with crude measures of how much knowledge they have accumulated:

> *Schools should become places in which teachers and students live together, talk to each other, reason together, take delight in each others' company. Like good parents, teachers should be concerned first and foremost with the kind of people their charges are becoming. My guess is that when schools focus on what really matters in life, the cognitive ends we are now striving toward in such painful and artificial ways will be met as natural culminations of the means we have wisely chosen.*

(Noddings, 1991, p161)

We should remember that all forms of communication are social processes grounded in the negotiation of *common*, shared understanding. Even the most detached transmission of information always requires the 'sender' to draw on assumptions about how the 'receiver' can be expected to respond. What will be too obvious to be worth mentioning? What will be familiar, interesting, challenging, confusing or irritating? Arriving at a common understanding is much easier in situations which can be co-regulated by all participants; where responses can be monitored and misunderstandings can be repaired almost before they happen. When this is not possible, when communicating with a child's family by means of an entry in a diary, a newsletter or notices and signs, for example, it is all the more important to draw on available knowledge about how a particular form of words might be (mis)construed. If we have taken time to get to know people we can tap into implicit, intuitive knowledge about how they can be expected to respond, allowing us to role-play communication in our heads. Time invested in 'idle' chat with children, colleagues and parents can allow us to get to know them (and let them get to know us), adding to the store of intuitive awareness which will inform our communication with them in the future. We do not feel the need to keep checklists of what we have learned about people in the course of friendly chat because we trust the automatic processes which allow us to sift out information about their personality, likes, dislikes and interests from the kinds of contributions they make (and don't make). Studying the earliest stages of communication may help us to think carefully about how traditionally cool professional discourses and practices can be warmed up if we are prepared to pay more attention to the human aspects of how we live and work in social communities; to enjoying as well as to achieving. Much of our thinking about education is grounded in a metaphor which represents learning as a hunt, the pursuit of knowledge, the acquisition of skills, but we also learn a great deal, especially about other people and their social relationships, by less purposeful, more intuitive 'picking up' of information as a by-product of social gatherings (Parker-Rees, 2010):

> *the main function of conversation is not to get things done but to improve the quality of experience.*

(Csikszentmihalyi,1992, p129)

Issues for debate

Is it possible for staff in group care settings to provide the levels of intimacy and familiarity which babies need if they are to engage in joyful, exuberant and playful interactions? See Biddulph (2006), Reddy and Trevarthen (2004) and Trevarthen (2004).

ACTIVITY 1

How much can video capture?

Make a short video recording of interaction between children under three years old (preferably under two) or between one child and an adult or older child. Make sure you obtain the parents' permission both to make the recording and to share it with a colleague. Two or three minutes will be enough but you will probably need to record much more in order to be able to pick out a short sample which is reasonably 'natural' (an adult encouraging a child to 'perform' will be less interesting). Watch the video carefully and try to record what is happening: a) as a transcript of what is said and b) with explanatory notes about gestures, body language, mood etc. to try to capture as much as possible of what was going on. Of course you cannot hope to capture exactly how the participants understood their interaction but you can try to explain what you felt (the difference between being there and just seeing the video). You may find it helpful to present both transcripts in parallel columns, one for each participant, so that you can show how their actions and speech overlap.

Share your observations with a colleague, as follows:

1. *Show your colleague just the bare transcript (no scene setting or explanations). How much sense can your colleague make of what is going on? Are they willing or able to comment on how the participants may have felt about their interaction?*

2. *Now play the video but minimise the window so that your colleague gets only the soundtrack. What additional information does this provide?*

3. *Now reveal all! Play the video with sound and pictures. How much is added to what your colleague was able to make of the soundtrack?*

4. *You could go on to give your colleague your full transcript (with explanatory notes) and talk about how you 'read' the interaction before playing the video one last time. How is our understanding of social interactions changed when we are able to tune in to contextual information?*

Now switch roles and see what you can make of your colleague's piece of video. This should help you to appreciate how much we rely on non-verbal channels of communication of which, in everyday life, we are scarcely aware. Be prepared to have your interpretation challenged and to challenge your colleague's interpretation of his/her piece of video. How could you determine whose interpretation best fits the limited perspective captured on video?

ACTIVITY 2

Looking below the surface

Develop the habit of standing back from different kinds of social interaction (lectures, discussions, gossip, arguments) to monitor what is being communicated. What do people express through the way they speak, what they emphasise, what they ignore, facial expressions, posture, etc. and how much of this is picked up by others? You may find that it is easier to note what you feel about what is going on and then try to work out what may have informed that feeling. Be warned that if your friends feel that you are analysing their interaction, they may object!

FURTHER READING

Carpendale, J I M and Lewis, C (2006). *How Children Develop Social Understanding*. Oxford: Blackwell.

This is an excellent review of research in child development, with a strong focus on children as social agents.

Tortora, S (2005) *The Dancing Dialogue: using the communicative power of movement with young children*. Baltimore, MD: Brookes Publishers.

Tortora explains her use of sympathetic movement to engage with children who cannot be reached through language.

Hoff, E and Shatz, M (eds) (2006) *Blackwell Handbook of Language Development*. Oxford: Blackwell Publishing.

This collection of chapters by experts in the field provides an excellent review of research into language development. One of the editors, Erika Hoff, has also produced a fourth edition of her comprehensive book Hoff, E (2009) *Language Development*. Andover: Wadsworth/Cengage.

4 Children's health and well-being: investing in the health of the nation

Norman Gabriel and Philip Selbie

Introduction

What do we mean by children being healthy and experiencing a good quality of life? And how can we better promote children's health and well-being? In this chapter we will first examine the dominant medical discourse of children's health and why it is important to look at some of the more holistic perspectives on children's health and well-being. We will apply a relational approach to understanding children's health, looking at the multi-dimensional aspects of children's health and well-being: an individual child is not a self-contained entity or unit, divided into separate compartments like 'mind' and body', 'reason' and 'feelings', but an integrated human being embedded within a structure of a particular society:

> There is no zero-point of the social relatedness of the individual, no 'beginning' or sharp break when he steps into society as if from outside as a being untouched by the network and then begins to link up with other human beings ... the individual always exists, on the most fundamental level, in relation to others, and this relation has a particular structure specific to his society.

> (Elias, 1991, p27)

Second, this relational view of well-being will also be related to the long-term dynamic aspects of social processes, especially the way we view the formation of the welfare state, which has usually been explained by factors such as social conflict within an individual state. We will argue that the organisation and structure of society is to a large extent determined by the intensity of the struggle between states. A crucial difference between inter-state and intra-state relations is the presence and the restrained use of the means of violence. At one level it is strictly forbidden to be violent and to kill people; at another, it is demanded as a duty to prepare for, and to use, violence in relations with other humans (Elias, 1987, p80).

We will then use Elias's relational perspective to illustrate how some of the major historical conflicts have influenced state policies on children's health in Britain: the Boer War (1899–1902), World War One (1914–1918) and World War Two (1939–1945) exposed weaknesses in the military strength of Britain as a world power and drew attention to the poor social and health environment in which children lived. Adults looked for a better future for their children and this influenced the way in which social reformers and politicians attempted to alleviate the worst aspects of these conditions. And lastly, we will critically review some of the major government policies on children's health that New Labour has introduced since coming to power in 1997.

The biomedical model of health

Fisher and Goodley (2007) refer to a linear medical discourse which gave rise to the bio-medical model of the nineteenth and twentieth centuries. This model emphasises medical interventions and tends to uphold professional hierarchies. With experts protected by the establishment of professional boundaries, narratives that did not contribute to the pursuit of scientific progress were usually discouraged in the 'delivery' of health care. The role of patients' own narratives was often reduced to a process of eliciting information regarding specific symptoms of disease or of abnormality (McLaughlin, 2005). The task of the doctor was to link these pieces of information into a definitive diagnosis that could be attributed to specific biological causes. This growing preoccupation with 'normality' led to the construction of illness as individual forms of pathology. In this process the medical profession came to exert almost complete jurisdiction over definitions of 'normality' and 'abnormality' (Lawrence, 1994).

A good example of how this medical discourse is used to assess children's health is the height and weight growth chart that was first introduced in the early twentieth century. It is still used today by doctors and health visitors to check a child's development and is currently being used to track obesity nationwide. Measurements are made of a child's height and weight at different points in time and these are then plotted against predetermined growth lines which define the boundaries of normality for low, medium and high growth rates. Although the chart's measurements are supposed to depict a child's unique development, the significance of this uniqueness is derived from comparison with the population as a whole. The 'normality' or 'abnormality' of each individual child is measured and within this, age is crucial, for it will determine which 'healthy' or 'pathological' height and weight trajectories are charted. For Burman (1994), these different development stages are used to ascribe different versions of childhood: clearly defined markers of normality are constructed, against which children are judged. Armstrong (1995) has also argued that this wide-scale surveying of the child population gradually began to define certain limits of normality for children's bodies – 'normality' for children had become firmly linked to a collective model of age-based change and development, inscribed upon the individual bodies and minds of 'the child' (James and James, 2004).

Holistic views on health and well-being

In 1948 The World Health Organisation defined health as 'a state of complete physical, mental and social well-being', not merely the absence of disease or infirmity. But what is the relation between 'physical', 'mental' and 'social' well-being? According to Smith and Morris (2005) health services in Britain often fail to see the child as the 'whole person' with developmental, physical, mental and social needs that are very different from those of an adult. However Casas (2000) is critical of this concept of 'developmental' needs or the related idea of fostering children's 'rights'. He argues that this leads to an approach that identifies 'risk factors' – circumstances where children may need professionals to intervene to address the disadvantages they face and to protect them from harm. Such 'risks' can become problems associated with individual children, rather than located within the structures of society. As an alternative, he suggests that the concept of 'quality of life' is useful in considering children's health because it refers to children's happiness and satisfaction with their lives. A key concept here is resilience: resilient children somehow manage to grow up healthy and happy despite major setbacks they may face in their childhoods (Stainton Rogers, 2004).

And what do we mean by 'well-being'? We can focus on either the constituents of well-being, for example, indices of health and welfare, or the determinants, for example, access to food and clean water and educational provision (Dasgupta and Weale, 1992). Stainton Rogers (2004) advocates a quality-of-life analysis that is much more holistic – which looks at children's experiences, circumstances, values and priorities as a whole, recognising that there can be considerable variation in what matters for individual children. For Pugh (2005) the promotion of wellness or well-being requires an ecological approach, one that is grounded in work with young children in their families, within the community and culture in which they are growing up. Roche (2001) also argues that we need to take into consideration the position of children, emphasising the development of children's abilities through participation in the processes that affect their own lives:

> *To have access to decent education and health services is a necessary condition for Quality of Life – but it may not be sufficient. Whilst it is obviously of fundamental importance to have access to such services, it does not address the issue of how those services are experienced and seen by all children. While the concept of quality of life retains its concern with the welfare of persons, it at the same time stresses the perspective of children and seeks to understand the way in which different children are affected by oppressive ideas and the uneven distribution of social resources.*

> (Roche, 2001, p82)

Dinham (2007, p183) suggests that 'the idea of well-being is generally helpful in providing us with a glimpse of something important: the basic conditions for happiness and fulfilment as a right. In addition, it is conceptually useful in drawing into direct relationship the social, psychological, *spiritual* and physical dimensions to which many discussions refer'. In 2007, a UNICEF report on child well-being in rich countries identified forty 'quality-of-life' indicators, measured across six dimensions of children's lives such as 'material well-being', 'health and safety', 'education', 'peer and family relationships', 'behaviours' and 'risks' and notably placed the UK at the bottom of an overall ranking of 21 countries (UNICEF, 2007a). The inclusion within the report of a dimension to children's lives entitled 'young people's own subjective sense of their own well-being' emphasises Roche's view that the views of children themselves must be taken into consideration if we are to gain a deeper insight into children's well-being today.

The 'Good Childhood Inquiry' (Layard and Dunn, 2009) also set out to gather the views of children and young people about what constitutes a 'good childhood'. This inquiry, based upon evidence from 5–17 year olds in areas of life deemed significant to them such as 'Family', 'Friends', 'Schooling' and 'Mental Health', drew upon contributions from over 35,000 people and set children at the heart of its remit: 'adults need to understand that children can form and express their views in coherent ways ... We must continue to promote participation as a right not a gift' (Layard and Dunn, p7). This report concludes that there are some valuable foundational elements that need to remain firmly in place to sustain a sense of well-being and hence a good childhood for a significant number of children in the UK today. Children themselves said what they want more than anything else is love and, if they are well cared for, then that is what they learn to give. The report comments that 'for this to happen, they need parents and teachers who are unselfish and from whom they learn the secret of harmonious living; putting human relationships above all else' (Layard and Dunn, p151).

We now want to move one step further by suggesting that good relationships and the concept of 'relatedness' are at the heart of studies conducted to find out more about children's understanding of well-being. Camfield and Tafere (2009, p123) concluded that the most important aspect of children's well-being in the international studies they reviewed was the quality of their relationships with others: 'in particular, well-being is dependent on whether children feel *valued and secure*, if they can depend on *good quality family relationships*, whether they enjoy *comfort and openness* in their relationships, and finally, if they feel *included and respected*.

Hay and Nye's (2006) research on the spirituality of children also observed high levels of perceptiveness in children's conversations about their relationships to themselves, other people, to the world as well as to the 'transcendent': relational consciousness 'is so deeply a part of being human that in one sense it merely requires someone to direct our attention for it to become obvious' (Hay and Nye, 2006, p154) .They argue that this potential to exercise compassion and concern for others, which would seem so significant to children in their relationships at home and within society, is based upon a spiritual dimension to life. Yet if we do not acknowledge and then nurture it as an important part of our 'being' then surely we will fail to support that which makes a significant contribution to our children's sense of 'being well'?

Hart (2003, p69) also suggests that children's ability to exercise concern for others is important evidence of the spiritual in their lives: 'developmental theorists typically tell us that children are self-centered and incapable of real empathy or compassion; they have not developed sufficiently to really put themselves in someone else's shoes'. Indeed, this is part of the more visible side to children's nature but children do not have to wait for adulthood to act unselfishly. 'Their openness allows them to experience deep interconnection with the world, and their compassion can arise very naturally' (Hart, 2003, p69).

Children are curious about finding meaning and being valued in their lives and this is important to them if they are to live well and experience a holistic sense of well-being. A child's sense of identity, of discovering answers to questions such as 'who am I?' is fundamental to the search for meaning and the development of a sense of self-esteem and personal well-being. If we are to value the 'whole child' and support the development of their relationships we should not ignore these issues in relation to their health and well-being. Dr Rod Mackenzie, our good friend and former colleague at the Rolle School of

Education in Exmouth, aptly summarised some of the important ways we can develop an integrated sense of well-being:

> *Disciplined practice should be rooted in creative traditions of activity, experience and inquiry. There should be integrated work of real quality in the arts, sciences and humanities, developing a sense of wonder towards the mystery of life and creation. This would be to sustain a sense of wonder toward the mystery of life in a secular age, whilst also connecting with older wisdom traditions. Both freedom and responsibility should be nurtured and a capacity to care for the self, others and the world.*

Investing in children's health

So far, we have considered some of the important experiential dimensions of children's health and well-being and what children themselves think about their own well-being. However, these concerns about children's well-being are intimately connected with large-scale investment by European states in the health of young children. In the latter half of the nineteenth and the early twentieth centuries, in an age of growing nationalism and imperialist wars, the health and fitness of the population became an important concern for different political establishments.

As Rose (1990, p121) writes:

> *In different ways, at different times, and by many different routes varying from one section of society to another, the health, welfare, and rearing of children has been linked in thought and practice to the destiny of the nation and the responsibilities of the state.*

To a large extent the destiny of the nation-state is determined by its relations with other states. This inter-state dynamic is a life-and-death struggle about the use or threat of the means of violence. When two survival units struggle for survival – whether it is about prestige or scarce resources – they are dependent on each other. This interdependence influences the character of the internal structure of society, which to a large extent is determined by the intensity of the struggle between states. The organisation of internal social structures can be explained only if one takes into account the compelling force that groups exert upon each other and their bilateral function for one another as enemies (Elias, 1978).

This struggle for survival and inter-state rivalry is part of a dynamic relationship with crucial unintended consequences for the health and well-being of children in different nation-states. In England, poor health among adult men was brought to light by the Boer War (1899–1902) when two out of five of those who volunteered to go to fight in South Africa were rejected because of poor physique (Cunningham, 2006). The level of recruitment and the poor performance of the British army were seen as an urgent national problem which was linked to the poor health of young children (Hendrick, 1994). And this was not solely a British concern – Heywood (2001) notes that in 1906 the medical expert Arthur Schlossman explained in a speech that tackling high infant mortality rates needed to be given a high priority since an increase in population would contribute to Germany's military strength, its labour force and its consumption. New statistical devices such as tables of infant mortality rates were introduced in response to government concerns to improve the health practices of the population by intervention in the private, domestic sphere:

> *The relationship between infant and mother ... rapidly became entangled in the web of analyses of domestic life ... the infant mortality rate became ... an important indicator of social well-being.*

(Armstrong, 1986, pp213–4)

Widespread ill-health, disability and early deaths among babies and children were reflected in the high infant mortality rate, which had risen since the 1880s (from 145 to 151 deaths under one year per 1000 live births, 1891–5) (Gorst, 1906). The decline in the birth rate, from 35.5 per 1000 of the population in 1871–5 to 29.3 in 1896–1900, was increasingly a concern for the British government, anxious about the defence and administration of the Empire (Dwork, 1987; Hendrick, 2003). The physical condition of the population was first raised by the Interdepartmental Committee on Physical Deterioration in 1904 and again in five further reports between 1910 and 1916. Such concerns led to the development of the Infant Welfare Movement with its emphasis on the physical aspects of child development and public health. At the heart of this movement was a network of voluntary facilities, clinics and welfare facilities whose main objective was to promote 'mothercraft', helping mothers to nurse their infant in their own homes. An initial visit from a woman doctor before birth was followed by visits from voluntary workers (Hendrick, 2003). This development of infant and maternity care continued during the First World War:

> *The European war has now given new emphasis to the importance of the child as a primary national asset. The future and strength of the nation unquestionably depend upon the vitality of the child, his health and development, and upon his education and equipment for citizenship.*

(Chief Medical Officer Report for 1917–18, xi, 99, p.vi, in Hendrick, 2003)

In 1914 the local government board offered grants to local authorities to cover expenditure for maternity and child welfare work, including salaries for health visitors (Dwork, 1987). The number of local authority health visitors increased from 600 in 1914 to 2577 in 1918 and the number of maternity and child welfare centres rose from 650 in 1915 to 1278 in 1918 (Hendrick, 1994). An important factor in this growing concern about mothers and babies was the fear of population decline following the death of huge numbers of men at the war front. The Maternity and Child Welfare Act of 1918 consolidated the rapid growth in infant welfare centres and it became compulsory for local authorities to establish these centres, thus confirming the Act's importance for public health policy.

World War Two and the National Health Service

A clear indication of the way in which World War Two focused attention on children's health can be seen in the large number of investigations carried out by the Ministry of Health and the Board of Education, with other government departments, to monitor the health of the population (Harris, 1995). Towards the end of 1940, for example, the Ministry of Food and the Ministry of Health initiated a regular programme of food monitoring to investigate changes in family diets (Bransby, 1946). The Board of Education conducted systematic surveys of changes in children's heights and weights and a large number of separate inquiries were undertaken into the effects of different forms of nutritional supplementation (see, for example, Magee, 1944).

The evacuation of children during the war also exposed the ineffectiveness of routine medical inspections conducted by the School Medical Service, bringing to light conditions that had existed among poor families across generations: uncleanliness, undernourishment, inadequate footwear and clothing. According to Hendrick (1994), the evacuation revealed the extent to which interwar housing schemes had failed to eradicate the slums and related problems such as overcrowding, lack of proper toilet and washing facilities and the presence of rats and other vermin. Significantly, it also raised concerns about the 'psychological health' of young children who were separated from their parents. The numbers of children whose parents were single, destitute or dead rose rapidly as fathers were killed in the war and mothers were drafted into work. Residential nurseries, designed to care for young children from the evacuation areas, became the catalyst for debates about the harmful effects of institutional care and the necessity of traditional family life. In its editorial entitled 'War in the nursery,' the *British Medical Journal* for January 1944 commented:

> *... in the years from two to five the battle between love and primitive impulses is at its height ... Destructive impulses let loose in the war may serve to fan the flame of aggression natural to the nursery age ... the Age of Resistance may thus be prolonged to adolescence or adult life in the form of bitterness, irresponsibility, or delinquency.*

(quoted in Riley, 1983, p1)

The experiences of World War Two – the evacuation of mothers and children, the retreat from Dunkirk and the shared horrors of the Blitz – brought about a fundamental change in attitudes towards social policy. It reinforced 'the war-warmed impulse of people for a more generous society' (Titmuss, 1950, 507–8) and facilitated the development of the welfare state. The social and welfare reforms introduced by the Labour government of 1945 brought significant financial and medical benefits to families, in recognition of the increasing demands placed upon their household budgets. These included a maternity grant for all married women and 13 weeks' maternity benefit for those who had been insured workers before pregnancy. Even more significantly, the new family allowance of five shillings a week, awarded for second and subsequent children, gave mothers some degree of financial independence. Under the new National Health Service, mothers were entitled to free antenatal and post-natal care, the right to be attended by a doctor or midwife at delivery and health visiting services during the first five years of a child's life (Davidoff et al., 1999).

Policies and initiatives for children's health and well-being

Since coming to power in 1997, the New Labour government has developed a number of key policies for the National Health Service that have affected the health and well-being of young children. The National Service Framework for Children, Young People and

Maternity Services (DoH, 2004a) is a 10-year programme intended to encourage long-term and sustained improvement in children's health by designing services around the needs of children. It set national standards for children's health and social care designed to 'promote high quality, child-centered services': these services are, for example, designed to promote physical health, mental health and emotional well-being by encouraging children to develop healthy lifestyles. More recently, the statutory introduction of the Early Years Foundation Stage (EYFS) into all early years settings, in September 2008, has heralded something of shift of emphasis in the aims of early years policy. Previous policy documents and non-statutory guidance had valued the importance of developing young children's personal, social and emotional development. However the EYFS demonstrates a much clearer commitment to the holistic health and well-being of young children. In the resource materials supporting the EYFS principle of 'A Unique Child', health is described as 'much more than having nutritious food and being free from illness'. Young children should be encouraged to 'lead healthy lifestyles,' and become 'physically, mentally, socially, emotionally, spiritually and environmentally healthy' (DCSF, 2008c, Effective Practice: Health and Well-being, p1). In *Every Child Matters* (DfES, 2003), five outcomes underpin the government's aim for every child, to be healthy, stay safe, enjoy and achieve, make a positive contribution and achieve economic well-being.

How can we begin to assess the effectiveness of these specific policies in enhancing children's health and well-being? Kurtz (2003) has suggested that it is difficult to relate changes to specific policies in the short term, and Axford et al. (2003) have argued that, for the most disadvantaged children, there needs to be more intensive provision, rather than low-level intervention. However, what is even more important is the extent to which children can be entrusted to take more informed decisions about a more healthy way to live. Within many of the initiatives and policy documents that have appeared since 1997, there is a clear commitment to seeking the views of children whose lives are affected by health service delivery – their participation is encouraged by *Learning to Listen: Core Principles for the Involvement of Children & Young People* (DCLG, 2001) and the *National Standards for the Provision of Children's Advocacy Services* (DoH, 2002). Hart (1997) has provided a very useful model for different degrees of participation by children in decision making, ranging from 'assigned but informed' decisions to those that are more child-initiated and shared with adults. He argues that only when children initiate an intervention and share decisions with adults are they then taken seriously at the level of political decision-making (see Chapter 9).

This form of participation is rare, since it requires adults who are attuned to the interests of children while current British government policy on child health is mainly based around investing in children as the next adult generation, rather than focusing on their current concerns and well-being (James and James, 2004). Despite the apparent inability of policymakers to seriously entertain such an idea there are certain initiatives that offer an alternative perspective. 'Child-to-Child' is an important attempt to empower children by promoting their participation in efforts to improve their health and well-being, developing their life skills and taking action, with the support of adults to promote health in their communities (Child-to-Child, 2010). The Child-to-Child Trust was formally established in 1987 and works in over 70 countries through both local partners and large international organisations such as UNICEF and UNESCO. UK based Child-to-Child activities began in schools in Northumberland and Durham local education authority areas in 2002. Children are encouraged to take action about their own health and the health of the local community as well as gaining an awareness of global health issues through links to a school in the developing world.

Conclusion

This chapter began by reviewing some of the attempts by medical practitioners to discover biological causes for some of the major diseases that affect children's lives. But the dominant biomedical model developed by the medical establishment not only created false divisions between children's 'minds' and 'bodies', but helped to establish measurement criteria by which children's development could be determined as 'normal' or 'abnormal' and thus subjected to professional and state control. The logic of individual measurement creates an impression that well-being ultimately resides within the individual person: the modern health user is required to be the responsible agent who exercises self-mastery. This notion of the empowered consumer appears to place the burden entirely onto the individual.

The development of New Labour policies in relation to 'normal' and 'healthy' are also framed within a contractual model of individualised relationships and universal 'standards' (Fisher and Goodley, 2007). National services and standards, based upon children's need for good food, positive adult–child relationships and opportunities for physical activity are supposed to be implemented by a more highly trained and multi-agency workforce of early years professionals. These standards are designed to 'drive up' and improve the long-term health prospects of children. What is surely of most concern is that many national initiatives and policies are still too 'instrumental', narrowly focused on improving outcomes by intervening in the lives of children and their families. An important distinction should be drawn between understanding well-being in terms of *how* children experience their lives compared with the instrumentalist view that emphasises *what* children should know and the skills they should possess. In working with children, it is important to consider whether our own practices are informed by a holistic view of health and well-being or whether they are to a significant extent influenced by a perspective based on assessing outcomes. The 2007 UNICEF report and the Good Childhood Inquiry are timely warnings that children have very different perceptions of their own health and well-being compared to the materialistic values so dominant in some of the richest nations of the world today (UNICEF, 2007a; Layard and Dunn, 2009).

A reconsideration of children's health also needs to be placed within the historical development of the relations between modern nation-states and the attempts by their governments to introduce welfare policies to improve the health of young children. We have suggested that in the nineteenth and twentieth centuries these policies were to some extent influenced by concerns that arose from the unintended consequences of wars, especially the First and Second World Wars. New groups of professionals – doctors, nurses, health visitors – were increasingly trained by the state to focus on the causes of the poor 'physical' and 'psychological' health of children, implementing policies that would help to ameliorate the worst aspects of their conditions. These policies have been further developed through national institutions like the NHS and more recently by New Labour in an attempt to intervene positively in the health and well-being of young children.

Keeping children healthy should not just be a matter of government investment that helps to prevent the onset of illness, but should be related to the quality of their life with other children and adults. We need to move beyond a one-dimensional concept of children's health towards a more 'holistic' concept of children's well-being, one that is based on the development of good relationships. Being healthy and being well is a relational process that involves living in happy and productive relationships. Children's positive experiences of well-being need to be nurtured and sustained in communities:

> *Today it is still somewhat difficult to convey the depth of the dependence of people on each other. That the meaning of everything a person does lies in what she or he means to others, not only to those now alive but also to coming generations, that he or she is dependent on the continuation of human society through generations, is certainly one of the most fundamental of human mutual dependences, those of future on past, of past on future, human beings.*

> *(Elias, 1985, p33)*

ACTIVITY *1*

Outline some of the major factors that affected your own well-being as a child. How might you begin to determine those which were the most important to you as an adult? To what extent have these perceptions influenced the ways in which you try to enhance the well-being of children, parents and colleagues?

FURTHER READING

Brancaccio, MT (2000) Educational Hyperactivity: the Historical Emergence of a Concept, *Intercultural Education*, 11 (2), 165–78.

This is an excellent article that discusses the way that unruly behaviour among schoolchildren became pathologised by scientific experts.

Hall, D and Elliman, D (2004) *Health for all Children*. (4th ed). Oxford: Oxford University Press.

An accessible book that emphasises the importance of health promotion for children and incorporates some of the recent government initiatives on children's heath.

Part 2

Working with children: extending opportunites for participation

5 Observing children

Jenny Willan

Introduction

The Statutory Framework for the Early Years Foundation Stage (DCSF, 2008a, p16) asserts that 'Ongoing assessment is an integral part of the learning and development process. Providers must ensure that practitioners are observing children and responding appropriately to help them make progress from birth towards the early learning goals'. This chapter looks at some of the issues around our day-to-day observations of young children to show there is much more to observing children than ticking boxes in a developmental checklist. Professionals involved with children – social workers, carers, parents, doctors, speech therapists, teachers – all make use of observation to gather evidence to make informed decisions about working with the children in their care. For early childhood studies students, learning to become competent observers is crucial. Close observation of children helps to link theory and practice and provides a base from which to challenge current theories and orthodoxies about children's development, behaviour and needs. Part of learning to be a good observer involves learning to stand back, to suspend judgement, to watch and above all to listen. Children have views of their own and part of any professional observation or assessment should be, whenever possible, to hear and take account of the child's own evaluation of the situation.

This chapter shows how observing children is a dynamic undertaking conducted within a context of continuous change – children change, situations change, observers change and theories change.

Ethnography and the role of the participant observer

Ethnography is the name given to a mode of study originally developed by anthropologists to study tribes and groups (Mead, 1934). At its simplest, it is an approach that records, analyses and interprets all significant details of a social structure or situation in order to understand something about the beliefs and behaviours of the group under scrutiny. Generally, the key feature of an ethnographic study is that the researcher takes the role of *participant observer* – acting alongside the other members of the group in as natural a way as possible. Ethnography takes account of the 'insider' perspective of the members of the group and examines the social structures and power structures that constrain and define their actions. In an early years setting, it can be a very useful approach – for example it might be used to find out how the adoption of a new routine affects different children in the group or it could be equally useful in discovering the dynamics amongst a team of adult practitioners. The ethnographic researcher respects all the different voices in the situation and tries to faithfully record the views expressed. At the same time, she tries to keep in mind the myriad contextual details which constrain the roles and behaviours and attitudes of all the participants (including her own).

The importance of context

We encounter children in a variety of contexts and each context will have an influence on the way we see them. Bronfenbrenner (1979) imagines the child living within a series of interconnected contexts. He distinguishes between the *microsystem* of the immediate environment of family or classroom; the *mesosystem*, which links home and school; the *exosystem*, which links the child to the outside worlds, for example the parents' working day; and the *macrosystem* of the larger social and political policies which determines the society in which the child lives. All of these affect children to a greater or lesser degree and influence the way they engage with their world.

We live in a complex web of interrelated dimensions – physical dimensions of time and space, social dimensions of status and place, emotional dimensions of self and others, cognitive dimensions of knowing and not knowing. All these dimensions are subtly and constantly shifting. It is our responsibility as observers of children to be aware of the situational features, including our own presence, appearance and language, which might cause them to behave in one way rather than another: 'The emphasis on the whole and on connections within and across systems can be very useful as one seeks to understand children in context' (Graue and Walsh, 1998, p48).

The Department of Health suggests a framework for gathering and analysing information about children and their families (see Figure 5.1). This framework provides a useful checklist for studying the child in context.

Figure 5.1 *The assessment framework (DoH, 2000, p17)*

There are general aspects of context to consider in all observations – time, place, gender, age, physical surroundings, relationship with the observer, emotional state of the child, the kind of activity through which the observation takes place. There are also specific contextual features related to particular observations. For instance, a study of the linguistic development of a group of three-year-olds would mean something very different if the children were the offspring of refugee immigrants rather than the children of native-speaking professionals. It would be essential to set each group in context if we wanted to understand anything meaningful about our observations.

Context can alter what the observer sees. For instance, a social worker may describe a child as quiet and withdrawn, while a parent describes him as noisy and boisterous. We can imagine a child who is an elective mute in adult company but the life and soul of the party with friends. We can contrast the four-year-old in Piaget's experimental situation who appears to be at a 'pre-operational' stage with the four-year-old in Margaret Donaldson's more relaxed setting who appears to be at a 'concrete operational' stage. What about the child required to give evidence of abuse – will he give the same evidence in the court video as he gave to his sister in the kitchen? Context can be a defining feature of behaviour and when we are observing children we need to search for all the significant features of the context that might have some bearing on what we are observing.

Values and beliefs in observational studies

Observation is something we all do throughout our daily lives but it is not as straightforward as it might seem – we all have a tendency to see what we are looking for and to look for what we already know. We need to be aware of our own perspective and to learn to take into account the perspectives of others. We often talk and think as if we believe that we 'know' what sort of person someone is, as if their character is set. Yet we have all had the experience of finding ourselves and others changing and adapting according to changing contexts.

In order to make the most honest observations and evaluations that we can, we need to take our own beliefs into account. We need to look inside ourselves with a clear and critical gaze to tease out the links between who we are and the judgements we make. As Bruner wrote (Bruner et al., 1956, p10) – in the days before feminist sensitivities about language came to the fore!:

> *The categories in terms of which man sorts out and responds to the world around him reflect deeply the culture into which he is born. The language, the way of life, the religion and science of a people; all of these mold the way in which a man experiences the events out of which his own history is fashioned. In this sense, his personal history comes to reflect the traditions and thought-ways of his culture, for the events that make it up are filtered through the categorical systems he has learned.*

This examination of self requires effort and will on the part of the observer. Many of the beliefs and assumptions we hold are deeply rooted in the person and in the culture and in the language and have been gradually laid down within each of us since childhood. Others are an expression of the *zeitgeist* – a general feeling in the air that seems to be current, common sense, the accepted view. Common sense and personal belief can both be poor underpinnings for professional judgement. Sometimes we need to define our terms with a fine degree of precision. What does it mean to talk about observing a child interacting with her 'teenage mother' in a mother and baby clinic? Do we mean the mother is aged 19 or below? Should we distinguish between unmarried and married teenage mothers? Should we distinguish between mothers who have chosen to be pregnant and mothers who have fallen pregnant by accident? What about teenage mothers in stable relationships? Teenage mothers in supportive families? Teenage mothers with educational aspirations? All of these contextual differences will have a bearing on the way we interpret our observations of 'teenage mothers' and this in turn will have an impact on the way we interpret the interactions between mother and child.

Consider the following questions.

- Are there some children we like more than others? Do we judge the children we like less harshly than the children we don't like?

- When we see a child playing alone, do we see a child who is a *loner*, a child who is *rejected*, a child who is *self-sufficient* or do we see a *rugged individualist*?

- When someone tells us a child comes from the *leafy suburbs* or from *a run-down council estate*, what effect does that have on our view of the child's potential?

- How do we feel when someone tells a child 'Act your age!'?

- Are we more understanding with children who are the friends of our own children than with children who are strangers to us?

These are the sorts of question that challenge habitual ways of thinking and confront underlying beliefs and values. When we are dealing with children, we have a moral duty to question our assumptions and values about childhood. Knowing the context of our own beliefs and values is a starting point for understanding the points of view of the adults and children around us.

Examining expectations about childhood

The way we were expected to behave as children can have long-term effects on the way that we, as adults, expect the children around us to behave. New parents, for instance, often discover that they are at odds with one another over their expectations about childhood. At the least it can be a source of intense irritation; at worst, it can be a cause of inconsistent parenting and major conflict. Parents may first discover a disjunction in their attitudes when they try to plan their first proper family Christmas or Diwali or Hannukah:

- 'we weren't allowed to open our big present until after lunch!'

- 'we always had to go to church/ temple/ synagogue'.

They may discover it when they hear themselves saying the words their parents said to them:

- 'no TV until after lunch!'

- 'no sweets between meals'

- 'when I was your age...'.

People who have a role in children's lives need to address the issues in their own childhood to try to uncover the links between what they were expected to do by their own parents and how they complied with or subverted that expectation. Different people respond differently to the experience of being a child. For instance, in childhood we were all controlled for our own good by a concerned adult. For some it felt like strong love and bred a sense of security. For others it felt like being thwarted and bred a sense of frustration with authority. For others it provided an example of how to behave once they had grown big enough and powerful enough. Some children enjoy being children; others feel their lack of power keenly and are impatient for childhood to end; others are unhappy or lonely; some feel diminished by the expectations of the adults around them; most feel a mixture of all these emotions.

Everyone has an echo of a childhood past which affects their attitudes to children in the present. Whatever your experience of childhood, you need to take into account the expectations that you have internalised when you are observing and reflecting on the children in your care. You may not have to abandon all your beliefs – but you will have to provide yourself with sound reasons for holding them. This can be a mind-expanding experience – as Socrates said, 'The unexamined life is not worth living!'

Observations and emotions

Observing children is not a neutral process. As we have seen, values, beliefs and expectations are all involved. So too are emotions. Both child and observer come with their own load of emotional baggage. The child being observed or assessed has feelings; so do the parents and carers and educators around him/her – and so of course does the observer. It is important to be aware of the emotional dimension of the observational context and to try to take it into account as part of the whole assessment process.

Not all emotions are easy to express in words. Much of our understanding of others is based on a reading of body language – a gesture, a flicker of the eyes, a facial expression, a stance, a way of moving, a tone of voice. Most children learn to respond to body language before and alongside spoken language and much of our understanding as adults involves reading the hidden messages behind words from the contextual cues provided by the speaker. But it is easy to get it wrong! Knowing the derivation of our own emotional reactions can alert us to our tendency to misapply them in certain situations. Take the sniff, for instance. In some families it denotes derision. In other families it merely indicates a runny nose. Some people have a powerful emotional reaction to the sniff; others barely register it!

Awareness of children's body language and of our own body language and its effects on the children we are observing is important. Some children such as those with visual or hearing impairment or non-verbal learning disorders or autistic spectrum disorders may learn body cues more slowly than their peers and may have difficulty in 'reading' the people around them and reproducing the relevant body language themselves. This can make communication and social relationships problematic and can skew our observations of what is going on.

We sometimes hear exasperated adults say 'Look at me when I'm talking to you!' They may be reading lack of eye contact as defiance or avoidance. But it may be related to something else. Boys are popularly reported to make less eye contact than girls. Some children, particularly those on the autistic spectrum, find eye contact painful (Diamond, 2002). Others avoid eye contact when they feel threatened. Others may avoid it when they feel shy and ill at ease. Work by Doherty-Sneddon (2003, 2004) on gaze aversion shows that young children (and adults) may need to break eye contact when they need to access internal representations, because the information from eye contact is too compelling (dazzling) to allow children to access the much dimmer images they are able to conjure up in their own minds such as memories, concepts, imagined scenarios.

As an observer or assessor, our role may be perceived as judgemental and this may set up a reaction in the child under scrutiny. We ourselves may react at an emotional level to the child under observation. To be fair in our observations, we need to take into account our own emotional context and that of the child.

Observation and language

As observers and writers of observational studies and reports, we have a duty to confront the way we employ our language. In communicating our observations to others we will need to choose our words carefully. This will be a particular concern to those of you who may find yourselves, in the wake of the Laming (2003) recommendations for multi-agency working, negotiating with parents and/or colleagues from other disciplines about referral reports in connection with a child.

Sometimes the purpose of observing children is to come to an assessment or evaluation – of their situation, of their understanding, of their ability, of their behaviour. As a consequence, we may have to categorise them in some way. The words we use can be powerful and emotive – they may even be damaging. Slotting people into tidy boxes, labelling them, summing them up in a few chosen words makes report writing quicker but it may not be helpful. Positive labels may help some children (not all), negative ones help no one. Labels are quick shorthand ways of summarising, but too often they can become substitutes for more sophisticated understandings. There may be equal opportunity issues. If interpretations seem to be based on stereotypical assumptions around sex, special needs, ethnicity, culture or class, then they must be challenged.

Where observational reports are passed around among colleagues and concerned professionals, they can quickly generate set responses and prejudice the way children are seen by others (Billington, 2006). They may even contribute to a self-fulfilling prophesy when readers of the report adopt a corresponding mindset towards a child. We can ameliorate some of the difficulties inherent in articulating our observations by checking them with the child or a carer or a colleague where this is appropriate. Through our exploration of differences in interpretation, we may come to discern our own values and attitudes and recognise how they affect the way we work. In order to become competent observers, we need to explore, acknowledge and confront our own values, beliefs, emotions and language. Testing our observations against another person's helps us refine our ideas and encourages us to be more objective and to stay alert to our duty of maintaining high standards of fairness.

Examining research perspectives

When we study children, we start from a particular perspective, a theory that underpins the way we ask our questions. This perspective is sometimes referred to as our *paradigm* (Kuhn, 1970). The dominant or *hegemonic* paradigm within which we conduct our study of children can affect the way we impose a pattern or interpretation on what we observe. For example, in 1948 Esther Bick pioneered a system of infant observation at the Tavistock Clinic. The close observation of neonates and infants was a compulsory part of the training for child psychotherapists. Student psychotherapists observed the interaction between mothers and fathers and their newborn babies and continued their observations at weekly intervals for a year. In the observation below, the student psychotherapist is trying to understand the baby's emotions during feeding. Because of the particular psychoanalytic paradigm through which he views the incident, he attaches a very particular significance to the way a baby is sucking – first at his mother's breast and then on his fist:

Observation at 12 weeks

Oliver sucked vigorously at the breast then lay motionless. He jerked his head away from the nipple as if he had forgotten that he had it in his mouth. The jerking hurt the mother and she jokingly said that if he did it again she would give him a 'big cup and a straw'. After feeding, Oliver grabbed one fist with the other and vigorously sucked on his knuckle.

Perhaps nipple and mouth were not felt to be separate, in that he may not have attributed a separate existence to the breast but felt it to be part of himself. Sucking on his knuckle may be evidence that he felt he possessed something like the nipple available whenever he wanted. This related to the devastating rage precipitated when Oliver woke up to find mother not there. Then, despite sucking his knuckle, fingers, and other parts of his body, he could not satisfy himself. It seemed hard for him to tolerate a space or the idea that he was dependent on something outside himself or the thought that he did not possess everything that mother had.

(Miller et al., 1989, p180)

The way we view children influences the way we study them, and the way we study them influences the observations we make. The inferences we draw from our own observations are subject to a kind of metaphorical framing, depending on our own particular paradigm as observer.

Doing observations

The early years workforce tends to be multi-professional (play workers, teachers, social workers, medical staff, police welfare officers) and multidisciplinary (education, sociology, psychology, medicine). To address these multiple perspectives, the Common Assessment Framework (CAF) has been introduced to enable professionals in all areas of child work to communicate effectively with one another about children of particular concern (for a discussion about the Common Assessment Framework see Billington, 2006). Students of early childhood, whatever their professional aspirations or discipline, are encouraged to learn techniques associated with systematically observing and studying young children.

There is a wealth of literature about observational techniques, some of which is listed in the further reading at the end of this chapter. There are many aspects of children's lives and development that might reward close observation and we have listed some of them below. This section provides a brief introduction to some of the study techniques students of early years might wish to use.

What to look at

All of the following provide fertile ground for observation – you can probably think of many more depending on your own professional interest. The 'look, listen and note' sections (pp24–114) of the Practice Guidance for the Early Years Foundation Stage (DCSF, 2008b) give lots of helpful pointers for what you might like to observe.

Physical development	Inside and outside play (use of space, boys and girls, preferences)
Communication skills	Gendered play
Emotional well-being	Activities (educational, play, imitative)
Intellectual abilities	Learning
Moral and spiritual development	Behaviour in different situations
Social relationships	Interaction in peer groups
Critical incidents (birth of a new baby, starting school, separating from a parent)	Interaction with parents
Comparisons of ages and stages	Interaction with different adults
Types of play (free play, directed play, solitary play, interactive play)	Special needs
	Special settings (hospital, sickroom, dentist, first day at nursery)
Patterns of play (play with materials, role play, imaginative play)	Special situations (tests, unfamiliar settings)

Ethics

Once you have decided what to observe, you need to run through a checklist of questions before proceeding to the next stage.

Do you need permission to observe?
Are there any risks?
Will your observation raise any ethical issues – anonymity or confidentiality perhaps?

How to be an observer

The observation style you adopt will depend on what aspects of a situation you want to observe. You need to think about how close you want to be to the children you are observing. Different styles suit different situations.

> When and where will you observe?
>
> Will you observe alone, with another adult, with a child, with a professional, with a parent?
>
> Will you observe one child or a group of children?
>
> Will you be part of the observation (participant observer) working alongside the child and involved in the activity or will you be a discreet observer at a distance?

Techniques for studying children

The next step is to choose an observation technique that fits your purpose – or be creative and come up with novel ways yourself. For example, observation with a child as co-observer is an area that is relatively untried and could be rewarding, raising new issues in the conduct of observations. Currently, there is an emphasis on listening to the child, and an acknowledgement that in the past assessments and evaluations have failed to take on board the views of children about their own predicament.

The following is a selection of tried-and-tested techniques – it is not an exhaustive list but it represents some of the most common approaches from the literature.

Narrative observation

This is a pencil-and-paper exercise providing field notes, a naturalistic record of the features that seem most significant to you at the time. Text message spelling can be useful. Examples might be to observe the arrival behaviour of a child at preschool or the interaction between a foster carer and child.

Focused or targeted observation

This is targeted on a particular child or activity. Sometimes we need to track a child to follow progress and development over a period of time. The Foundation Stage Profile (QCA, 2003a) produced by the Department for Education and Skills is a good example of one way of devising a target child observation. It provides a frame for constructing a comprehensive record of social, physical, emotional and cognitive development across a whole year. You may want to devise your own.

Duration and time sampling observations

These allow you to pick up on how long a particular behaviour or activity lasts or how frequently it occurs. For instance, you may have noticed that a child often seems to be staring into space, or that a mother rarely makes physical contact with her child. It could be useful to keep a record of the frequency and duration of each occurrence of the behaviour.

Interviews

There are three main types of interview – *structured*, *semi-structured* and *unstructured*. Structured interviews are verbally administered questionnaires based on the interviewer's predetermined areas of interest. They may prevent you from following up interesting leads but they are easy to analyse. Semi-structured interviews are based on predetermined questions but allow for follow-up discussion of significant points. Unstructured interviews are very flexible but may be difficult to control since the interviewer and interviewee bear equal responsibility for the direction of the talk.

Video, tape recording, photography

There are issues of permission, confidentiality and storage associated with electronic data recording. There are also plenty of opportunities for technical glitches! Managing the machinery at the same time as conducting interviews and observations can be rather difficult but recorded information can be a useful source for backing up field notes. There are some particular limitations of using recording equipment – clarity of sound recording, the narrow view obtained through a camera lens and the effects of self-consciousness on those recorded. But there are also possibilities not open to other forms of observation, such as replaying material to closely examine verbal and non-verbal interactions, or particular personality traits, or the roles played by individuals within a group.

Checking observations

Any study of children needs to be looked at 'from all sides round' – including, where appropriate, from the child's perspective. Part of the context, as we have seen, is the position and perspective of the professional doing the assessment. It can be difficult to reflect on one's own assumptions and expectations, difficult to step outside one's own views and knowledge and experience, to stand in the shoes of the child being observed.

In observation studies of children, it is advisable to collect data in as many different ways and from as many perspectives as possible. This is sometimes referred to as *triangulation*. Triangulation is a way of checking and cross-checking the validity and reliability of observations. There are several ways of doing this. Sometimes researchers use many data sources – child records, past reports, interviews with other significant adults; sometimes they ask several different people to make observations at the same time; sometimes they use several different methods to get at the same information – individual observation, group observations, interviews, video or audio recording. Using multiple sources allows you to check one source against another to provide richer data and a more reliable assessment.

A parent may be trying to get an infant to sleep through the night; a teacher may be having difficulty settling a child into a reception class; a social worker may be trying to decide whether a child would be better off leaving a difficult family situation – they would all need to be aware of the child, their own standpoint, the context and their own effect on the situation. Instead of saying, 'My child is a poor sleeper', the parent might need to think about feeding patterns and bedtime routines and their own expectations about sleep. Instead of writing a child off as clingy or difficult or shifting the blame to overprotective parents, the teacher might need to think about socialisation difficulties or a learning problem or her own behaviour towards the child. Instead of thinking in terms of problem families, the social worker might need to take into account the material circumstances of the family, what's happening all around them, the risks, the state of mind of the child and of course her own underlying assumptions about 'the best interests of the child'.

Whenever possible, a study or evaluation or assessment of a child should be done with the collaboration of a colleague. Collaboration allows the assessor to try out ideas, to have a sounding board, to listen to different views and responses. Working co-operatively provides support and alleviates the feelings of isolation and inadequacy that can well up where the responsibility for a decision weighs heavily. Collaborative consultation can also help to clarify issues and draw together ideas or suggest areas that need further thought. Whenever possible, always try to get a second opinion – your own may not be sufficient.

Conclusion

The EYFS profile is a good starting point for observing individual children and assessing their developmental needs. But it is not the whole story. Professionals should beware of being the outsider looking in and should remember that when we study children, we should try to stand in their shoes. We can't, of course, but we can provide ourselves with a more accurate picture if we refer to the contextual features operating around and within ourselves and the child under observation. This entails examining ourselves, hearing the child and taking into account the wider influences of family, culture and society.

ACTIVITY 1

With a colleague, choose one of the observation methods. Choose a child or group to observe. Obtain permission. Choose a focus that interests you. Now observe. Note down significant details of context, time and place of observation. Record anything that strikes you as significant in relation to your focus. Compare your observations – what was observed, what was said, what factors were most significant. Analyse what you have both written. Are there differences of emphasis? Is it possible to distinguish a particular paradigm at work? Comment on the significance of context, values, emotions and language in your two accounts.

FURTHER READING

For an interesting alternative veiw on the uses of observation try:

Billington, T (2006) *Working with Children*. London: Sage.

This book, written by an educational psychologist, explores the whole area of observation, assessment and report writing and questions the underlying assumptions made by professionals.

Clark, A and Moss, P (2006) *Listening to Young Children: the Mosaic Approach*. London: National Children's Bureau and Joseph Rowntree Foundation.

A simple and straightforward book which will give you lots of ideas for creative ways to observe, listen to and interact with young children.

Graue, ME and Walsh, DJ (1998) *Studying Children in Context: Theories, Methods and Ethics*. Thousand Oaks: Sage.

This book provides a theoretical underpinning for any work you might do in researching children, with chapters on the importance of context and the centrality of maintaining an ethical approach with your participants.

6 Providing an enabling environment

Philip Selbie and Karen Wickett

Introduction

One of the fascinating and unique aspects of working with babies and young children is that learning 'happens' and as it happens the learners become more engaged with their environment. At the same time they become more aware of themselves and their potential to discover and explore their surroundings. Learning appears to be a cyclical process; when observing very young children their natural curiosity to discover seems to indicate that learning is already 'energised', it feeds off itself and has the potential to continue indefinitely. The environment makes a significant contribution to this process and when the conditions are less than supportive, the quality of the process, if not the process itself, is threatened.

This chapter is partly about learning but more importantly it is about the 'places and spaces' in which this process takes place. Some of them are visible to us in the sense that we can see them, plan them and arrange them; however, we believe that some are not so clearly identifiable and so we will explore this idea further. We aim to highlight the significance and value of these places and spaces in supporting the learning process as well as encouraging practitioners to develop professionally at the same time.

The Early Years Foundation Stage (EYFS) identifies 'Enabling Environments' as one of its themes and suggests that practitioners are guided by the principle that 'the environment plays a key role in supporting and extending children's development and learning' (DCSF, 2008b: p5). Within these environments there should be opportunities for children and adults to foster relationships, to develop their thinking and ideas, to grow emotionally and spiritually, to contribute to the culture of the learning community and of course, to develop physically. The EYFS also states that 'the learning environment involves both the people and the space in which children develop and learn' (DCSF, 2008c: Effective Practice 3.3:1).

The learning environments practitioners encounter are as multifaceted, dynamic and evolving as the young children who inhabit them on their developing learning journeys. The recent Cambridge Primary Review (Alexander, 2010, p90) highlights the greater recognition that now exists 'of the inter-relatedness of the biological, social, emotional and intellectual aspects of children's psychological make-up and their dependence on the socio-cultural environment'. Children are very competent and capable learners, given the right linguistic and social environment. As the process of learning in the early years supports a child's progression from interdependence to independence, the environments where this learning happens play a considerable role in 'enabling the learner' or to put it another way, supporting the learner in 'being able'.

Enabling environments are the places and spaces where learning happens but of added importance is the contribution they can make to a young learner's developing awareness of him or herself as a competent individual. Allied to this view of the competent child is the recognition that learning begins first and foremost with the child or perhaps we should say 'within the child'. Learning is not something that can ever be done 'to the child' or 'for the child'; it is something that must surely be carefully revealed from within the child.

Starting with the child

Over forty years ago the Plowden report (CACE, 1967, p9) boldly declared that 'at the heart of the educational process lies the child' and championed the cause of play as a way of enabling the learning process for all children. Although there have been significant influences that have shaped early years practice in recent years, the principle of 'starting with the child' remains as powerful in guiding practice today as it did over forty years ago. All high quality learning begins by putting the learners at the centre and setting out to meet their needs.

The statutory introduction of the EYFS (DCSF, 2007a; 2008a-c) confirmed the growing interest by policymakers in the early months and years of learning and development. Echoing some of the spirit of the Plowden era, the EYFS has remained committed to keeping the child at the centre of the learning process. It also acknowledges the uniqueness of every young child and, most significantly, it recognises the status of babies as learners.

The EYFS also emphasises once more the importance of a play based approach when planning learning and it is important to note here the contribution that play makes to the environment as a place where powerful learning occurs. Young children messing about and having fun with practical objects has long been accepted as good practice in early years settings. Play makes a significant contribution to early learning and as Moyles (2005, p35) states, 'play is a means by which babies and young children explore their environment and the people that are special to them'. This idea is also a feature of the EYFS;

> *Play helps young children to be competent learners who can make connections and who can create and transform ideas and knowledge, because they are imaginative and expressive.*

> (DCSF, 2008c; Effective Practice 4.1, p2)

Whenever and wherever play is encouraged, babies and young children will be learning through exploration, at a practical level but also in self discovery. Learners will be discovering more about themselves and their own capabilities; as Friedrich Fröbel (1782–1852) stated long ago 'Play is the highest expression of human development in childhood for it alone is the free expression of what is in a child's soul' (Fletcher and Welton, 1912, p50).

The legacy of the early pioneers and the more recent introduction of government legislation that puts children and play at the heart of early learning is one thing but how do such aspirations become realised for young learners (see Chapter 13)? In addition, what relationship is there between policies on the one hand and the places and spaces that practitioners can utilise to ensure high quality, transformative learning experiences for children?

A principled approach

Most early years practitioners who work with or study babies and young children welcome the recognition by policymakers of the importance of the earliest years of a child's life and of the necessity to provide an enabling environment for them. However, there are challenges to overcome as the constant advice, intervention and expectations from government can be overwhelming at times. In order not to succumb to these external pressures practitioners should consider what they believe our youngest children might need in their earliest experiences in order to lead full and satisfying lives, not only in the future but also at the present time. As Nutbrown asks:

What sort of things might be good for them to do? What kinds of adults might be best suited to their needs and the ways in which they spend their time? These are important questions whatever our working context, culture or country.

(Abbott and Nutbrown, 2001, p112)

When making decisions which affect the learning environment, such as the type of resources to be provided or the role of the adult in children's learning, practitioners must be guided by their own principles. It is essential that practitioners understand and are able to articulate their principles for as Edgington (2004, p16) states 'teachers whose work is not underpinned by principles which they can back up with research evidence are less likely to be able to see a clear direction for the development of their practice'. Practitioners should be provided with opportunities to reflect on the decisions they make and to consider the principles that underpin their work.

Such a process will also support them in articulating their beliefs and their understanding of children as learners so they will be able to enter into dialogue with others and confidently explain their actions in a clear and informed manner. This is particularly important in times when increasing attention from policymakers can cause confusion for practitioners and result in them losing sight of their vision. The Cambridge Primary Review draws attention to this by stating early in its report that 'it is the principles by which productive teaching is underpinned which should first command teacher's attention' (Alexander, 2010, p7).

Competent learners

History has given us different images of the child as a learner, from Locke (1632–1704) who declared that adults played a crucial role in the learning process, to Rousseau (1712–1778) who claimed that children would develop naturally and that there should be minimal intervention by adults. Locke viewed the child's mind as blank or empty and in need of being filled, stating that: 'The senses at first let in particular ideas, and furnish the yet empty cabinet...' (Locke, 1824: para 146). On the other hand, Rousseau professed that children learn through experiences and exhorted adults to 'Give nature time to work before you take over her business, lest you interfere with her dealings' (Rousseau, 1762/1911, p71).

After the Second World War and as the new preschools of Reggio Emilia were beginning to develop, Loris Malaguzzi (1920–1994) stated that children are 'rich in potential, strong, powerful, competent and, most of all connected to adults and other children' (in Penn, 1997, p117). Those who let their principles guide their image of the child as a competent learner found a new opportunity to consider the interests of the children. One of the principles that guided Malaguzzi and his colleagues was that 'things about children and for children are only learned from children' (1998, p51). As the preschool buildings arose out of the desolation and empty destruction of the past, the future for the next generation was being built upon the needs of the present one.

There has been much debate in recent years about the concept of a child's 'readiness to learn' and we suggest that in some respects such a term has not always been helpful as while it is agreed that babies are born as 'competent learners' they are also born as 'motivated learners'. The two are interrelated and we may be distracted by the suggestion that children enter certain developmental periods when they are more ready to learn something than they were previously. As adults we can all too easily become preoccupied with what *we need* from the child rather than with what the *child needs* as an already competent learner.

Most recently, our view towards babies and young children as competent learners has been influenced by technology that has introduced us to new ways of examining the marvels of the brain. After it commences its lifelong, developmental journey in the womb a baby is born with a brain that contains most of the neurons or nerve cells it will ever have. This number will remain almost the same until around the age of 65 although a considerable amount of 'rewiring' of connections takes place after birth and especially in the early years. Babies who have already begun to make sense of their experiences in the womb are ready to make sense of their new world from the moment they are born and, as Gopnik et al. (1999, p142) state 'babies are born with powerful programs already booted up and ready to run'.

The Birth to Three Matters framework (DfES, 2002) built on this new understanding and recognised that babies were 'competent and capable' and this was developed further in the EYFS. The theme of the 'Unique Child' states that 'Every child is a competent learner from birth who can be resilient, capable, confident and self-assured' (DCSF, 2008b, p5). We might even ask whether babies, young children and, for that matter, adults are ever not predisposed to learn. Indeed, Gerhardt (2004, p18) states;

> Each little human organism is born a vibrating, pulsating symphony of different body rhythms and functions, which co-ordinate themselves through chemical and electrical messages.

More recently, neuroscientists have suggested that babies and adults have very similar mechanisms for learning. The Cambridge Primary Review (Alexander, 2010, p96) highlights the fact that 'the difference between children's and adults' learning, according to Goswami and Bryant (2007), is not the structure of their brains but their relative lack of experience, metacognition and self-regulation'.

Recognising the journey

All young learners have their own unique experiences (DCSF, 2007a; Fisher, 2008) which they bring to their setting and these experiences have shaped their understanding of themselves and of the world around them and will have enabled them to practise and develop skills. When planning the learning environment, practitioners need to take into account these unique journeys. Within the EYFS one of the commitments of the theme 'Enabling Environments' states that 'All planning starts with observing children in order to understand and consider their current interests, development and learning' (DCSF, 2007a, card 3.1). More recently practitioners have begun to gain a richer insight into a child's world by gathering documentation based upon such things as conversations, photographs, video, and children's drawings.

Margaret Carr developed *Learning Stories* (2001) as a framework to document children's learning. Practitioners record in writing what they see and photographs are used to support the writing. After the learning story is written it is analysed using five domains of learning dispositions; these are *Taking an Interest, Being Involved, Persisting with Difficulty, Expressing an Idea or a Feeling* and *Taking Responsibility*.

Carr claims that this process 'sharpens the focus on important features of children's learning' (Carr, 2001, p137) which then enables practitioners to listen to the children, have open minds and plan learning environments informed by the children's interests, development and learning. Therefore, 'they help practitioners to construct a learning community with shared values, and they extend that community out to the families' (Carr, 2001, p141). Including parents in this process of planning and assessing learning through discussion gives value to the culture of the home and the community as partners in the learning process. Not only does this approach recognise and value learning as a process but it also helps us 'to bring learning into view, so that it can be seen, reflected upon and discussed' (Luff, 2007, p192).

Dahlberg et al. (1999, p146) emphasise this when asserting that 'observation' is 'mainly about assessing whether a child is conforming to a set of standards' compared with 'documentation' which is 'mainly about what the child is capable of without a predetermined framework of expectations and norms'. Such an approach is a welcome break from some past practice which relied too heavily on narrow and often subjectively written practitioner observations in order to plan for the next steps in learning. Practitioners should actively make sense of observations in order to understand a child's preoccupations and consider the child as one who 'is active in their own development and is a person in their own right' (Abbott and Langston, 2005, p9).

In a sense we all have our own 'story' that informs who we are and how we respond to situations and, equally importantly, how we relate to the learning opportunities presented to us. This is no different for babies and young children and the EYFS recognises this when it states;

> The environments in which children grow up have a strong influence on what they do and can accomplish. These environments are made up of a multitude of different influences such as places, cultures and people that each child comes into contact with from day to day, month to month and year to year.

> (DCSF, 2008c: Effective Practice 3.2:1)

Having considered the centrality of the unique child, a principled approach and an informed view of the learner, we now turn our attention to asking where it is that these 'spaces for learning' exist and what are the different ways they support learning for babies and young children?

Enabling environments inside and outside

Whether it is in the womb before birth, in the home or in the garden, in the role play area or in the sandpit, a physical place is naturally where we can observe learning taking place. First hand sensory experiences which involve young children in doing practical things such as sitting or standing, looking or listening, talking or touching provide opportunities for learning to take place. In a literal sense learning happens in a physical space; it is located in a place *somewhere.*

Places such as these support the process of learning, sometimes with the involvement of an adult who may plan the resourcing, but on many occasions these places enable learning by virtue of their very nature. They are 'cradles for learning'; places which encourage the natural curiosity of young children to explore and discover the potential of the environment as well as the potential within themselves.

Maria Montessori (1870–1952) quickly recognised the powerful potential for learning that could be realised by matching a supportive environment to a strong disposition to learn. In her work with young children in the 'Casa dei Bambini' in Rome at the beginning of the twentieth century, Montessori recognised the power of the environment to both enable as well as hamper the learning of young children. She was astounded to observe that many schools were poorly equipped and not suitable for young children and so quickly set about 'having school equipment made proportionate to the size of the children that satisfied the need they had of moving about intelligently' (Montessori 1948/1967, p46).

Montessori believed in 'setting the child free' by removing obstacles to their natural desire for independence and mastery of their world both physically and intellectually. This was developed further as Montessori observed that the children she worked with were particularly attuned to a sense of order during the first two years of life. These early discoveries provided the foundation for the development of the Montessori Method which continues today to place emphasis on the physical environment and practical activities during the first six years of a child's life. Montessori referred to this as the period of the 'absorbent mind' which 'reflected her belief that children in this stage were engaged primarily in absorbing sensory perceptions and information from their environment' (Gutek, 2004, p50).

The importance of the outdoor space, and in particular the garden, was evident in the writings and practice of early pioneers such as Friedrich Fröbel in the nineteenth century and Margaret McMillan and Susan Isaacs in the twentieth century. McMillan believed that a healthy body was necessary for a healthy mind (Bilton, 2002, p26) and set up her first open air nursery in Deptford, London in 1914 arguing that 'the best classroom and the richest cupboard is roofed only by the sky' (in Ouvry, 2003, p5). As the twentieth century came to a close the use of the outdoors for early learning on a widespread scale received relatively little attention from practitioners who, for a variety of reasons, from poor funding to insufficient training, often failed to exploit the enormous potential of the nursery garden.

However, the use of the outdoors has regained greater recognition again following the introduction of the EYFS, as there is a clear recognition that 'outdoor play is central to young children's learning, possibly more to some children than others' (Bilton, 2002, pxii). Not long before the introduction of the EYFS, the 'Learning Outside the Classroom

Manifesto' (DfES, 2006c) set out the government's vision of enabling every young person to experience the world beyond the classroom as an essential part of their learning and personal development. One of the aims of the document was to support the potential for learning from direct experience coupled with the belief that *how* and *where* young children learn was as important as *what* they learn.

Within the EYFS, the outdoors is now valued as much as the indoors and therefore practitioners are encouraged to plan both outside and inside learning environments, so that children 'have the confidence to explore and learn in secure and safe, yet challenging, indoor and outdoor spaces' (DCSF, 2007a; card 3.3). The outdoor learning environment is no longer seen purely as a place for children to release excess energy while practitioners take a step back. Instead it is now recognised as a valued learning environment in itself, where children should be able to spend considerable time learning, developing, playing and exploring alongside involved practitioners. Just as practitioners observe and plan for children's learning inside, there is now an expectation that this practice will continue outdoors too. For example, if a child is observed enjoying making marks inside then they should also be able to make marks outside through the provision of paintbrushes and buckets of water or through encouragement to explore naturally occurring resources such as sticks and muddy puddles.

The outdoor environment adds a valuable dimension to the learning opportunities available to children and gives them direct first-hand opportunities to develop their learning independently as well as with others. Growing acknowledgement by practitioners of the potential for learning in the outdoor environment is helping to counter the public perception that many children today are deprived of healthy outdoor activity. In addition, it helps to underline the notion that conceptual boundaries between learning inside and learning outside may exist in the minds of some adults, but only in a small minority of children.

Enabling environments in the community

The 'Learning Outside the Classroom Manifesto' also stated that settings need to 'identify ways of encouraging parents, carers and the wider community in learning outside the classroom activities' (DfES, 2006a, p20). For instance a piece of research undertaken by one of the authors explored how to extend children's learning using the resources of the community. Practitioners had observed that a group of three-year-old boys were interested in motorbikes so they arranged to take them to a motorbike shop.

During the visit the boys took pictures of the motorbikes, helmets and other pieces of motorbike paraphernalia. They returned to the nursery and developed the storyline of their play by including what they had learned during the visit to the shop. Not only were practitioners making links with the community but they were also enhancing the boys' experiences with their families, as one father told a practitioner that he often took his son to the motorbike races. This child had instigated the motorbike theme with his friends. From these opportunities to make links between the setting, the community and home, the children gained some long term, deep learning experiences about themselves as learners and about their world. Their new learning was embedded in a context which made sense and which built on their existing understanding and experiences.

The EYFS encourages practitioners to recognise the wider context of a child's learning and development, for instance in their local community and home life, 'Working in partnership with other settings, other professionals and with individuals in the community supports children's progress towards the outcomes of *Every Child Matters*' (DCSF, 2007a: card 3.4). Beyond the immediate boundaries of the setting there are many opportunities, such as the one described, to extend children's learning and make connections between learning within the setting and in the community.

Environments as enabling places

We have identified some of the environments where learning happens and what those environments might look like and so it now remains to explore how environments 'enable' young children's learning. Learning in the outdoors will, by its very nature, provide more space and greater sensory stimulation and practitioners may use these features in order to support the learning process. The womb is another rich learning environment for the developing foetus and is one that naturally supports the learning process even before a baby is born. However, to what extent can some learning environments be more consciously arranged by practitioners and contribute more deliberately to the learning process?

Loris Malaguzzi is well known for his belief in the environment as the 'third educator'. This aptly describes the important role played by the environment in partnership with children and adults as they in turn co-discover learning in a way so crucial to the Reggio Emilia philosophy. Every Reggio school has a space known as the 'atelier' which might be described as a workshop or studio where children and adults discover and research their interests together. These studios are designed to engage children in skills and techniques; they are places where children master the skills needed to realise creative ideas and bring projects to life. Many individual classrooms also have an atelier, an environment which supports adults as they observe children investigating and expressing themselves as the learning process becomes visible and can be documented and shared with others. It is a feature of the Reggio philosophy that 'young children are encouraged to explore their environment and express themselves through all of their available expressive, communicative and cognitive languages' (Edwards et al., 1988, p7).

Whether it is purpose built or a carefully utilised space within a refurbished building, every Reggio school is designed with attention to detail and a creative use of light and colour. Each school has a central piazza designed for children and adults to meet and perform together while the space for eating together is generally at the heart of the school and close to the open plan area where food is prepared. There is a deliberately planned relationship between the function and beauty of the architectural spaces and the potential for learning in the children and adults that inhabit them. Bishop (in Nutbrown, 2006, p73) expresses this relationship well when he states;

> *The unique qualities of each building come not from the formal arrangement of parts but from the pragmatic relationship between person and place, detail and material, building and building, building and site.*

The contribution of the environment to enabling young children's learning is also a feature of Steiner Waldorf Kindergartens where emphasis is given to ensuring that the space in which children play is carefully arranged by the practitioner to maximise the interaction with the environment and thereby the child's learning. Early learning experiences will develop in a space that is conducive to child-initiated activities and Steiner practitioners recognise that 'everything which surrounds the child, both visible and invisible, has an impact on the child' (SWSF, 2008, p5). Young children use all their senses to gain an understanding of their worlds and their worlds exist within environments where resources, furniture and toys are made of natural materials such as wool, wood and stone. As the beauty of the environment is highly valued 'very careful consideration is therefore given to the detail of the quality of all aspects of the kindergarten environment to ensure that it is gentle to the eye, ear and all the senses' (SWSF, 2008, p3). As the very youngest children make the transition from home to school, Steiner practitioners seek to make the learning spaces as 'homely' as possible in order to ease the child's transition from one environment to another.

'Rhythm and repetition are crucial' (SWSF, 2008, p6) within these environments and the rhythms of the daily routine ensure the children feel secure and confident, as they know what will happen next. The children themselves determine the length of sessions and the repetition of activities and daily routines also supports a sense of security, allowing the children to revisit, practise and deepen their developing skills and learning. The benefits of the rhythms and repetitions of the day and the importance attributed to the learning environment are evident in the words of a Steiner practitioner below:

> It (the room) tells you when it's done... It just shines when everything is in its place and it sounds ridiculous I know.... but ... the room speaks. If something is out of place it jars... keeping the place clean and just the care of it, it speaks, it sings.

> (Drummond and Jenkinson, 2009, p8)

Steiner learning environments offer young children infinite opportunities to imagine and consider possibilities.

This contrasts with some learning environments that are characterised by a sense of 'visual busyness' and seem to reduce the learner to little more than a consumer of information rather than one that is curious and capable of contributing to the culture within the environment. Tarr (2004, p3) makes this point after encountering learning environments for young children filled with displays, mobiles and bright colours to the point where 'the mass of commercial stereotyped images silence the actual lived experiences of those individuals learning together'. Enabling learning environments should make a positive contribution to young children's learning although naturally it must be left to the informed and sensitive practitioner as to how this is done.

It is perhaps worth concluding this section with the words of the seventeenth century Moravian educational reformer Jan Amos Comenius (1592–1670) who recognised over three hundred years ago the significance of the learning environment when he wrote:

> The school itself should be a pleasant place, and attractive to the eye both within and without. Within, the room should be bright and clean, and its walls should be ornamented by pictures.

> (Comenius, 1657/1923, p131)

Relationships as enabling environments

When young children feel safe and know that there is someone nearby that they can depend upon, they quickly develop the self-confidence to attempt new challenges. They are prepared to take risks in their learning, they explore and experiment, relate well to others and becoming increasingly independent. The EYFS promotes the use of the 'key person' system as good practice in the early years and it is the work of the skilled practitioner to identify an individual child's needs and organise routines and a pattern to the day that will help the child predict what is likely to happen and when. In such environments, practitioners use not only the physical space and resources to enable learning but also the relational space that exists between themselves and the child, taking careful account of the child's well-being and in particular their emotional needs.

The EYFS emphasises this feature of the learning environment through the theme of 'positive relationships' where there is a clear emphasis on the need to value the human above the material resources that are more typically associated with the learning process:

> *Babies and young children are highly interested in people: they learn about the situations and things around them through their contact with significant people.*

> (DCSF, 2008c: Effective Practice 3.3:2)

There is a sense too in which a supportive environment which places a strong emphasis on the quality of relationships between practitioners and young children requires the adult to be available to the child at an emotional level. In other words, in the same way the adult is learning about the child, the child needs to be able to learn about and interact at an emotional level with the adult. According to Gerhardt (2004, p18) 'the baby is an interactive project not a self powered one'. This can be demanding for a key person who is supporting several young children's learning at the same time and so requires careful monitoring by setting managers. However, when warm, trusting and respectful relationships are able to flourish this leads to a powerful and enabling environment for learning.

Such an emphasis on relationships is a feature of the New Zealand early childhood curriculum *Te Whāriki* (Ministry of Education, 1996) which, like the EYFS, puts *Relationships* alongside the other broad principles of *Empowerment, Holistic Development* and *Family and Community*. Where it differs from the EYFS though is in the notion that 'children learn through responsive and *reciprocal* relationships between, people, places and things' (Ministry of Education, 1996). One of the unique features of the country's first bi-cultural curriculum is the emphasis on relationships and holistic development that reflects the Maori culture from which so much of its design and philosophy is drawn.

The title *Te Whāriki* implies 'a woven mat for all to stand on' and recognises that children learn in a holistic way, with many different views or 'threads' co-existing together. It is also worth noting here that early childhood settings in New Zealand are able to create their own curriculum by 'weaving' threads drawn from the four principles and in this way have flexibility to be responsive to the needs of young learners.

Such relationships need to be established but they also require nurture, development, enhancement and maintenance if babies and young children are to learn and develop to their fullest potential. Almost without question we value 'positive' relationships but how often do we stop to think about what such relationships create space *for* or, put another way, what might evolve or develop for both partners within a good relational environment? It might be a greater understanding of the other person and what they bring to the relationship; it might be a greater sense of 'unity' with the wider world or it might just be time to think together.

Anning and Edwards (2006, p60) note 'caring and reciprocal relationships are central to the co-construction of mind and this is markedly so throughout the early years of life'. Adults play a familiar role in the co-construction of meaning with young children; this might be conceived of as a collaborative journey towards, and the ultimate discovery of meaning. In the same way, two explorers might seek hidden treasure in a dark cave; one holds the map while the other holds the torch. The treasure might be likened to those outcomes or products of learning that are there to be 'found' once the environmental conditions are right. They are the recognisable frameworks of meaning that help us all to make sense of our world.

However, our understanding of the role of adults in an enabling environment can be taken a step further. If we are truly respectful of young children as 'powerful' as well as strong and competent learners we should be prepared to step back and let them show us their power as well as their competency. We must allow ourselves to be surprised by their abilities while at the same time we must let them lead us to meaning that exists in spaces that we may not be familiar with. Hyde (2008, p162) refers to these as 'spaces between the frameworks of meaning. These are enticing spaces. They are full of opportunity and choice'.

Hyde suggests that the role of the adult here is still one of a guide on a journey of discovery but one who accompanies children into such spaces and offers support in a much more passive sense. These spaces are important environments that adults need to facilitate for young children by providing times of quietness, stillness and reflection. Hyde (2008, p162) goes further by suggesting that these are spaces 'of possibility in so far as spiritual questing involves those who engage with it in search for authentic ways of being in the world and of relating with Other'. Young children are sensitive to the natural created world and they experience awe and wonder as well as responding to beauty and love. These experiences are often equated with a sense of the spiritual that can be mysterious or threatening to adults. We would argue that it is important that we allow children to nurture their own spirituality by being available to them in their quest to learn more of what it means to be human.

Conclusion

Within this chapter we have explored a variety of practices and learning environments for young children's learning from within and beyond England and the UK. These enabling environments have been informed by practitioners who recognise the complexity of providing for young children's learning and believe that the child is a unique competent learner. In addition, it is accepted that the practitioners are learning alongside the child; children are learning about their worlds and adults are learning about children as learners. This is work which requires high levels of skill and dedication from those who work with young children and care deeply about helping them to learn and develop as unique individuals.

There continues to be a vigorous debate about the necessity for a universal and standardised framework such as we now have in the EYFS. Not least, whether certain aspects of it deny children the opportunity to learn at a pace that takes full account of their individual needs. However there is much to celebrate; not least that within the EYFS the unique child is valued, play is promoted and practitioners are encouraged to put the child at the centre of planning for learning. The EYFS also states that 'the bedrock of enabling learning is to create an environment that is flexible and varied enough to respect and respond to individual needs' (DCSF, 2008c: Effective Practice 3.2:2).

Developing a genuinely enabling environment in the early years is not an easy task. It requires recognition not just by practitioners, but also by external agencies and policymakers, of the multifaceted nature of the term 'environment', as well as an appreciation of the complexity of the different forms that environments can take. It is therefore the responsibility of all those involved with the provision of enabling environments for babies and young children to be informed and up to date with current research and practice.

In addition, practitioners must have a reflective attitude towards their beliefs and principles in order to gain an insight into what guides decisions and develops their understanding of young learners. Policy and legislation must also be interpreted in a way that suits the needs of the children, families and communities with which practitioners work. Babies and young children now have a legal entitlement to be at the centre of the policies which guide those that care for and support their learning in the early years. Most important of all, they deserve rich and diverse learning environments which will enable them and develop their potential as competent, motivated and powerful learners.

ACTIVITY 1

Think of a place or an environment where you feel comfortable and relaxed and then let your thoughts wander freely.

Is it inside or outside? What are the colours, smells and sounds surrounding you?

How does this inform your thinking about creating a learning environment?

ACTIVITY 2

Reflect upon your own personal learning journey to date. Which experiences did you learn most from? What did you learn? Where did this learning take place? Who was there? What was their role during the experience?

Consider how these learning experiences shaped your principles and beliefs.

ACTIVITY 3

Case study

In the early 1990s a practitioner managed a day nursery based upon her belief that children learn best through play. In 1996 the government introduced the Desirable Learning Outcomes and Ofsted Inspections. Gradually the practitioner realised the setting was not providing the learning environment she wished and the practice was being compromised. Instead of long periods for children to play, they were expected to do more formal activities.

The practitioner returned to university to explore young children's learning further. Her studies gave her the opportunity to reflect and gain a deeper insight into her beliefs and attitudes about children's learning which had informed her principles. She found that her studies not only supported her principles with evidence from reading and research, but also enabled her to articulate and share her principles and understanding of children's learning with others.

After completing her degree she felt more able to provide the learning environment for children and adults that reflected her principles.

Questions

1. Having read the chapter, how has it developed your view of an enabling environment for young children's learning?

2. How would you begin to provide an enabling environment informed by your principles?

FURTHER READING

Fisher, J (2008) *Starting from the Child: Teaching and Learning from 3 to 8*, 3rd edition, Maidenhead: OUP.

This practical and inspirational book discusses how recent research continues to shape our understanding of early learning and would be a natural source of further reading to link theory and practice. The book contains many ideas for practitioners to consider when planning to build on children's competence as learners and to develop appropriate learning environments.

Papatheodorou, T & Moyles, J (eds) (2008) *Learning Together in the Early Years: Exploring Relational Pedagogy*, Abingdon: Routledge.

Relational pedagogy is at the heart of this book which draws together contributions from a variety of international experts in early years education. Many of the chapters discuss how young children and adults relate to each other, culture and their environment and how these interactions affect teaching and learning in the early years.

7   Tackling inequality in the early years

Ulrike Hohmann

Introduction

Equality of opportunity, or the lack of it, has an impact on everybody's life. Children, parents and early years practitioners are affected by structures of inclusion and exclusion and play an active part in developing inclusive and anti-discriminatory practice. This chapter unravels some of the complex issues attached to the notion of equal opportunities and the implications for work with young children. Early years practitioners have to be aware of the political and social context within which the demands for tackling inequalities develop and of a variety of arguments that are used to support or criticise attempts to define equal opportunities for children and their families. The examples in this chapter are mainly drawn from the 'classical' areas of discrimination: class, ethnicity, gender and ability. This is not a comprehensive list but serves as a starting point. As some forms of undue discrimination are curtailed, new forms emerge. For example, many unaccompanied asylum-seeking children are falling through the gaps in equality legislation (Wirtz et al., 2009) and there are disturbing reports about young children suffering mentally and physically when forced to live in immigration detention centres (Lorek et al., 2009).

The general context

The Children Act 1989, *Every Child Matters* (DfES, 2003) and a number of Education Acts from 1944 onwards emphasise the rights of children in Britain to equal opportunities and protection from unfair discrimination. On an international level such concerns are addressed by the United Nations Convention on the Rights of the Child. As well as needing to work within this legal framework, early years practitioners are expected to be active in promoting equality of opportunities and anti-discriminatory practice for all children. One of the overarching aims of the Early Years Foundation Stage is:

> *providing for equality of opportunity and anti-discriminatory practice and ensuring that every child is included and not disadvantaged because of ethnicity, culture or religion, home language, family background, learning difficulties or disabilities, gender or ability.*

> (DCSF 2008a, p7)

In addition to concerns about children and equal opportunities, there are concerns for adults' equal opportunities. The Early Years Development and Care Partnerships (EYDCPs) are charged with the responsibility of providing equal opportunities for men, for people with disabilities and for older people who work in childcare settings and with actively encouraging their participation.

Equal opportunities and early years employees

Early years practitioners who become employers, for example as proprietors of a private nursery or manager in a children's centre, have a duty to implement equal opportunities and anti-discriminatory practice for staff as established in a number of Acts. Most important are the Equal Pay Act 1970 (amended 1984), the Race Relations Act 1976, the Race Relations Amendment Act 2000, the Disability Discrimination Act 1995, the Human Rights Act 1998, the Special Educational Needs and Disability Act 2001, the Racial and Religious Hatred Act 2006, the Work and Families Act 2006 and the Age Discrimination Act 2006. Employers encounter the practicalities of equal opportunities when they employ new staff or when conflicts emerge between employees, or employer and employees. At the time of writing there were attempts to combine these major pieces of legislation and many statutory instruments into a single act, to allow better understanding and easier application and the Equality Bill was at the Committee Stage in the House of Lords.

Equal opportunities: creating the ethos

Providing equal opportunities is not just a matter of legislation. It is unlikely that the legal framework can be brought to life without staff in early years settings having a cognitive and affective commitment to equal opportunities. Equal opportunities for young children are predicated on two main arguments. Firstly, there is a moral obligation to provide children, like everybody else, with equal opportunities. Because children are not in control of their own lives but are dependent on their parents for their social and economic position, it is incumbent upon society to protect their rights and treat them equally. For example, Child Benefit is a universal benefit for all children, rich and poor, and any increases to address poverty will be equally applicable to all children. In contrast, adults' eligibility for benefits may be connected to employment, training or actively seeking work because adults are perceived as being largely in control of their own social and economic position. Secondly, there is the argument that sees children as our future and as the makers of future societies. This argument is connected to a belief that we should aspire to provide children with the social competence to respect other groups and individuals (Lindon, 2006; Siraj-Blatchford, 2010). This approach looks towards the future in its desire for a particular version of a just world that has not yet been reached but that, with suitable nurturing, may be achievable in future generations.

Definitions

Equality of opportunities appeals to our sense of justice, but it is not an easy notion to work with. It lacks a clear definition and is used in different contexts and for a wide range of purposes. Equal opportunities can be based on 'minimalist' or on 'maximalist' principles. The 'minimalist' position aims to create 'level playing fields' for competition, to avoid unjust discrimination; it results in unequal but fair outcomes. For example, providing free nursery education for all four-year-olds could be interpreted as providing the necessary conditions for fair competition in school, leading to fair competition for university places in the future. The 'maximalist' position attempts to rectify both discrimination and disadvantage and aims to create equal outcomes (Alcock et al., 2002; Blakemore and Griggs, 2007). An extreme way to accomplish this might be through a generous citizen's income, payable to all individuals independent, for example, of age and of labour market participation. The New Labour government has adopted some characteristics of the 'maximalist' principles in declaring its aim to abolish child poverty through a system of benefits available to all lower-income families with children.

In the field of early childhood studies, the definition of equal opportunities depends on how we see children and their role in society. Early years provision can fulfil a number of functions depending on how narrowly equal opportunities are defined. They may be defined as the duty to prepare children for future competition in the educational system and in the labour market. They may be defined in terms of eliminating the disadvantages experienced by certain groups of children, for example by those from ethnic minorities, by boys or by children with disabilities. Equal opportunities may focus on the provision of an environment free from discrimination, to be enjoyed by children here and now. Projects like Sure Start combine all these aims by providing high-quality preschool education and play in high-quality buildings situated in areas of disadvantage. In addition it is hoped that elimination of disadvantage for preschool children may result in long-term benefits for society in terms of reductions in crime and unemployment. Tackling multiple disadvantages early in the lives of children may help break the cycle of social exclusion. The short-term costs will be more than offset by a reduction in the long-term need for social welfare and benefits, by reduced levels of crime, and by an increased level of income tax received by the Exchequer (Glass, 1999). Lessons learnt from Sure Start inform the 3,500 new Centres of Excellence promised by 2010 (HM Treasury, 2004). By December 2009 the number of Sure Start Children's Centres had already passed the 3,000 mark (UK Government, 2009).

The complexity and the interdependence of possible disadvantages are captured by the capabilities approach which focuses not simply on people's freedom from harm but on what they need to enjoy the freedom to flourish as human beings, ensuring they have genuine autonomy to shape a life worth living. In order to tackle inequality for children it may be helpful to map children's situation. For this purpose Burchardt et al. (2009) have drawn up a special capabilities list for children, building on three types of inequality: of outcome, process and autonomy. These are set out in ten domains: Life; Health; Physical Security; Legal Security; Education and Learning; Standard of Living; Productive and Valued Activities; Individual, Family and Social Life; Identity, Expression and Self-respect; and Participation, Influence and Voice.

Challenging discrimination

The legal framework and set of standards pertaining to children and early years provision provide some indication of the kinds of disadvantage and discrimination at work in Britain; for example, gender, ethnicity, physical and mental ability, and perhaps overlapping these, language and religion. They enshrine the belief that we all have an obligation to challenge sexism, racism and 'ableism' (a term linked to discrimination on the grounds of disability). Gaine (1995, p27) defined racism as 'a pattern of social relations and structures, and a discourse (a linguistic and conceptual process of defining and positioning) which has specific outcomes operating against less powerful groups defined 'racially'. This definition may be adapted to each of the different forms of discrimination by replacing 'racism' with 'sexism', 'ableism' and so on. This exercise can help us to distinguish between children who are more likely to start from a disadvantaged position and those who suffer unfair discrimination. This distinction between disadvantage and discrimination also helps us to keep in mind that patterns and relationships change over time and can be demonstrated through example – for instance, through the idea of 'sexism'. Children in Britain grow up in a society where women and men have equal rights. However, women do not have financial equality with men. In spite of the fact that women have equal voting rights, equal pension rights and equal employment rights, that they are present in large numbers in the labour market, and that fathers are spending more time with their children (Hatten et al., 2003), women still earn on average 22 per cent less than men. The gap between men's and women's earnings in full-time employment is continuing to narrow but is increasing for those in part-time work (ONS, 2009a). In addition, despite their equal rights, women are far less likely to be in powerful positions such as company managers, civil servants and politicians.

A good example of the importance of distinguishing between disadvantage and discrimination is the academic achievement of boys and girls. Recently girls' examination results at all levels have been better than boys'. What does this mean? Does it mean that boys are not well served by the present system of schooling? Do we need to redress the balance with some gender-specific strategies (Arnot et al., 1998; Skelton and Hall, 2001; Francis and Skelton, 2005)? Or does it mean that educational settings are now discriminating against boys? What does it mean for the future? Does it mean that once this generation of pupils has reached the labour market, women will progress faster up career ladders and earn more money than their male contemporaries? Or will gender-specific power relationships continue to cancel out educational achievements?

Working with ambiguous concepts of equal opportunities

An example of ambiguity in interpretation of equality of opportunity is the approach towards children whose first language is not English. Some would argue that these children are disadvantaged in relation to their English peers and, in order to create a 'level playing field', they would benefit from additional English language support. Once these young people have achieved an approximately equal command of the English language they are in a better position to compete in school and later in the labour market and in further and higher education. This perspective has led to a demand in some quarters for parents to speak English at home to 'overcome the schizophrenia which bedevils generational relationships' (Blunkett, 2002: p77). On the other hand, research has shown that bilingual children who are supported in the development of their home language go on to achieve higher standards in English (Cummins, 1984; 2000; Smidt, 2008). Children growing up with more than one language and receiving support in developing language skills also achieve more highly in other areas of the curriculum (Brown, 1998). Early years practitioners need to be aware of these issues when they are devising programmes for children whose first language is not English.

What are the wider implications of equal opportunities for early years settings? Providers of care and education for young children are required to comply with equal opportunities legislation. However, discrimination takes place in quite subtle ways. It can be difficult to translate theories of equality into actual practice. Siraj-Blatchford (2010) observed that some children are disadvantaged because some early years staff have a poor understanding of children from diverse backgrounds.

For example, the two concepts 'race' and 'ethnicity' are often confused – not only by early years practitioners. The term 'race' rests upon beliefs about the importance of supposed biological differences; these differences are then linked to differences in intelligence and social behaviour. Genetic differences determining skin colour are minimal and do not support 'race' as a scientific argument. Individual differences within a group are much greater than between groups. Some people argue that race is a purely social construct based on observed physical and cultural characteristics of individuals (Banton, 1987). The concept 'ethnicity' moves away from biological explanations and includes the historical, social and cultural context in which people live. An ethnic group is seen as a group of people who hold a sense of identity which may arise from a distinct history, nationality, language, norms, beliefs and traditions. This is expressed in many different ways and is often quite striking at the level of detail. For example, the food we eat, how we prepare it and what counts as good table manners vary enormously. Norms and traditions can be accepted as just 'doing things differently'. Not all of the emerging conflicts can be avoided by working on becoming more and more flexible and accepting of differences (Anning and Edwards, 2006). Also, when children need protection, care pathways may be counter to the belief systems of their parents, for example regarding mental health services and social care and welfare interventions and, in the interest of the child, parental wishes and feelings may be overridden (EHRC, 2008).

At other times norms and traditions come into conflict with the law of the host country. For example, the practice of taking child brides is illegal in Britain but may be condoned among certain ethnic groups who live here.

Chris Gaine, a former teacher in a predominantly white school, was interested in how teachers continue to claim that racism is not a problem in their school. He identified a number of reasons why teachers and other professionals do not see racism. They may ignore racism because they may be unwilling to challenge their own prejudices; they may not have been confronted directly with racism themselves; or they may believe that dealing with racism is not their business. They may feel reluctant to approach such a sensitive and potentially explosive issue (Gaine, 2005; 1995). This reluctance to confront discrimination may also be a problem for practitioners in early years.

Creating equality of opportunity in early years settings

One starting point for creating equality of opportunity in early years settings is for practitioners to look more closely at how children relate to each other. Literature on children and equal opportunities provides many examples of children using gender, race, religion, language and the sexual orientation or the economic position of their parents to call children names or to exclude them from their activities (DCSF, 2008a; 2008d; Brown, 1998; Claire et al., 1993). Accidental eavesdropping on children and anecdotal evidence suggests that not much has changed. Why do children do this? Some illumination is provided by research into gender. Broadly there are two schools of thought. One explains gender differences in biological terms (nature), the other explains it with reference to socialisation (nurture). Practitioners who are more convinced by biological explanations, such as different hormone levels or gender specific brain functions, may be more inclined to accept and accommodate the view that boys do not behave like girls and vice versa. Those who lean towards explanations linked to the socialisation process are interested in how gender roles are constructed and how they change over time and across different contexts. However, others argue that 'nature' and 'nurture' are so interdependent that attempting to disentangle them is unhelpful (Head, 1999). From a very early age, children learn what boys and men do and what girls and women do. It has been suggested that when children display 'gender appropriate' behaviour they are rewarded by adults, who may not be aware that they treat boys and girls differently. At the same time others argue that children are active in constructing their own gender roles, forming their gender identity by acting out behaviour that they perceive to be opposite to that displayed by the opposite sex. This explanation emphasises the fluidity of the concept of gender and of children's attempts to 'try out' roles (Skelton and Hall, 2001). In the same way that children identify with and construct gender roles, they also learn and construct attitudes towards ethnic groups. Milner (1983) found that by the age of two children notice differences in skin colour and between three and five they come to learn, regardless of their own skin colour, that it is 'better' to be white than black in Britain. This has implications for working with young children – the challenge is to find ways of supporting children's growing sense of self in an atmosphere where everyone is valued.

Children's developing understanding of self and others

What is known about children's development of gender identities may be adapted to other areas of their identity. Children develop an understanding of themselves and of others from a number of key sources: their parents and wider family, their peers, their early childhood settings and their neighbourhoods. The task of early childhood settings is to foster positive attitudes and behaviour by engaging in anti-discriminatory practice and including all children and families. Writing about the effects of racism on young children, Derman-Sparks (1989) states that early childhood educators have a responsibility to prevent and oppose any damage from racism before it becomes established. Many textbooks on early years refer to, or have sections on, equal opportunities. They appeal to practitioners' duty to implement anti-discriminatory practice (Bruce and Meggitt, 2006; Lindon, 2006; Pre-school Learning Alliance, 2001; Woods, 1998) or provide lists of recommendations for becoming an inclusive setting (Hyder and Kenway, 1995). However, what do we mean by 'inclusive'? What exactly does a multicultural setting look like? Is there a danger, for example, in introducing children to other cultures through studying what might be termed 'exotic' (romanticised and perhaps even incorrect) versions of different cultures

(Houlton, 1986)? Practitioners planning to use persona dolls as a tool to introduce young children to people from minorities, have experienced some difficulties in challenging their own stereotypes (Farmer, 2002). Is it possible that in our endeavour to include as many different ways of living together as possible, we are distracted from thinking more deeply about the stereotypes we may actually be promoting (Woods, 1998)?

Challenging adult stereotypes

To unravel these questions, we need to recognise that we all operate with stereotypes. All adults hold deep-seated ideas about gender, ethnicity, age and so on, and about what constitutes appropriate behaviour within their cultural and/or religious framework. Children pick up both positive and negative attitudes and behaviours. In order to help children to unlearn misconceptions and stereotypical thinking that they may have absorbed (Brown, 1998), early years practitioners need to become aware of their own stereotypical assumptions. Stereotypes are oversimplified generalisations which often, but not always directly, have negative implications. Take for example the stereotypical assumption that black people are good at sport. For the athletic black child it can be a great source of reassurance and identity. But stereotypes like this can undermine the confidence and feelings of self-worth of black children who are not good at sport. Additionally, they can have negative implications for black children who are steered towards sporting achievement but get less support for academic achievement. The effect on white children could be negative, too.

Inclusion and exclusion

How do we know whether our beliefs, values and practices are based on stereotypes? Asking this question is itself a good starting point. The question forces us to think more widely about the concepts and debates around, for example, sex and gender, race and ethnicity, and integration and inclusion. An understanding of the theoretical models which explain differences can be useful. These theoretical frameworks can help us to explore issues of inclusion and exclusion, discrimination and anti-discriminatory work and to examine areas of equal opportunities in relation to our own life.

As important as it is to look at the stereotypes individuals hold, it does not mean that the context within which they are formed, accepted and spread is less significant. More effective anti-discriminatory practice can be supported by using the PCS analysis (Thompson, 2006). The 'P' of PCS stands for the personal, including prejudice and practice, which is embedded in the cultural, reflected in commonalities, consensus and conformity (the 'C'). 'C' also includes the 'comic' or humour. Jokes are powerful in passing on stereotypes and can be very hurtful but humour is also a potent strategy against oppression. The personal and the cultural are embedded in 'S', the structural, for example existing social divisions and the struggle over these, and 'S' is reflected in legal frameworks. None of these perspectives by itself can explain existing discrimination or show ways to move towards more acceptable practice.

A good example of how theory informs practice and supports reflexivity is provided by two models of disability which have held sway over the past century. For much of the twentieth century, the cause of a disability was seen as physical and residing within the individual person. This perspective is referred to as the 'medical model'. The medical model understands disability as the outcome of disease, trauma or a health condition. Disability is the outcome of a 'tragic event' and there is no cure. Disabled people cannot participate fully in society and are dependent on others. Until the 1970s many children with any form of disability were seen as 'ineducable' and removed from their parental homes to spend their lives in institutions. After the Education Act of 1970 made local education authorities responsible for the education of all children, children with impairments most frequently found themselves in special schools, segregated from mainstream education (Wall, 2006).

In contrast to a focus on the individual, the 'social model' of disability looks at the context within which impairments become disabilities. Disability is seen as a socially created problem. Features in specific physical environments and in the culture and prevalent attitudes can present barriers to full participation for individuals. For example, it is not the inability to walk but the lack of an affordable wheelchair, and the lack of ramps or lifts that prevent a partially paralysed child from gaining easy access to a school built on different levels. Another barrier can be bullying (DCSF, 2008d). Within the social model the problem of disability demands a political response. This perspective requires the development of social welfare strategies that support autonomy and promote independence.

Segregating children with impairments into institutions was widely criticised. The first move to end this segregation was to 'integrate' children with disabilities into mainstream schools. Integration sometimes takes the form of a special school and a mainstream school sharing premises; sometimes schools offer separate lessons for children with special educational needs but allow for shared break times; sometimes schools offer some shared lessons. These forms of integration of children in mainstream services are all informed by the medical model. The focus is on the individual child: he or she will be assessed by a specialist; the diagnosis will specify expected outcomes and recommend an individually tailored programme. Ainscow (1995) suggested that this definition of integration merely means making a few additional arrangements for individual children with disabilities and has little overall effect on their opportunities for becoming full members of the group.

Since the late 1980s, 'inclusion' has superseded 'integration'. 'Inclusion', based on the social model, focuses on the classroom, looks at teaching and learning factors and aims to create an adaptive, supportive regular classroom which will benefit all children. In the context of school education, inclusion is a 'process of increasing the participation of students in, and reducing their exclusion from, the cultures, curricula and communities in local schools' (Centre for Studies on Inclusive Education, 2002, in Wall, 2003). This definition does not emphasise the active part children with disabilities can play. Farrell (2001, p7) argues that 'for inclusion to be effective pupils must actively belong to, be welcomed by and participate in a school and community – that is they should be fully included'. So, inclusive education is the outcome of a collaborative approach by the whole school community. This should include a more critical examination of the use of teaching assistants. They are often used to substitute for teacher's time resulting in children with SEN having less access to support from more highly qualified teachers (Lamb, 2009).

Currently, the government shows a strong commitment to inclusion (DCSF, 2009a; DCSF, 2008a; DfES, 2006b; Cabinet Office, 2005; DfES, 2004b). However, from the perspective of children with disabilities and their families there is plenty of room for improvement. A review of service provision for children with disabilities and their families showed that they face a lottery of provision and access, often depending on how hard parents can push; they have to rely on a patchwork of services, which sometimes offer too little, too late (Lamb, 2009; Audit Commission, 2003b). An inclusive approach may meet resistance from specialists in special schools because they feel their expertise is overlooked. There may also be resistance from teachers and practitioners from mainstream services because they feel ill-equipped to implement inclusive practice (DfES, 2004e). It appears that there are still tensions between the medical model and the social model of disability.

Conclusion

In terms of 'natural justice', equality of opportunity is like apple pie and motherhood – it appeals to all of us. But equality of opportunity is not an easy concept to work with. It requires a lot of hard thinking on the part of practitioners. And that requires us to abandon common-sense beliefs based on uncritical stereotyping. Critical reflection offers an opportunity to think more widely and to examine our vision of the future for our children. This chapter has traced some of the ways in which we can think critically about equality of opportunity.

Debates around equal opportunities involve arguments about 'nature' and 'nurture'. Although it has been pointed out that 'nature' and 'nurture' are intertwined and that to some extent this relationship cannot be undone, it is still valuable to examine the arguments and decide what is and is not acceptable. To use the minimal genetic differences between people of different skin colour as justification for discrimination is not acceptable, nor is it acceptable, for example, to prescribe medicines which may have been tested only on a limited sample of the population (one size fits all). However, exploring the medical needs and differences of children with disabilities can positively inform the process of becoming an inclusive day centre or school. Inclusion and exclusion, discrimination and anti-discriminatory practice are processes which take place on a number of interlinked levels. Equal opportunities cannot be achieved by stopping short at the individual level, by blaming cultural differences or by declaring that social structures are fixed (Thompson, 2006).

This chapter has used a number of examples of discrimination to draw out common patterns. It can only provide a brief introduction. Focusing on areas of conflict and difficulty can give the impression that a mass of interdependent problems must be tackled before we can develop truly inclusive practices. However, benefits achieved by thinking through and practising ways of letting positive relationships grow, where children, practitioners, parents and friends gain, cannot be highlighted strongly enough. Early years practitioners play an important role in supporting discussions and practices that allow everyone to be part of creating an inclusive setting: colleagues, children, parents and the community. Equality of opportunity cannot be prescribed through legislation alone and, as early years practitioners, we have a duty to involve ourselves in the long process of developing satisfactory anti-discriminatory practices. The theoretical and practical engagement with inclusion has a huge potential for developing satisfactory relationships within and between communities.

ACTIVITY **1**

Tackling inequality in your nursery

Imagine that you are a member of staff who has recently been given responsibility for equal opportunities in a Children's Centre in a predominantly white rural community. What elements would you include in a policy document supporting equal opportunities for the children and parents? What obstacles do you foresee in changing attitudes and incorporating the policy into practice?

ACTIVITY **2**

Getting in the picture

Select a range of media intended to entertain and educate children, like picture books, television programmes, DVDs and children's songs. How are gender, ethnicity and class relationships represented? Do they pick up issues like disability, migration and different family forms? If yes, how are children and adults represented? You will find some ideas on how to analyse these representations in Saunders (2000) book Happy Ever Afters: a storybook guide to teaching children about disability. *What would you change?*

FURTHER READING

Malik, H (2009) *A Practical Guide to Equal Opportunities*. 3rd edition. Cheltenham: Nelson Thornes.

Hyacinth Malik provides an easy to read introduction to key terms and major themes of exclusion and inclusion. Key points, case studies and activities help the reader to engage with the themes of disability, gender and race and how to tackle inequalities in early years settings.

Nutbrown, C and Clough, P (2006) *Inclusion in the Early Years*. London and Thousand Oaks, New Delhi: Sage.

This book offers a readable account of inclusive practice in early years, making links to relevant theories. The strength of the book is the wider focus on talking about exclusion of children, their families and communities, including staff working in early childhood settings.

Channel Four (2003–2009) Born to be Different, Series 1–6

The series follows six children born with a disability from birth in Britain. This documentary presents an empathetic account of the experiences of the children and their families.

Part 3

Multi-professional practice: developing empowering communities

8 Working with colleagues

Caroline Leeson and Valerie Huggins

Introduction

Recent changes in welfare and education policy and practice have encouraged early years practitioners to stop thinking of themselves as 'just a teacher', 'just a social worker' or 'just an early years worker'. Thus, to be an effective early years practitioner now requires both an ability to understand the theoretical constructs of collaborative practice and the possession of skills that facilitate working positively with others from different professions and perspectives, often in difficult or complex circumstances.

In this chapter, we will explore some of the key issues in effective collaboration with colleagues as we seek to demonstrate the interrelatedness of the core skills of communication and team working. We will be arguing that the concept of colleagues should be taken in its widest sense, encompassing friends, clients and families as well as professional and work colleagues. We believe it is particularly important that we do not exclude children's voices throughout this debate on working together. It is our position that young children are capable of participating in simple and complex decision-making and should be actively involved. Regarding children as 'victims' or 'threats' (Hendrick, 2003) interferes with our ability to view children as colleagues and it is our contention that this has to be addressed as no amount of policy or political encouragement will further the interests of children until our restrictive beliefs about their abilities and status are challenged.

The current early years context

Early years practitioners can no longer confine their attention to their own setting; they are expected to have a holistic concern with children in wider family and social contexts. For instance, in the course of a single day, a young child may now be cared for by their parents, by a childcare team, by after-school club play-workers and by a child minder. The statutory guidance underpinning the new Early Years Foundation Stage (DCSF, 2008a) recommends that in such a situation there has to be an effective sharing of relevant information between all the practitioners involved and the parents in order to ensure continuity and to improve the outcomes for the child. Where a child and family are experiencing particular difficulties such interagency sharing is even more critical. All this necessitates collaborative working with colleagues and therefore depends on the development of sophisticated understandings and skills.

Within the past 10 years Government initiatives have made collaborative, multi-agency working a requirement and given it a structure nationally, regionally and locally. The *Every Child Matters* (DfES, 2003) agenda, implemented through The Children Act 2004, Child Care Act 2006, Early Years Foundation Stage (DCSF, 2008a), Early Years Professional Status

(CWDC, 2007) and the Children and Young People's Workforce Strategy (DCSF, 2008h), emphasises the necessity for agencies to work together as fully integrated services, meeting the needs of children and families with a seamless service provision based on 'a shared perspective, effective communication and mutual understanding (Jones and Pound, 2008). Furthermore, *Every Child Matters: Change for Children* (DfES, 2004b) advocates a lead professional approach to simplify and strengthen the support for families with particular needs. A single Lead Professional now liaises with the family to co-ordinate the work of other colleagues and to ensure there is clear accountability. So, early years practitioners from health, social care, welfare, education and the criminal justice system now work in a legislative framework where a multi-agency approach is required (Dunhill et al., 2009).

Structurally, Children's Trusts have been established within each local authority to bring together health, education and social services for children and young people to work in partnership under a Director of Children's Services, underpinned by the Children Act 2004. The subsequent Children's Plan (DCSF, 2007b) has strengthened the work of Children's Trusts through the Apprenticeship, Skills and Learning Act 2009, giving Local Authorities a statutory duty to implement the Children and Young People's Plan in their area. There has also been a commitment to establish a Sure Start Children's Centre for every community by 2010, to provide health and family support services at a single point of contact and 3000 centres are already in place. Two thirds of schools also now offer extended provision for school-aged children.

In response to all these new demands, the DfES has identified a Common Core of Skills and Knowledge for the Early Years Workforce (DfES, 2005) which includes communication, teamwork and assertiveness within multi-agency working. The Children's Workforce Development Council (CWDC) has established a new role, the Early Years Professional (EYP) (CWDC, 2007) is to lead effective, collaborative practice in settings, as well as the National Professional Qualification for Integrated Centre Leadership (NPQICL) training for early years leaders. One limitation of the EYP Status is that the standards are very education-based. An early years status that was equally relevant for practitioners from other professional backgrounds would have helped to promote partnership working through shared training and a co-constructed approach.

Coping with such huge structural change to Children's Services at national, regional and local level has not been easy. The original Early Excellence Centres pioneered a model for integrated services that were responsive to the needs of local communities through collaborative working which was then developed further in the Sure Start Local Programmes. However, we note that the subsequent national roll-out of Children's Centres has, at times, imposed a particular way of working on a group of professionals that has not fitted the requirements of the community, being driven by national targets that may not be appropriate to local priorities and has thus perhaps not met community needs.

Working together in partnership

The challenge has therefore been to work in an integrated and effective way, within an environment of structural change and variations in policy, while valuing the contribution of all the participants. This requires a shared vision and compatible way of working to enable a diverse range of people to work in partnership.

Partnership is not a new term; it has been a key word for early years policymakers since the late 1980s (Hornby, 2000) and has been used to mean the increased involvement of families, children and carers and the sharing of power between these groups and early years practitioners.

There are proven benefits of working in partnership though these have sometimes been assessed in terms of increased 'efficiency' rather than in terms of how this improves outcomes for children and families. Working in partnership can increase the creative facility of agencies to provide bespoke services to children and families and can improve understanding of local needs and pressures as well as supporting the sharing of skills, roles and services.

In the past, it was possible for early years practitioners to pay lip service to the idea of working closely and collaboratively with colleagues, whilst in practice resisting fiercely at both a conscious and unconscious level. This is no longer a sustainable position. But Government policies will not in themselves bring about harmonious and effective collaboration. It is still necessary for early years practitioners to be clear about who their colleagues are and how to work with them, to be aware of the considerable barriers to collaboration that exist and to know how to build and sustain positive partnerships.

Who are our colleagues?

In the past we have been prone to define 'colleagues' very narrowly – often as those with very similar professional backgrounds or who work in the same setting. The integrated approach to work within the early years sector means we have to reconsider the term. For the purposes of this chapter we are taking colleagues to mean all the people who interact and work together towards a common, identified goal. This would therefore include practitioners of all kinds working within the setting and in the wider community, as well as the children and their families.

Professionals as colleagues

Within the early years sector, people work together in a variety of situations, teams and frameworks – multi-agency projects, care management teams and strategic decision making groups (Atkinson et al., 2002). The Children Act 2004 and the new Children and Young Peoples Workforce Strategy (DCSF, 2008h) are intended to promote multi-disciplinary work in order to improve services to families identified as needing intervention and assistance. However, there is evidence that professionals are still defending their specialisms for fear of becoming deskilled and are jockeying to maintain their own power bases (Barker, 2009). As a consequence, they may fail to see the potential of collaborative work, where all positions and perspectives are valued and service provision can be seamless and meaningful.

Looking at the social psychology of work enables us to identify the cultural positions people start from and to understand the complexities of working effectively with colleagues. We should be mindful of the sense of duty that is often attached to people's attitudes to their work as well as the issues of power and territory that affect decision-making processes and subsequent action. Any developments in terms of working together have to recognise that early years work is people-based and therefore highly dependent on interpersonal relationships as well as on understanding how people operate and how they think about their work.

Links between agencies and participants need to be developed in such a way that everyone is valued and respected – this includes children and their families. We cannot assume that all stakeholders will share the same view, therefore the development of respect for all points of view is paramount (Fitzgerald, 2004). Building such respect requires significant consistency and continuity in the make up of teams. There is a need within multi-disciplinary work at all levels for members of each team to build stable relationships with their partners in other teams. Consistency of personnel is vital to build trust and respect, to nurture shared understandings and to develop a kind of multi-disciplinary attachment. Sometimes more than one person from each service team will need to be involved and to be informed about the work being undertaken so that they can be part of a pool of familiar faces. Children's Trusts are beginning to work towards this goal, taking seriously the need for participants to know and trust each other fully (DCSF, 2008a).

If we are to develop effective multi-agency teams, appropriate styles of leadership are critical (Jones and Pound, 2008; Purcell, 2009). We are beginning to see some tentative shifts in leadership approaches (refer to Chapter 9) from top-down managerial models towards distributive, transformational models that offer opportunities for leadership to be shared throughout the team (Duffy and Marshall, 2007). Such a shift helps to develop environments for effective and meaningful partnerships, with shared language, vision and direction (NCSL, 2004), by empowering and valuing the contributions of all parties.

Children as colleagues

When considering working together we often overlook the children themselves. Too often we see children as helpless and incapable of making decisions for themselves: 'A factor that sustains adult-child power relationships is a belief that adults have superior knowledge.' (Robinson and Kellett, 2004, p84). Children can feel a sense of powerlessness when they are not party to decisions that affect them and this may have serious repercussions throughout their lives (Leeson, 2006; 2009). It is reported that adults who find it difficult to make relationships often reveal that they were not involved in even the smallest decisions as children and the resultant self-doubt has left them unable to make choices for themselves (Dallos in John, 1996). Decision-making has implications for building resilience and the way in which a situation is dealt with, the impact of the situation and the degree to which the child is involved can have lifelong implications (Daniel et al.,1999). Being able to practise and become competent in decision-making is crucial to emotional well-being and the development of integrated persons (Clarke and Clarke, 2003). Research into school councils (John, 2003), children experiencing divorce (Neale, 2002) and children being involved in decisions about their health (Thurston and Church, 2001) all points to children's ability to discuss objectively and appropriately the important decisions that have to be made about their environment and their lives.

Nevertheless, there is a tendency for professionals to believe that children are dependent on their parents and that parents will act as responsible advocates for them. This may not always be the case – a series of enquiries into abuse of children, including Jasmine Beckford

(London Borough of Brent, 1985), Victoria Climbié (DoH and Home Office, 2003), Child B (Samuel, 2007) and Baby P (LSCB, 2009) all show how children can get lost in adult agendas, no longer seen as separate beings with their own story to tell. The argument is often made that children cannot be involved in discussions as they are not fully cognisant of all the facts. But how often do adults have all the necessary information? Adults make decisions, plan and act according to their beliefs at the time. We would argue that children should have the same opportunity. Sometimes our underlying attitudes towards children prevent us from viewing them as valued members of the community or as colleagues working with practitioners to enhance their environment and/or community. It may be an anxiety about relinquishing our own power and control; it may be about pressure of time, or poor skills or limited resources. Certainly, regarding children as colleagues would require a shift of focus away from adults delivering care to children to adults and children working together to provide a caring environment for the benefit of all.

Viewing children as colleagues and co-constructors of our world has significant repercussions for the way we work together as adults, the way we shape our work and the way we maintain relationships with one another. We therefore welcome the insistent calls for children to be regarded as colleagues, as active participants in decisions that affect them (Cairns, 2006; Lansdown, 2010) and the quality of their lives and experiences. We note that this is beginning to be evidenced in government policies such as the Early Years Foundation Stage (DCSF, 2008a) where children are encouraged to take a lead in the learning process, and the Children's Plan (DCSF, 2007b) which promotes the role of children in helping to shape the services available for them and their families.

Parents as colleagues

Until recently the purpose of working with parents was largely seen as compensating for their perceived inadequacies, both in terms of their parenting skills and their limitations in understanding and providing for their children's needs. Thus the practitioners had all the power and the parents' participation in the relationship was very much in the role of recipients. This inequality potentially reduced the impact of their involvement. However, there has been a significant shift in models of working with parents towards one of empowerment (Whalley, 2008, p132), where parents are seen as colleagues and 'professionals actively promote parents' sense of control over decisions affecting their child.' Devereux (2003, p86) argues that:

> *Working in partnership is not just about the two very different spheres of home and setting. It is also about people from different cultures learning to work together for the good of the child.*

In order to do this, practitioners have to accept caregivers as having equal, though different, expertise – in their child and their family culture. Only then can parents move from a compensatory involvement to a fully participatory one (Whalley, 2001). Such full participation is crucial if we are to achieve the wider benefits of working with parents.

These benefits are considerable. Desforges and Abouchar (2003) confirm that parental involvement in early years settings and schools has a positive effect on children's achievement. This is supported by the Effective Provision of Pre-school Education (EPPE) case studies which show how 'parents and staff can work together so that *learning environments* of home and pre-school are harmonized and stretched' (Pugh, 2006, p176). The role of parents as partners is now also enshrined in the new Early Years Foundation Stage:

> *Parents are children's first and enduring educators. When parents and practitioners work together in early years settings, the results have a positive impact on children's development and learning.*

(DCSF, 2007a, Card 2.2)

Another of the key findings of the EPPE project is that the quality of the home learning environment is more significant in promoting children's intellectual and social development than parents' occupations or qualifications (Pugh, 2006).

This challenges many professional assumptions about the limitations of less advantaged families and underlines the importance of working with all parents as full colleagues. But it is still a huge challenge to combine and balance the practitioner's expertise in child development and learning with the parents' expertise in their child and their family culture, in order to produce the best outcomes for the child.

The personal and cultural assumptions of some families may be very different from those of the practitioners due, for instance, to diverse religious beliefs or different views of the purpose of early years education. These differences are not always easy to resolve but the arguments for establishing a genuine partnership with parents, both from research and from current policy requirements, are overwhelming. Parents are our colleagues and we must find ways of respecting and making full use of their contribution. Bax (2001) suggests that practitioners should be sensitive to the parents' right to participate in the range of services on offer at any level that they choose. They also need to consider imaginative ways to empower parents in their local context to enable them to participate (Whalley, 2008).

Obstacles to effective partnership

The dangers of *not* working in partnership have been highlighted in many inquiries into child deaths. The child abuse inquiries mentioned above have all found evidence of professionals' significant and systematic failure to work together effectively through the meaningful sharing of information and successful interagency working. Research consistently shows a number of key factors that prevent or inhibit successful interagency collaboration (Atkinson et al., 2002; Lumsden, 2005; Anning et al., 2006; Harris and Allan, 2009):

- Territorialism and role identifications, discussed above, including unhelpful stereotyping of each other's roles and reactions which leads to mutually unfulfilled expectations and disrespect for the expertise of others;

- Status and power – working together can incur a perceived loss of status for key personnel who see their opportunities to exert power and authority curtailed or questioned;

- Failure to share responsibility is apparent in the child abuse enquiries mentioned above;

- Competition for resources is inherent within a managerialist system;

- Different professional and organisational priorities;

- Different value systems and attitudes towards children and their families;

- The use of professional jargon that erects ideological barriers between professions;

- The lack of ability or willingness to reflect on personal practice.

The Early Years Foundation Stage (DCSF, 2008b) puts partnership with parents at the heart of effective practice. It advocates that all parents should be involved in their child's learning and outlines various strategies to encourage practitioners to develop an effective partnership by showing respect, understanding the role of the parents, listening, being flexible, giving time, valuing different perspectives and collaborating in a genuine way. These expectations can be difficult to achieve, especially if families have had bad experiences with other professionals. Lumby (2007) found that some professionals were reluctant to engage in partnership with parents because of anxieties about their professional role and their reluctance to share governance and power, echoing some of the barriers to collaboration between professionals. Practitioners should therefore reflect upon how their own attitudes and values may create barriers to working as colleagues with parents, as well as with other professionals.

Managing conflict by the facilitation of more collegiate ways of working should be one of the goals of effective partnership (Anning et al., 2006; West-Burnham et al., 2007). On the assumption that every parent wants the best for their children, we should ask what is making the partnership so hard to maintain instead of abandoning the idea as soon as it becomes difficult.

Making partnerships effective

Atkinson et al. (2005) have identified a range of key factors for successful multi-agency working and argue that the most important is the commitment and willingness to work together. However, as Fitzgerald (2004, p21) argues

> *For partnership to be maintained it is vital that there are effective strategies in place to facilitate two-directional communication and support.*

But what are these effective strategies? Let us start with something simple. How do we refer to our partners? As clients, service-users, patients, mums and dads, cases ... colleagues? All of these terms are value-laden; some have negative connotations, implying a weaker or inferior position in relationship with the 'professional'. So we need to think very carefully about the labels we use and how we can promote partnership and collegiality.

> *To work together all parties need to have a shared sense of what partnership means to them all.*

> (Fitzgerald, 2004, p7)

Defining what partnership means to us will affect the way we work – and will inform our attitudes and our policies. Miell and Dallos (1996) suggest that partnership may be difficult with some families because they see professionals as coming from privileged backgrounds in terms of class, race, education and, frequently, gender and therefore as having higher status.In many respects this is valid – in addition to the social capital accrued through education and training, a social worker acting in a professional capacity is an agent of the Local Authority, supported and protected by all their structures and value systems.

> *In entering into a relationship with a professional body, individuals appear to be negotiating from a position of disadvantage and they are, to some extent, obliged to comply with the professional's definition of their needs.*

> (Miell and Dallos, 1996, p299)

We must work to break down such perceptions if we hope to build genuine partnerships. There are various theoretical frameworks for supporting the development of such partnerships. In education, Holt (cited in Fitzgerald, 2004) devised a 'ladder of empowerment' that agencies can use to identify an appropriate level and type of partnership. In social welfare, the 'continuum of service user participation' (Martin and Henderson, 2001, p162) serves a similar function. Both frameworks measure how meaningful and genuine the partnership is for both the professional and the families involved. They demand that we look at any situation and ask whether the plan we are developing is one of genuine empowerment and autonomy or one of lip service to a required code of practice. For a partnership to be effective, everyone needs to see how they fit into the partnership and what they bring to it in terms of an agenda, motivation, emotion, information and ways of working. The five outcomes of the Every Child Matters agenda help to facilitate this process, in that they provide a shared vision for practitioners from different agencies and parents alike to work towards (Stacey, 2009). They can then discuss their roles and responsibilities in the effective implementation of policies and approaches that will promote the health and well-being of each child (Jones and Pound, 2008).

Fostering good communication

In this context, more effective multi-directional communication is needed, not just between the families and the professionals but between the professionals themselves. The formal structure of the Common Assessment Framework (DCSF, 2009b) has perhaps supported this process by enabling better communication between the people involved with a family, through a clarification of their roles and responsibilities within the team around the child. It is this sort of relationship-building within a community of practice (Phillips, 2009) that fosters effective communication and empowers people.

By recognising the different perceptions of the child/family which stem from their particular professional background (Anning et al., 2006), professionals working within a multi-agency team can enjoy the benefits of having a much richer knowledge base that enables the development of a much clearer picture of the needs of the child, and improved identification of how best to support the family (Stacey, 2009). Therefore, all participants and organisations involved in the care of a particular child should work hard to understand each other's points of view, to respect and value the differences and the similarities between those views, and to share information effectively, always operating from the assumption that everyone is working together for the good of the child and their family. We acknowledge the enormous challenges in trying to coordinate communication, identifying points of contact, negotiating meanings and assumptions and overcoming the constraints and demands on organisations and individuals (Brechin, 2000). The Laming Reports into the death of Victoria Climbié (Laming, 2003) and updated following the death of Baby P (Laming, 2009) have both highlighted the ongoing problem of how differing jargon, cultures and motivations prevented agencies in both instances from working together in meaningful ways. One of the authors can still remember the first multi-agency meeting she attended and her feeling of inadequacy as she struggled to get to grips with someone else's acronyms. Leiba (2003) talks about the 'codification of communication' between professionals, where conditions and connotations in one professional code can exclude others.

Good communication skills are therefore crucial. Good communicators express their meaning in all sorts of ways - through body language, through 'paralanguage' (the way they say things and the way they listen) through appropriate choice of vocabulary, through the medium in which they choose to communicate and through using their own experience to encourage and promote dialogue. Good communicators also listen with attention and empathy, actively seeking to understand and appreciate the points of view of others (Ellis and Fisher, 1994). Co-location of services within Children's Centres and Extended Schools has supported this process, as personal relationships between professionals are built up through daily conversations and exchanges, but it is a long and slow process that requires considerable support and nurturing.

Conclusion

Vocational training for health workers, social workers and teachers is increasingly concerned with effective communication and working in partnership in all its different forms. All professionals working in the early years field are expected to liaise closely with one another for the benefit of the children in their care. Team building between agencies and within early years settings depends on a willingness to listen and a willingness to change.

As practitioners working with young children and their families we must challenge ourselves, our assumptions and our ways of working if we are to achieve effective working relationships. Most importantly, we have to address how we interact and communicate with others. We should be promoting the importance of working together and actively seeking ways to improve our ability to do so. We may need to reconceptualise the way we regard young children. We must develop awareness of how we can renegotiate the roles and relationships we have with existing colleagues and of how we can involve new people. Most importantly of all, we have to develop trust between all who are working together for young children, making full use of formal and informal mechanisms to do so.

ACTIVITY 1

Over the next month, look through newspapers, journals and periodicals for coverage on health, education, police and welfare issues. See if you can identify some of the following:

- *Political bias*
- *Examples of good and poor collaborative practice*
- *Involvement of family and child in decision making*
- *Quality of the working relationship between agencies*
- *Communication issues*

From this, begin to develop your own idea of what contributes to effective collaboration between early years practitioners and of how partnerships may be helped or hindered by government policies.

ACTIVITY 2

Compile a portfolio of your own experiences of the following:

- *Communication*
- *Teamwork*
- *Partnership*
- *Emotional literacy*

Examples of your own practice could come from work situations, group living, leisure activities or study experiences. What do these experiences tell you about these topics and your own skills? How have your experiences shaped your attitude towards working with others? What will you now seek to change?

ACTIVITY 3

Prepare a presentation on one of the early years service professions. We would suggest you look at a profession you might work with in the future rather than the profession you think you might like to join. Try to find out about:

- *The history of this profession; when it was first created and how it has developed. How has training changed and what historical developments might help to explain the identity and nature of the profession? Are there key people who have pioneered the creation or development of this service?*
- *The laws which underpin the expectations placed on this group of professionals.*

continued

ACTIVITY **3** *continued*

- The current situation with this profession in terms of training, numbers, working patterns and ideologies.

- The hierarchy or accountability structure for this profession.

- Any professional bodies which support, monitor or police the actions of their members within this profession.

- The role this profession has in helping care for young children and their families. How is this role manifested?

- The responsibilities of this profession, to whom they report and any specific duties they have to perform.

- Any developments in the pipeline for this profession.

- Any other information that you feel it would be useful to share with your audience.

FURTHER
READING

Anning, A (2005) Investigating the impact of working in multi-agency service delivery settings in the UK on Early Years practitioners beliefs and practices. *Journal of Early Childhood Research*, 3(1), pp 19–50.

An important article exploring beliefs and practice and the ways in which these are affected by experience of multi-agency working.

Dunhill, A, Elliott, B and Shaw, A (2009) *Effective Communication and Engagement with Children and Young People, their Families and Carers*. Exeter, Learning Matters

An essential guide to communication.

Siraj-Blatchford, I, Clarke, K and Needham, M (2007) *The Team Around the Child: Multi-agency Working in the Early Years*. Stoke-on-Trent, Trentham Books

An excellent discussion of the history, contemporary practice and the future of multi-agency working.

9 Leadership in early childhood settings

Caroline Leeson

Introduction

Leadership has emerged as an important issue for all early childhood professionals, not just for those who hold leadership or management positions (CWDC, 2007). According to Earley and Weindling (2004) how leadership is carried out is crucial in terms of the ultimate effectiveness of the organisation. Therefore the development of leadership skills has become increasingly important for all early years practitioners no matter what stage they are at in their career. This chapter seeks to explore the significant steps which can be taken to facilitate effective leadership in early childhood settings and will offer a critical examination of the current theoretical models used.

Over the last few years, the early years sector has embarked on an interesting journey towards a creative and innovative form of leadership which has been influenced by several, diverse drivers for change. Firstly, some serious reflection has taken place leading to the recognition of the importance of effective leadership in welfare services for young children and their families. This acknowledgment has therefore created a demand to take leadership seriously and improve the calibre of leaders. For example, Lord Laming's report into the death of Victoria Climbié (DoH and HO, 2003) was the first enquiry into the death of a child to criticise the calibre and expertise of leaders and managers in all services for young children rather than placing the blame on front line staff. The collective failure of leaders to lead with vision and to take responsibility for managing their staff was seen as a major contributory factor in the events leading to Victoria's death. The Audit Commission (2003a) was equally critical of the failure of local government to grasp the nettle of corporate governance, suggesting that, even at the highest levels, leaders are poor at communicating their vision and promoting their services effectively.

As a consequence, the Every Child Matters agenda (DfES, 2003) and the Children Act 2004 sought to address these criticisms by developing an expectation that managers should manage more effectively, accept accountability and be more proactive in developing multidisciplinary training opportunities for all front line staff and that all of this would take place in a multi-professional context. However, this has not been easy. Laming revisited his original recommendations in 2009 and found that few had been fully implemented. Questions of how individual professions work together and how this collaborative practice can be effectively led have still not been adequately addressed. Laming recommends:

> The Department for Children, Schools and Families should organise regular training on safeguarding and child protection and on effective leadership for all senior political leaders and managers across frontline services.

(2009, p20)

Development has been slow; we have only very recently seen training emerging for those working at a strategic level with the new DCS leadership programme (National College, 2009) beginning to identify what great leadership looks like, enhancing ability and confidence and thereby creating a greater vision of the different strategies and approaches across local authorities. The National Professional Qualification in Integrated Centre Leadership (NPQICL) National College for School Leadership (NCSL, 2004) and Early Years Professional Status (EYPS) (CWDC, 2007) are also recent qualifications that are a welcome development. However, they are targeted at specific settings and individuals. They are not, as yet, universal courses accessible by all who will take a leadership role.

Secondly, we have seen a substantial development at national level of policy, strategy and legislation highlighting and promoting the need for good quality and effective leadership. Indeed, the context within which services for children and families currently operate might be characterised as one of constant change in a fast moving world with ever shifting goalposts. There has been a continuous stream of national strategies, government initiatives and related policies since the Labour government took office in 1997. These have been introduced at national level and gradually implemented and interpreted at local level impacting upon provision and services (DfES, 2004c; DfES, 2007; CWDC, 2007; DCSF, 2008f). For example, several sections of the National Childcare Strategy (DfEE, 1998b), including the setting up of Early Excellence Centres, Sure Start local programmes and Neighbourhood Nurseries, gave the impetus for settings to become multi-disciplinary and multi-functional. This precipitated an expansion of the functions, roles and responsibilities that early childhood professionals are expected to undertake.

In the Early Excellence Centre pilot programme's Second Annual Evaluation Report (DfEE, 2001), it was suggested that Early Excellence Centre Heads had to develop their management and organisational skills to manage the diverse range of services within their settings. The report highlighted that already these heads were under significant pressure and finding their role extremely complex and demanding as they tried to deal with increasing management responsibilities and competing demands from parents, children, the community and LEAs.

In the Government's Green Paper, *Every Child Matters* (DfES, 2003a) a key strategy involved plans to establish Sure Start Children's Centres 'in each of the 20% most deprived neighbourhoods' in the country by 2006. This continued the push towards integrated services. The intention was that these centres would 'combine nursery education, family support, employment advice, childcare and health services on one site' to provide integrated care and education for young children (DfES, 2003a, p7). Most recent legislation such as the Child Care Act, 2006, gave parents a voice in the planning and delivery of services that suited their needs as well as the right to expect high quality provision. It also placed a responsibility upon Local Authorities as strategic leaders to enhance partnership working across all sectors.

As a consequence of the above drivers for change, there has been a period of significant investment in the early years sector with many diverse environments and settings for children and families being established that require the development of different models of leadership. One of the keys to early intervention and effective protection for 'disadvantaged' children has been 'on the spot service delivery';

Professionals are therefore encouraged to work in multi-disciplinary teams based in and around schools and Children's Centres, providing a rapid response to the concerns of frontline teachers, childcare workers and others in universal services.

(DfES, 2003a, p9)

This move towards integrated services, with its concomitant complexities has created demand for debate on the most appropriate leadership styles and tone for these new ways of leading, managing and developing services for all service users (Lawler and Bilson, 2010).

It seems that multi-professional working requires strong leadership with powerful, motivating vision (Jones and Pound, 2008; Earley and Weindling, 2004), the type of leadership articulated by the leaders of the new SureStart Children's Centres (NCSL, 2004) in practice.

However, the idea of flexible, integrated services is not a new one. For example, a number of Nursery Centres were set up in London and other cities in the late 1970s, which offered state nursery education with wrap-around day care facilities and, often, a range of other services to meet the needs of their local communities. These centres did not become a widespread phenomenon and the staff working in them were definitely challenged to find new ways of working in partnership across different services such as education, social services and health. Individual practitioners today are also attempting to communicate and resolve issues starting from very different backgrounds and perspectives. Thus, we have seen a steady move towards integration for all public services with early years services at the forefront of this shift leading the way and finding new paths. Helping everyone involved to 'think outside the box' or developing a box big enough or flexible enough for everyone to think inside is therefore a major challenge and it appears we may still be a long way from fully embracing the need for visionary leaders who will effectively promote the needs and aspirations of young children and their families. Having been personally involved with NPQICL in the Southwest and hearing the voices of Children's Centre leaders, it appears to me that there is still a long way to go to achieve this objective. Currently, the main message seems to be 'do more with less' as the Children's Centre agenda is rolled out and the picture is still unclear as we enter a new parliament concerned with tackling a serious budget deficit.

One of the key difficulties for the development and articulation of leadership in the early years is the lack of theory to assist with the understanding and practice of leadership. Rodd (1994; 1998; 2005) argued that, although there is 'an abundance of literature on leadership as it pertains to business, industry, human services and education in general, little has been written specifically for the early childhood profession' (1998, pxi). Furthermore, leadership happens within a cultural context yet is most often written about as a culturally neutral, universal truth (Coleman and Campbell-Stephens, 2010). Thus, considerable work has had to be done to rethink some of the models of leadership and management that already exist within Local Authority bureaucracies and to establish new ones that reflect the aspirations of recent reports and recommendations and which facilitate working together with the child at the centre of practice.

A crucial question posed by the current debate on leadership and the development of services has to be, do we want leaders 'to fix things' in Early Childhood settings or is there/should there be a different way forward? Should there be more emphasis on a collegial approach that has, at its core, the opportunity for all practitioners to develop leadership skills whatever their job description or level?

Certainly, it appears that all practitioners should be enabled to develop theoretical and practical frameworks for leadership and management appropriate to contemporary early years provision based on knowledge of relevant theory and research. A criticism of the new Early Years Professional Status (CWDC, 2007), designed to establish leadership skills and abilities throughout the children's workforce, may be that this important theoretical underpinning is not sufficiently developed for the role to be truly effective. Currently, only the NPQICL qualification encourages the development of theoretical perspectives by offering participants the opportunity to engage in dialogue about what leadership means to them in their setting.

What is leadership?

We have had a fascination with leaders for centuries, attempting to establish and understand what defines the leader as opposed to the led, gaining insight and trying to encapsulate strong and weak characteristics in order to test/predict or identify those who may lead in whatever field we are engaged in. Leaders are seen as having a profound effect on whatever organisation they are in charge of, sometimes beneficial and sometimes detrimental. Leadership is often considered to involve influencing the behaviour of others, often to persuade them to follow a path defined by the leader. Thinking about 'best' leaders and 'worst' leaders in history is an absorbing occupation often engaged in by those attempting to make sense of the role of the leader.

Leadership theories have come, predominantly, from the field of industry. Throughout the twentieth century studies have focused on contributing towards a body of knowledge in order to give the world of business an understanding of what to look for and to enhance in the leaders they employ. These theories have increasingly been used in other fields, and during the last twenty years in particular, have been scrutinised and developed within the areas of education and social welfare.

Leadership theories can be broadly divided into the following categories: trait theories; behavioural or style theories; contingency or best fit theories and transformational theories. They are not necessarily exclusive, as Van Maurik (2001, p3) explains;

> *Although it is true that the progression of thinking tends to follow a sequential path, it is quite possible for elements of one generation to crop up much later in the writings of someone who would not normally think of himself or herself as being of that school. Consequently, it is fair to say that each generation has added something to the overall debate on leadership and that debate continues.*

Trait theory

Trait theory formed the basis of most leadership research up until the 1940s. Attempts were made to identify various personality traits or personal characteristics which, if present in an individual, would indicate his or her suitability as a leader. Key traits were usually identified by studying successful leaders in history, for example Julius Caesar, Alexander the Great, Mohandas Gandhi, Martin Luther King. Workers in this field developed tests that could predict which of the people applying for a leadership position possessed the desired traits and, therefore, were the most employable.

Using tests to establish whether people have particular identified qualities proved attractive to the business world for two reasons. Firstly, the predictive quality was regarded as promising less risk of employing the wrong person. Secondly, the innateness of trait theory suggested that money need not be spent on training leaders to do their job as eventually their skills would shine through.

Although there have been many criticisms of trait theory, aspects are still incorporated in training to support leaders (for example head teachers) in education today. McLelland's (1987) seminal work on human motivation is currently used by the National College (NC) where traits are described as 'non-conscious drivers'; that is, they influence our behaviour throughout many aspects of our lives including our working lives.

The major criticism of trait theory is that it is too simplistic, that other factors also need to be taken into account. So researchers began to focus on leaders' actions rather than just their attributes, considering the situations that leaders find themselves in and how to predict the traits or qualities required to deal with particular situations.

In summary, trait theory is based on an assumption that traits are innate rather than learned; that leaders are born rather than made. Experience, however shows us that this is not the case, not all leaders are born leaders. Studies of successful leaders show that they do not all have identical qualities. Most of the early research focused on male leaders in history. What does this say about women leaders, particularly pertinent in the early years field where the vast majority of leaders are women? Consequentially, the focus shifted from thinking about the leaders themselves to issues of leadership and what *styles* of leadership could be identified and described.

Behavioural theories of leadership

Writers who had become dissatisfied with the limitations of trait theory began to identify a range of leadership styles which could be used to develop tests to measure people's ability to lead and manage. The focus was now on how leaders behaved. Dozens of leadership styles were identified by many writers using different words to describe essentially similar behaviours. Influential writers such as Blake and Moulton (1964), for example, developed a Managerial Grid to assist in this identification process with the assumption that there is a best style of leadership. Likert (1967), another key writer in the field, suggested four different styles which incorporated some of the main ideas around at the time.

These leadership styles were:

- *Exploitative/authoritarian*, where leaders manipulate their subordinates and are used to prescribing tasks in the expectation that they will be obeyed without question by their staff;

- *Benevolent/authoritarian,* where leaders are used to being in charge and have a paternalistic approach to their employees;

- *Consultative* leadership, where employees are asked their opinion prior to leaders making decisions; and

- *Participative* leadership, where employees are involved in the decision-making processes.

Likert's typology, however, was based on the assumption that individuals are fixed with a particular style; therefore unable to shift from one style to another when the task and/or personnel change.

In the 1930s Lewin identified three different leadership styles; autocratic, laissez-faire and democratic. Autocratically led teams were those where the physical presence of the leader was required in order to get the work done. 'Follow me, I am right behind you' summarises a laissez-faire approach to leadership. Democratically led teams were those who could be given autonomy and responsibility and could be trusted to do their work without being constantly overseen. In order to be successful, the leader would need to be able to adopt the most appropriate style. Style theories, therefore, did offer the opportunity to begin to understand what has happened when leadership appears to go wrong, such as a particular style has been used that was inappropriate for the team or the task that was being carried out.

Tannenbaum and Schmidt (1958) were interested in the processes of decision making and continued to work on defining the autocratic-democratic continuum. They outlined a spectrum of situations and styles that could be used to identify the leadership requirements at any one time. Context was beginning to be recognised as important. This proved useful as it began to show that, over time, leaders might need to move from one style to another as teams developed in competence and that an autocratic leader would not be successful with a team of capable people who would wish to develop their own autonomy.

Neugebauer (1985, cited in Rodd, 1994 and 1998) related styles of leadership specifically to early years contexts with typologies of the Task Master, the Comrade, the Motivator and the Unleader, suggesting that the third was the most effective in these contexts. Again a useful thought as we see a move towards an increasingly autonomous workforce in early years with higher expectations regarding qualifications/experience and calibre of personnel.

A serious criticism of style theory is that people rarely lead using just one style. This approach did not take into account the changing contexts and situations that leaders might find themselves in. Frequently leaders have a variety of styles available to them that they feel comfortable with and are able to use; hence the development of contingency theories.

Contingency and situational theories of leadership

Contingency or situational leadership theories were developed to look at the ways in which leaders adapt their leadership style to be effective in different contexts, what Fiedler and Chemers (1974) term 'leader-match'. Thus, the idea of 'best fit' emerges where leaders are chosen by the organisation as being most effective in a particular situation given the structure of the task, the characteristics of all the people involved, both leaders and led, and the nature and quality of the relationships between them. Contingency theory gave the opportunity to look at the situation and its impact upon leaders rather than on the traits of the leader and their impact upon the situation (Northouse, 2009). Furthermore contingency theory recognises, for the first time, that leaders do not have to be effective in all situations (Northouse, 2009); all things to all people.

With regard to situational leadership, Hersey and Blanchard (1977) identify four styles that leaders might use to lead in different situations taking account both of tasks to be done and the relationships between the leader and others in the organisation. These were:

- *telling* – a style often required in situations where the task is repetitive or needs doing quickly;

- *selling* – a style that encourages and motivates people to do the tasks required;

- *participating* – a style required when the competence of staff is high, but unacknowledged by them so tasks still need facilitation, supervision and support by the leader;

- *delegating* – a style used where high staff motivation and competence means they are able to get on with the task without supervision or direct support.

In order to be successful according to contingency or situational leadership theory, leaders and their organisations need to be skilful at reading the requirements of the context in which they work (Telford, 1996). A key question, therefore, is what style and traits can be utilised so that the best will be achieved in given situations?

Transactional and transformational theories

Burns (1978) developed another set of ideas by distinguishing between transactional leadership (getting things done) and transformational (visionary) leadership. According to Burns, transactional leadership, coming primarily from management literature, can best be described as management techniques that are now recognised as effective, good and proper management. It is, therefore, about the use of negotiation with the led, an exchange of services for various kinds of rewards (both extrinsic and intrinsic) in order to reach a point of mutual satisfaction resulting in completion of the task.

Important aspects include setting up procedures, clear job descriptions, appraisal of performance, management by clarifying objectives, and so on. The effectiveness of and, therefore, the importance and use of praise, recognition and the delegation of responsibility is also acknowledged in this style of leadership.

Transactional leadership, though, can still be seen as a top-down rather than a bottom-up model of leadership. Transformational leadership is defined by Burns as moving beyond this. In transformational or visionary leadership, the leader and led work together on common objectives towards common aims.

Bass (1985), however, was critical of Burns' view that the two theories were oppositional. He preferred to see them as complementary and useful to each other and expanded and refined ideas about transformational leadership. Van Maurik (2001) suggests that the two should be looked upon as progressing from one to the other as demands upon leaders were becoming increasingly complex towards the end of the twentieth century. Working from transactional towards transformational leadership helps and enables both leaders and led to navigate around high levels of uncertainty in unstable and uncertain times. It is hardly surprising with constant and rapid change being a key characteristic of life through the 1980s and 1990s that interest in transformational leadership rose to the fore at that time.

Research on emotional intelligence has provided a further dimension to models of transformational leadership. Goleman et al. (2002) set out why it is imperative to have emotionally literate leaders. These are leaders who are aware of their own emotions, are committed to the professional development of themselves and others, are empowering, trusting, optimistic, have a life outside the working environment and look after their own physical and emotional well-being (McBride and Maitland, 2002, pp198–199).

Key aspects of transformational leadership are that it is about hearts and minds, about empowering people to learn and to seek change and improvement, not about controlling them. It is a people oriented approach rather than focused mainly on tasks or products. It is about trusting those with whom you work, transforming feelings, attitudes and beliefs and having an impact on the culture of the organisation. Anyone should be able to lead (Owen, 2000).

Collaborative leadership

Now, in the twenty-first century, definitions of effective leadership refer to shared, distributive, collaborative, invitational and collegiate ways of working. All of these qualities build on aspects of transformational leadership. Rodd (1994), Owen (2000) and Telford (1996) all advocate that anyone can take on a leadership role, given the right context and opportunity; 'Leadership, at its best, is a shared venture engaged in by the many.' (Telford, 1996, p9).

Nias et al. (1989) were among the first to develop ideas about collaborative leadership within the school context, where leaders and led have shared values, beliefs and attitudes which assist them in working towards the overt goals of the organisation. Continuing with the context of schools, Southworth (1998) argues that as there is much to manage and less time for any individual to lead, schools actually need many leaders, who take and share leadership roles. He argues that this has implications regarding shared headship, otherwise there will just be a redistribution of management tasks rather than shared leadership. This may well be pertinent to leadership in multi-disciplinary and multifunctional integrated early years settings.

Owen (2000) takes the view that it is an important part of the human spirit to wish to lead and to be able to do so. She identifies leaders as only being successful if they have effective structures around them; a relevant point, when we consider the anxieties surrounding multi-disciplinary working in child protection. Bolman and Deal (1991, in Telford, 1996) consider transformational leadership in four contexts or frames in order to help us understand the theoretical underpinning of all leadership theories:

- *structural*, which includes the formal roles and relationships of the workplace;

- *human resource,* which focuses on the needs of the individuals within the workplace;

- *political* described as the internal politics and power struggles; and

- *symbolic* or the culture of the workplace.

Again, from within the world of education, Telford (1996) argues that 'collaborative' leadership takes from all four frames, using them to analyse the tasks and work towards achieving the vision of the school.

Ethical leadership

Espoused by Bottery (1992), ethical leadership looks at the responsibility of the leader to think about how their setting fulfils its purpose. He argues that the legislation that frames the setting and its task is highly relevant and needs to be taken into consideration when embarking on any leadership decision making. What *is* the setting *for*? Ethical leadership is, therefore, seen as acting with moral purpose.

> *Leadership in general must maintain an ethical focus which is oriented towards democratic values within a community. This has to do with the meaning of ethics historically – as a search for the good life of the community..... ethics here refers to a more comprehensive construct than just individual behaviour; rather it implicates this and how we as a moral community live our communal lives.*

(Foster, 1989, p55)

How does ethical leadership manifest itself in action? The answer to this question is particularly relevant to Early Childhood services where success depends on the interrelatedness of working with people, for people. Rodd (1998) for example, identifies four key areas within ethical leadership. These include:

- the promotion and protection of children's rights;

- the provision of a high quality and economically viable service which does not compromise children's rights;

- administration of services in accordance with the profession's ethical principles;

- employment of an early childhood code of ethics to guide the resolution of ethical dilemmas.

Interestingly, we still do not have written codes of ethics in the UK to inform workers in all early years settings.

Distributed leadership

A 'new kid on the block' (Hartley, 2007), distributed leadership has gathered considerable momentum in a very short time. Distributed leadership is the sharing of the responsibility of leadership by several people often at different levels within an organistaion (Gronn, 2002; NCSL, 2006). Thus, distributed leadership takes account of the context in which it occurs and focuses on the interaction of the leaders and followers in getting tasks done. There is a recognition that tasks may be too complex for one person to successfully complete as well as respect for the different skills and attributes of others who may be better placed or equipped to fulfil certain leadership functions. Distributed leadership has become popular as it is flexible, negotiable and adaptable, moving away from a focus on the leader as an individual with particular skills and attributes towards the effective sharing of tasks that need to be done (Earley and Weindling, 2004). In the complex, multi-professional world of early years, it is not hard to see why distributed leadership has been embraced by some of the key writers (Aubrey, 2007; Jones and Pound, 2008) and organisations (National College). According to Aubrey (2007), distributed leadership allows for collaboration, inter-action and interdependence, thus enabling the development of powerful and sustainable learning communities. However, distributed leadership has come in for a great deal of criticism. Both Harris (2007) and Hartley (2007) suggest that the move towards distributed leadership is a fashionable trend and its lack of conceptual clarity is a serious handicap; it is too flexible to be taken seriously as a substantial model of leadership. Furthermore, crisis situations demand a more assertive, some would say coercive (Fullan, 2002, cited in Aubrey, 2007) style of leadership that does not seem to sit easily with the more egalitarian distrib-uted leadership framework.

The emergence of authentic leadership

Another 'new kid on the block' is authentic leadership which takes inspiration from the work of Goleman (1998) amongst others and is therefore a leadership from within that relies upon self awareness; relational transparency; balanced processing and an internalised moral perspective (Champy, 2009) that enables the leader to be immune to the pressures of the role by giving them the facility of being true to themselves. Authentic leadership recognises the complexity of modern leadership and the demands that are made on indi-vidual leaders to reach even greater heights in managing complicated situations (Avolio and Gardner, 2005). Taking account of the sociological concept of emotional labour (Hochschild, 1983) where people are expected to act in certain ways according to the demands of the organisation, authentic leadership seeks to find a path that leaders might follow that protects them from exhaustion and burnout by encouraging them to lead as they see fit, being authentic and true to themselves. Authentic leaders are defined as:

> *those who are deeply aware of how they think and behave and are perceived by others and being aware of their own and others' values/moral perspectives, knowledge and strengths; aware of the context in which they operate and who are confident, hopeful, optimistic, resilient and of high moral character.*

(Avolio, Luthans and Walumba, 2004, cited in Avolio and Gardner, 2005, p321)

Like distributed leadership, authentic leadership promotes followership by fostering the development of authenticity in others within the organisation. Through the use of conscious personal reflective dialogues, leaders are able to develop skills of professional effectiveness as well as being ethically sound and value based in their decision making (Begley, 2001).

Conclusion

Despite the contested arena of what theoretical model of leadership should be used in early childhood settings, there is a discernible consensus as to what constitutes effective leadership:

- that there should be a shared, articulated philosophy based on values and principles (Whalley, 2006a; Siraj-Blatchford and Manni, 2006; Jones and Pound, 2008);

- that there should be a distribution of leadership tasks throughout the organisation (Siraj-Blatchford and Manni, 2006; Moyles, 2006; Jones and Pound, 2008);

- that leadership should be visionary, inspiring others and leading the way, finding innovative and creative paths (Earley and Weindling, 2004; Siraj-Blatchford and Manni, 2006; Moyles, 2006; Jones and Pound, 2008; West-Burnham et al., 2007);

- that the leaders should facilitate the co-construction of the environment with those who share it (Siraj- Blatchford and Manni, 2006; Jones and Pound, 2008);

- that leadership should promote the foregrounding of relationships as most important (West-Burnham et al., 2007; Curtis and Burton, 2009);

- that the development of an ethic of care to underpin the service provision is crucial (Osgood, 2006; Curtis and Burton, 2009);

- that the importance of followership should be recognised (West-Burnham et al., 2007);

- that the cultural context is regarded as relevant and key in shaping the style of leadership and its manifestation (Fleer, 2003; Tobin, 2005);

- that leaders are change agents (Sylva et al., 2004; Earley and Weindling, 2004; Moyles, 2006; Jones and Pound, 2008; Curtis and Burton, 2009);

- that it is important to be a reflective practitioner (Moyles, 2006; Jones and Pound, 2008; Urban, 2008; Curtis and Burton, 2009);

- that there are certain valued personal qualities, not least the ability to be authentic and encourage authenticity in others (Sylva et al., 2004; Moyles, 2006; West-Burnham et al., 2007; Jones and Pound, 2008; Curtis and Burton, 2009);

- that leaders have to be effective communicators (Sylva et al., 2004; Siraj-Blatchford and Manni, 2006).

There is a sense that leadership theory has moved from the 'hard' world of industry and business towards a more 'touchy/feely' world where people are valued for themselves, not just the work they do. This is perhaps vital and maybe inevitable as we have developed complex working worlds, trained and developed our staff to higher competencies and created more service oriented businesses as opposed to ones dealing in inanimate products.

However, I am concerned that this paradigm shift does not seem to be articulated in practice. For example, Aubrey (2007) talks about the difficulties of effective leadership where the structure is hierarchical, but the culture is collaborative. Furthermore, the role of chief executive as opposed to the role of leading professional seems to be the leadership model promoted by many Government reforms and policies. The requirement to balance the books is therefore taking precedence over the inspirational aspects of leadership. This can clearly be seen in policies that allow businesses to take over so called 'failing' schools, hospitals and other public services, where they have no intrinsic understanding of the setting, but know how to balance the books.

I think this raises questions as to whether it is possible or feasible for leaders to also be managers. Does this lead to job overload? We are already seeing evidence of this within education and within the first cohort of Early Excellence Centres. Thus we must ask what the new Government's agenda will be in 2010 as well as what we are trying to achieve by improving the leadership of early years settings.

In addition, I would suggest that we should engage in a meaningful debate as to what early years settings are there for. Are settings designed to allow today's workforce to go about their business knowing their children are being educated and cared for or to enhance children's experiences in the here and now? Moss & Petrie (2002) present a cogent argument that 'childhood is an important stage of the life course in its own right, which leaves traces on later stages' (p101). If we believe this then there are huge implications in terms of new sorts of relationships between children, between adults and between children and adults. Clear statements about our philosophy need to be central to the debate on what sorts of leaders we want.

I would argue that leadership in early years settings should be inclusive for all participants; staff, children, parents and leaders. Leadership is about learning, becoming wiser and more knowledgeable. This does not necessarily mean knowing a lot of things, but is more to do with knowing about oneself and acting in the right way given particular situations, developing learning cultures for staff and parents as well as children. We do not need superhuman leaders as they cannot be emulated by the many:

> *Even the most talented leaders require the input and leadership of others, constructively solicited and creatively applied. It's time to celebrate the incomplete – that is, the human – leader.*

(Ancona et al., 2007, p101)

ACTIVITY *1*

During the next few weeks read a variety of national and local newspapers and collect articles that demonstrate aspects of leadership. These could include references to politicians, football managers, celebrities, local initiatives, businesses, public services, etc.

Try to identify for yourself components of successful leadership to discuss in a small group.

ACTIVITY 2

In a small group, plan an early years setting of your choice. Consider the following aspects:

1. *outline the vision, purposes and aim of your particular setting;*

2. *describe, in detail, the services you will offer; the market you seek to serve and the premises you will require;*

3. *identify the staffing implications of your plan, in terms of numbers, roles, qualifications, terms and conditions;*

4. *identify how your setting will meet the needs of you, your staff, the children, their families and the wider community;*

5. *develop a short term and long term plan of what steps would need to be taken to create your setting.*

This could form the context for an assignment discussing key leadership issues related to your particular setting.

FURTHER READING

Ancona, D, Malone, TW, Orlikowski, WJ and Senge, P (2007) *In Praise of the Incomplete Leader.* Boston, MA: Harvard Business Review, pp92–102

This article is inspirational: it reminds us how important it is to be human and that leadership is not about having all the answers, but about enabling and promoting the development of communities.

Woodrow, C and Busch, G (2008) Repositioning Early Childhood Leadership as Action and Activism, *European Early Childhood Education Research Journal*, Vol.16(1), pp83–93

This paper discusses the tension between the preferred models of leadership espoused by early years leaders and the demands of corporate childcare and the commodification of services. Using feminist work in the areas of leadership and professionalism, the authors argue that there are new opportunities for further development of early years leadership.

Whalley, M (2006) *Leadership in Integrated Centres and Services for Children and Families – a Community Development Approach. Engaging with the struggle.* Paper given in Wellington, New Zealand, June 2006

Margy Whalley has been at the forefront of leadership development in early years settings and led the creation of the NPQICL. Her values and principles have facilitated discussion about new ways of leading that have taken the leadership of children's centre's in new and meaningful directions involving whole communities.

10 The benefits of comparison: recent developments in the German early years workforce

Ulrike Hohmann

Introduction

Who we think children are, who we feel should be responsible for the care and education of the youngest members of a society and what skills we think are necessary to do this well, are all questions which touch on wider social issues. Current shifts in thinking indicate changing relationships between children and adults and offer a rationale for new policy developments. This chapter explores the freshly revived debate around the training and education of the early years workforce in Germany. It explores the drivers of demands to lift training and education of *Staatlich Anerkannte Erzieherinnen* (the largest occupational group within this field) into higher education and identifies some barriers. This qualification and professional title is often shortened to *Erzieherin* (singular) or *Erzieherinnen* (plural). The literal translation is 'state-approved (child) raiser'. The discussions emerging in this process highlight the effects of demographic shifts observed in the developed world, show tentative signs for divergence in the experience of childhood across Europe and, in the tradition of comparative research, inform comparisons and contrasts with the development of Early Years Professional Status (EYPS) in England. A cross-national, comparative perspective has a number of benefits. The 'difference view' and the 'import-mirror view' as suggested by May (2001) refer to the analysis of how other countries solve a particular problem, for example, how changing demands on early years services can be met. Exploring differences by taking 'insider' and 'outsider' positions aids the formulation of new questions and can pinpoint more precisely which conditions support or hinder particular developments. We can begin to ask questions about what would happen if we were to import a certain set of policies and practices into our national or local context. Related to this perspective, cross-national comparison acts as a mirror or lens which can sharpen our focus on our own positions and practices while inviting us to challenge background assumptions which are specific to our national context and which might otherwise be taken for granted.

The chapter is informed by a pilot study in one of 16 *Länder* (singular, *Land*) of the Federal Republic of Germany undertaken during autumn 2006, which accessed opinions of a number of stakeholders, qualified *Erzieherinnen* and students enrolled in one of the first German BA courses in pedagogy of early childhood in Freiburg and also by recent developments in early childhood settings. I will begin by explaining and exploring some of the concepts used when reflecting on the relationship between parents, children and the early childhood workforce. Recent developments in early years pedagogy would not have been deemed necessary without the perception that childhood itself has changed, mainly due to socio-economic changes and demographic developments which will be addressed briefly. This will be followed by a broad overview of the German care and education system for children before they reach compulsory school age, and then of the training and education of practitioners. The rest of the chapter will explore the newly revived debate about education and training issues in Germany and will extract three perspectives that contribute to a better understanding of early childhood services.

Erziehung, Betreuung and Bildung: raising children, care and education

On a formal level, relationships and responsibilities are defined and reflected by the legal framework, which sets out rights and duties connected to kinship and family formation and laws regulating childcare and education. The discourse of childhood in a society is powerfully expressed through language. For example, relationships are defined by making decisions about whether to talk about 'children' or 'kids' (defined in my dictionary as baby goats); parents, mothers and fathers, or mums and dads; or addressing staff in early childhood settings as 'Auntie Jane' or 'Mrs Smith'.

In Germany much of the understanding of childhood and responsibilities is reflected through the use and the definition of the words *Erziehung, Betreuung* and *Bildung*. In contrast to the new *Länder* (in what used to be the socialist German Democratic Republic (GDR)), the old *Länder* (in what was West Germany), relied successfully on a particular definition of the traditional family with gender-specific tasks. Since this was generally accepted until recently, the structure and availability of childcare and education services appeared sufficient and congruent with people's expectations. The family is seen to be mainly responsible for *Kindererziehung* (literally translated as 'child-raising', sometimes translated as 'upbringing') reflecting primary socialisation tasks and *Betreuung* (best translated as 'care') during the earliest years of childhood. These expectations are discussed publicly and reflected in a number of family support policies. Around a child's third birthday attendance at a kindergarten or day centre has been seen as beneficial in supporting parents in their task – at least until recently. A new law (*Kinderförderungsgesetz*) provides the framework for extending early years provision and from 2013 guarantees a childcare place for children aged one to three years for parents who need it. *Bildung* (education) is the focus of school and to some extent of kindergarten, though relying on different forms of didactics. Education was more widely acknowledged as part of the purpose of kindergartens in the former GDR. More recently the task of providing educational opportunities in all early years services has been emphasised and now all *Länder* have drawn up early years curriculum guidance, although with varying content and relying on a range of approaches (Oberhuemer et al., 2009; Jaszus et al., 2008).

The three different concepts *Erziehung, Betreuung* and *Bildung* are useful for the discussion of future challenges regarding the socialisation of children and planning of services. The 12th Children and Youth Report (BMFSFJ, 2005) states that the boundaries between childcare services and school need to become more permeable. The aim is to move from viewing care, socialisation and education as a hierarchy of priorities towards approaches that integrate all of the three elements wherever children are cared for. For example, family has to be recognised as the basic and essential location of education and education needs to have a firm place in early childhood services for the youngest children. School has to embrace an ethos that acknowledges that it provides care and socialisation as well as education.

The threefold definition of children's needs stands in contrast to the debates in English speaking countries where differences between care and education are sometimes used to differentiate between the responsibilities of parents and the state in bringing up children.

Demographic changes

As in many European countries the fertility rate of women in Germany has declined, leading to more one-child households. Women's employment rates have risen and there is more demand for childcare for working parents. However, 20 years after the unification of the two German states, marked differences remain, making it difficult to speak of one Germany. There are different perspectives on how to balance work and caring commitments and how to divide tasks within households. The economic situations of the old and new *Länder* and continuing differences in structures of early childhood services lead to heterogeneous experiences for children and their families. Although there is a general trend towards more one-child families and children growing up with one parent or in step-families, there are significant differences to be observed in the old and new *Länder*. Additionally over the past three decades the proportion of children with migration backgrounds has grown (BMFSFJ, 2002, 1998). Now around a third of young children in Germany have some kind of migration background (Statistisches Bundesamt, 2009b) and 30 per cent of children who do not speak German at home attend day care facilities where more than half of the children are in the same situation (Autorengruppe Bildungsberichterstattung, 2008). Against this backdrop, demands on education in early childhood settings evolve because linguistic proficiency is an essential condition for social integration and educational achievement. Closely linked to the changing face of childhood in Germany is the increasing proportion of children growing up in poverty (Bertram, 2008). The pilot study shows that *Erzieherinnen* are acutely aware that this state of affairs imposes new demands on their skills and expertise. Growing knowledge about the long-term effects of disadvantages during childhood fuels the call for more and better institutional support for parents or even for demands to compensate for the alleged lack of interfamilial socialisation. In the light of the complex demographic changes that have taken place recently, it is not helpful to blame the family or another social institution, like the kindergarten, for disadvantages children experience in this manner. However, a commitment to well tailored and multi-level interventions during the early years is seen as an important step towards breaking the vicious circle of lack of education and poverty.

The childcare system

In Germany, provision for children before they reach compulsory school age (at six years) is traditionally divided into two main sectors. Children up to the age of three years are cared for in what is called a *Krippe* (literately translated as 'crèche') or they are looked after by a family day care provider (childminder). Overall, 20 per cent of children under three years took up a place in day care in March 2009 (Statistisches Bundesamt, 2009a). Provision in the old *Länder* is low, with places catering for only 14.6 per cent of children, but continues to be comparatively good in the new *Länder,* serving 46 per cent of this age group. From the age of three until they start school, children have the right to a kindergarten place and the provision is high, with 91 per cent in the old *Länder* and almost 95 per cent in the new *Länder* in 2009. However, only around a fifth of these places were full-time in the old *Länder* whereas two thirds of kindergarten places in the new *Länder* were offered on a full-time basis (Autorengruppe Bildungsberichterstattung, 2008). Places in *Krippe* and *Kindergarten* are subsidised but parents have to contribute, on average, 23.6 per cent of the cost. There are considerable differences between *Länder* and within *Länder* (OECD, 2006a). Only a relatively small proportion of children of compulsory school age have access to after school care (*Hort*), however, again there is better provision in the new *Länder*. Over recent years a softening of the rigid boundaries between these three (*Krippe, Kindergarten* and *Hort)* sectors has taken place, especially where these are housed in the same building under the same management (OECD, 2006b) and where some children are cared for in mixed age groups.

The workforce in day centres and kindergartens is overwhelmingly (97.4 per cent) female (Autorengruppe Bildungsberichterstattung, 2008), as in other European Countries (EGGE, 2009). The small proportion of men is most likely to be found in settings working with school aged children or children with disabilities (Autorengruppe Bildungsberichterstattung, 2008; Leu, 2005; Riedel, 2005). There is growing awareness that a better gender balance in early years services could have benefits for the care and education of girls and boys and most staff would prefer to work with both men and women in the nursery (Rohrmann, 2009).

In general, the younger the children, the lower the level of qualification held by staff working with them. About two-thirds (64 per cent) hold the qualification *Staatlich Anerkannte Erzieherin.* Providing a translation of this qualification and status in a meaningful way is beset with difficulties. However, attempts to do so may help to explain some of the ethos of this profession and the early years sector. Literally translated, they are 'state-approved (child) raisers'. The noun *Erzieher* derives from the German word *Erziehung* (see above) and describes the tasks of taking care of children and of supporting the socialisation process. If the word 'pedagogue' did not have a negative ring in English, it would be appropriate to call them state-approved (kindergarten) pedagogues. It seems to be less appropriate to call them kindergarten teachers, since the teaching profession is strongly protected by professional closure in Germany and driven by a quite different ethos.

After achieving lower secondary school qualification (corresponding to GCSEs) *Erzieherinnen* undergo three years' vocational training at a *Fachschule (FS) für Sozialpädagogik* (College for Social Pedagogy) including one year of work-based learning which is sometimes followed by a one-year internship. *Erzieherinnen* are qualified to work with children and young people of all ages in all kinds of settings. However, the training focuses on children between three and six years of age. The second largest group working in day centres are *Kinderpflegerinnen* (the name can be translated as 'child carers' – but also implies a suggestion of nursing). The professional title *Kinderpflegerinnen* is awarded after two years of vocational training and a one-year internship. Leaders of day centres are most likely to be social pedagogues who studied at a *Fachhochschule (FHS) für Sozialpädagogik* (university of applied science for social pedagogy). Social pedagogues are qualified to work with children and adults in all kinds of settings and can offer support in a wide range of adverse situations. Due to the federal structure of Germany and the education system, the content and more specific structures of the three training and education pathways vary from *Land* to *Land*.

The qualification framework of the early years workforce is considerably less fragmented than in Britain. One of the effects is that *Erzieherinnen* and social pedagogues have a professional habitus in common that is firmly grounded in the principles of social pedagogy. Both can be described as all-round professions because they work with people of all ages and personal situations (Prott, 2006).They base their work on a holistic understanding of children and adults, being aware of the complex interdependence of 'head, hand and heart' and the influence of historical and sociocultural context. *Erzieherinnen* draw much of their conception of their professional status from the approach developed by Friedrich Fröbel (1782–1852), viewing kindergarten as a pedagogical institution and utilising games and play to educate children. It is through play and art that *Erzieherinnen* and social pedagogues build relationships and they are skilled in using group processes to support development and well-being (Cameron and Boddy, 2006).

Demands on training and education

The context of demographic and socio-economic changes and the debate about characteristics and skills needed by the childcare workforce raised concerns about the levels of qualification. The *Erzieherin* of today has little in common with the *Kindergärtnerin* who educated and cared for children 50 years ago (Beher et al., 1999). Additionally, due to reforms of child and youth policies a much broader range of tasks and responsibilities has emerged for *Erzieherinnen* (Robert Bosch Stiftung, 2006; BMFSF, 2005; GEW, 2005). The demands for more and better knowledge of child development are voiced frequently and the training and education of *Erzieherinnen* has been the focus of attention. The changing work context demands that the qualification *Staatlich Anerkannte Erzieher/Erzieherin* should enable these women and men to engage successfully in continuous professional development, allowing them to base their daily work on the findings and insights of research. It was felt that modelling training too closely on school risked losing important elements of being able to apply theory to praxis and using theory to reflect on practice. Additionally, this form of teaching and learning did not promote self-study and self-development sufficiently. Although the deficit in the qualifications and training of *Kinderpflegerinnen* and *Erzieherinnen* has been repeatedly stated over the past 35 years (for example, Rauschenbach et al., 1995) and the trade union GEW has demanded education at graduate level since 1993 (GEW, 2005), this has not led to any significant reforms and improvements in college courses or to a policy decision to entrust higher education institutions with the training and education of the early years workforce (Thole and Cloose, 2006).

In contrast to Germany, the UK has a multitude of qualifications on a number of different levels. As in Germany, the demands for training of the early years workforce at graduate level emerged in the early 1990s and degrees in Early Childhood Studies have been offered in a number of universities in the UK since then (Abbott and Pugh, 1998). These degrees now form part of the highly complex National Framework of childcare qualifications. The British government contemplated whether improving the quality of the early years work-force should be achieved by increasing provision of early years qualified teachers or by developing a new profession along the lines of the continental 'pedagogue' model (HM Treasury, 2004). The decision was taken to promote a new Early Years Professional Status (EYPS) and in September 2006 the first candidates began assessment for EYPS.

Moving on: the Italian double momentum

In Germany, the new impetus to reform the qualification path of *Erzieherinnen* comes from two separate developments not directly connected to the early years sector. Firstly, one strand of the German discussion was prompted by the unexpectedly negative results of the PISA (Programme for International Student Assessment) study which emphasised the potential of very early childhood and raised concerns about the lost early years in the German system. The second factor was the Bologna process, which aims to standardise training and education across Europe and to make it more accessible by modularising and organising higher education as a coherent system of Bachelors and Masters programmes.

Some in Germany are concerned that lifting training into higher education institutions could exclude a group of young people, particularly women, from this education because they cannot meet the entry requirements. Instead of changing the location of qualifica-tions, closer co-operation between the different institutions (*FS, FHS* and universities) and, for example, offering some form of core qualification, shared by *Erzieherinnen* and pri-mary schoolteachers, could be a more palatable compromise (Oberhuemer et al., 2009). The dean of one of the *FS* for social pedagogy explained that this should not be regarded as a stance against change and different structures of teaching and learning, instead he is convinced that a close co-operation with institutions training primary schoolteachers is a more realistic way forward. Since 2007/08 the teacher training college he had in mind has offered a BA course in early childhood and elementary education. The argument for integrating the training and education of *Erzieherinnen* and primary schoolteachers gains additional weight from questions about whether existing teaching staff at *FS* are able to teach at higher education level, and from the perception that staff at *FHS* are not involved in social sciences and education research and therefore cannot offer the whole univer-sity experience. Attempts to create up to twelve Chairs in Early Childhood and Elementary Education in established universities had resulted in only three by 2010 (Speth, 2010). Early childhood and education is a new field of academic interest which lacks a pool of experi-enced academics and has not yet gained momentum in building up a recognised body of research and knowledge. However, this kind of development would provide the necessary teaching and learning environment, at higher education level, for the early years workforce.

One of the major barriers to changing the level of qualification demanded of members of the early years workforce is the anticipation of increasing costs if core practitioners become graduates. It has been argued firstly, that not all *Erzieherinnen* need initially to be educated to graduate level (Thole and Cloose, 2006), secondly that the costs of training are not higher than in Fachschulen and, thirdly, that the resources freed by a lower take-up of kindergarten places due to the declining fertility rate in Germany can be spent on increasing staff wages (Pasternack and Schildberg, 2005). This may calm concerns of politicians, providers and parents but how and how much public money is spent on the care and education of children is still a political decision. Decisions like this should be driven by a belief in the content of a new qualification route and the possible effects on the quality of early childhood services and the outcomes for children (Rauschenbach, 2006). In England, similar concerns about the financial impact and rising costs of childcare due to the employment of graduate staff led to the implementation of the Transformation Fund (HM Treasury, 2004).

Another aspect of the discussions (about whether the positioning of training and education within the higher education sector is a move in the right direction) is the question of what skills and characteristics are needed by people working with young children and how they are best acquired. Characteristics like patience, empathy, humour, openness, creativity and the ability to reflect, but also emotional stability and assertiveness, were listed as essential for their work by *Erzieherinnen* in the pilot study. Many of these characteristics are sometimes described as 'female' and linked to caring attitudes and practices (Sevenhuijsen, 1998; Noddings, 1993; Tronto, 1993). In the German context they are often subsumed under the heading 'motherliness'. These skills and attitudes are seen to be strengthened, at least to some extent, by the experience of motherhood. The importance attached to motherliness, and the common agreement about ways to promote it, led to its being seen as a kind of 'natural' qualification, so that women who have children of their own are given easier access into some of the training colleges (Ahnert, 2005).

However, much of the literature positions care in the private, unpaid domain (Graham, 1991) and neglects the question of whether all aspects of care in the public domain could be taught and learnt. Motherliness could be seen as a dark side of the profession if it influences practice without reflection and if the requirement of motherliness means that the profession has a lower status (Rabe-Kleberg, 2006).The newly emerging debate about the training and education of *Erzieherinnen,* and about the best location for it, may help to provide some answers. The *Erzieherinnen* in the pilot study explained that what proved to be useful in their work was knowledge and insight gained from psychology, particularly child development. Pedagogy and practical exercises, including those tapping into personal experiences, were valued. Other studies show that the current education and training at *FS* appears less suitable for fostering the ability to access academic knowledge and to make use of insight gained by research in the disciplines of psychology, pedagogy and other social sciences (Thole and Cloose, 2006). After all, colleges aim to make scientifically based knowledge accessible to their students in contrast to universities which have the task of supporting the development of research skills and knowledge construction.

Although the debate around moving the training and education of *Erzieherinnen* into higher education institutions uses powerful arguments about improving the quality of services (Robert Bosch Stiftung, 2006), a closer look at the funded pilot projects shows that there is no agreement about the form this move should take. Courses vary regarding their location, teaching and learning mode, entrance qualifications, titles and final awards (GEW, 2005; Thole and Cloose, 2006). Five years after the pilot project started, an online search tool developed for potential students held information on 55 BA courses and 10 Masters courses across Germany (Dreyer and Hildebrandt, 2009). This development may challenge the opinion that a general move to higher education is unrealistic. However, the range of variations already observed during the pilot stage shows that proposals to co-operate or to fuse *FS* and *FHS* and proposals to provide common core elements for the training of both *Erzieherinnen* and primary schoolteachers (Diller and Rauschenbach, 2006) have not been readily picked up. Considering the traditionally different training routes, differing professional identities and different purposes of early years care and education and school, this is not surprising. For example, elementary education (as the stage before schooling is called) is firmly grounded in inclusive ideas. In contrast to this value the German schools system has a strong selective element.

The development of training and education of the early years workforce in Germany seems to be leading to a greater fragmentation. If these new qualifications lead to a concentration on only a narrow range of work roles, for example managing a daycare setting, the profile of the workforce may become similar to that in England. The motivation of the first cohort of students on the BA Pedagogy of Early Childhood at the *Evangelische Fachhochschule Freiburg* arose from the perception that the previous qualification as *Erzieherin* was too superficial and did not allow them to acquire sufficient knowledge as a basis for their practical work. Students hoped for personal development and to increase their employability, both in Germany and abroad. They perceived themselves as trailblazers and enjoyed their role, though they also had feelings of uncertainty (see also Fröhlich-Gildhoff, 2006).

It appears that in Germany *FS*, *FHS* and universities compete against each other and the attempt to develop new training and education routes has shown that some practical problems are not solved yet. At the time of writing frameworks of academic standards for the training and education of *Erzieherinnen* and related jobs were just emerging (Speth, 2010; Gerstenberger et al., 2008). Decisions have to be made about who is qualified to teach and assess new qualifications and what is going to happen to the existing workforce. If, as appears very likely, a strong element of training and education is going to be based in work experience, mentors in settings may not yet have qualifications at the level the students are working towards and may therefore not be deemed suitable to supervise them (Prott, 2006). The potential challenge and tensions arising from this may also be relevant for the English EYPS as at first it will be difficult to find enough assessors who are qualified to judge whether candidates have met the required standards. The developments in Germany highlight three perspectives that can also be used to explore the state of affairs in other countries. Firstly, the debate about the purpose of childcare has not been resolved. The new balance of the three elements *Erziehung, Betreuung, Bildung* will depend on how the needs of parents, children and employers are prioritised. The German government has clearly expressed its intention to inject more education into care settings. This is often perceived as downward pressure from school which risks introducing unsuitable ways of working with young children. It may also influence what is considered the best approach to help childcare workers or pedagogues to integrate tacit, functional and professional aspects of their knowledge. When tacit and functional knowledge are emphasised, training can be offered by lower-level institutions and can be assessed by 'vocational-industrial qualifications'. A stronger emphasis on professional knowledge leads to demands for more professional academic education (Cameron and Boddy, 2006).

Secondly, do the proposed reforms lead to a greater specialisation of pedagogical roles and, therefore, the fragmentation of an all-round profession? This would work against the professional ethos of balancing *Erziehung*, *Betreuung* and *Bildung* – an ethos commended by the OECD (2006a; Prott, 2006). For each of the possible solutions, either specialisation of roles or further integration of an all-round profession, new career and training paths will need to be developed.

Thirdly, the debate highlights questions about how to link theory and practice but has not provided answers. One can be forgiven for having the impression that this is a chicken-and-egg discussion. However, preferences for particular sequences of development of practical skills and of theoretical knowledge will inform decisions about the level at which training and education are best situated, as well as choices about the content and the structure of programmes.

An interesting twist in the debate about how theoretical knowledge and practical experience interlink is highlighted by tensions that emerged among the first cohort of the BA Early-Childhood Pedagogy degree in Freiburg. The group of students had to work through conflicting perceptions – for example that a qualified *Erzieherin* with work experience would already know all there was to know about the value of play. Opportunities to reflect on previously learnt theories in the light of experience, to examine newly learned theories from a number of angles and to share different students' perspectives allowed the group to develop new insights and to value this learning opportunity. Similar differences in perspective have been observed when people with and without previous work experience and/ or vocational training study together on a degree course and it remains to be seen if this might lead to tensions in England as candidates for EYPS join higher education courses.

ACTIVITY 1

Use information on EYPS (e.g. from www.cwdcouncil.org.uk) to explore the following issues.

What is the purpose of childcare services in England? Which elements of the standards suggest that they are 'vocational-industrial qualifications' and which suggest a requirement for 'professional education'?

ACTIVITY 2

How would you describe the interplay between Erziehung, Betreuung *and* Bildung *in England and how do they link to different kinds of qualifications?*

Think about one of the themes of the Early Years Foundation Stage (a unique child, positive relationships, enabling environments or learning and development) and explore your experience of linking theory and practices.

FURTHER READING

More information on Germany and international perspectives relevant for early childhood can be found in:

Boddy, J, Cameron, C and Moss, P (eds) (2006) *Care work: Present and Future*. London and New York: Routledge.

The authors critically examine current themes in care work and look at the changing face of care work and care occupation for those working with children, young people, adults and the elderly.

Gelder, U (2003) Carving out a niche? The work of Tagesmütter in the new Germany, in A Mooney and J Statham (eds) *Family day care: international perspectives on policy, practice and quality*. London: Jessica Kingsley.

The chapter draws on my doctoral research (when my name was Ulrike Gelder) with family day care providers in one town in the north-east of Germany, to explore how the service has developed and some of the tensions created by combining the public role of childcare worker with the private sphere of home and family.

Oberhuemer, P, Schreyer, I and Neuman, M (2009) *Professionals in Early Childhood Education and Care Systems: European Profiles and Perspectives*. Opladen & Farmington Hills: Barbara Budrich.

This text provides information on the social context of childcare and educational services in a number of European countries. Cross-national themes and issues on training, provision and policy have been emphasised for comparative analysis.

Schweiwe, K and Willenkens, H (eds) (2009) *Child Care and Preschool Development in Europe: Institutional Perspectives*. Basingstoke: Palgrave Macmillan.

Public provision of care for children below school age is a pressing policy issue in European countries. This book traces the two competing approaches to childcare and shows historical and social roots. One focuses on facilitating women's paid involvement in the workforce. The other focuses on the educational needs of children.

WEBSITES

OECD reports on a number of countries can be accessed at

www.oecd.org/document/3/0,2340,en_2649_201185_27000067_1_1_1_1,00.html

Part 4

Comparing children's worlds: making the familiar strange

11 Adults' concepts of childhood

Norman Gabriel

Introduction

This chapter will look at some of the influential sociological perspectives on childhood, discussing their claims that children should be considered as active 'beings' in here-and-now situations, rather than as future adults. What are the social constructions and institutions which shape the experiences of being a child? Children experience a variety of different childhoods; we will examine some of the challenges and structural changes to two of the most important social institutions that children experience, families and schools.

We will then explore adults' concepts of childhood by tracing the historical forces that have helped to shape different constructions of childhood. A central concern of this chapter will be the way that different concepts of 'nature' have been used to define what we mean by childhood. If children are defined by their own innate 'nature' or 'natural' needs, then a number of assumptions are made about childhood in order to distinguish its unique qualities from adulthood:

> *The relationship between children, childhood and nature has existed at a number of different levels. It is as complex as our ideas about nature itself: the state of childhood may be seen as pure, innocent, or original in the sense of primary; children may be analogised with animals or plants, thereby indicating that they are natural objects for scientific and medical investigation; children could be valued as aesthetic objects ... but they could equally be feared for their instinctual, animal-like natures.*

(Jordanova, 1989, p6)

These different assumptions of what we mean by 'nature' will be considered in more detail by focusing on one very important area: the 'moral' upbringing of children and changing patterns of parental advice which have evolved since the eighteenth century.

And lastly, we will argue that although sociologists of childhood have highlighted some of the important issues that young children face as they grow up in British society, there is a tendency for them to narrowly focus their attention on the 'immediate present', neglecting some of the long-term historical processes that have led to changing conceptions of the relationship between adulthood and childhood.

Sociological perspectives on childhood

During the 1960s, childhood was seen as a preparation for adulthood: the child was seen as an 'incomplete organism', developing in response to different stimuli. Within the boundaries of child-rearing psychology, what was important was finding ways of turning the immature, irrational and incompetent child into a mature, rational and competent adult. These dominant principles at the heart of developmental psychology have been referred to by Smart et al. (2001) as the 'embryonic model', one where children are considered to be in a state of permanent transition, either within or between stages. Defined as potential persons, they are valued more for their future as adults than for their present lives as children. Such a 'futures' orientation (Cockburn, 1998) tends to place overriding importance on what children will become when they reach adulthood rather than focusing on their day-to-day lives as children.

In the new social studies of childhood that emerged in the 1970s and early 1980s, researchers began to rethink childhood and challenge the view that children were passive recipients of care and education. Sociologists of childhood challenged this view by emphasising the present tense of childhood, children's active participation in constructing their own lives and their relationships with family and friends. According to James and Prout (1997), children should be viewed as social actors, as participants in complex relationships with others. In the early years of human life a different framework is needed to understand the institution of childhood: '… children are not formed by natural and social forces but rather they inhabit a world of meaning created by themselves and through their interaction with adults' (James et al., 1998, p28).

A key aspect in James and Prout's (1997) framework is their commitment to developing a more sensitive awareness of different versions of childhood and children's experiences as children construct their own lives. These authors have criticised the belief that there exists one universal childhood, a 'standard' childhood based on the experiences of children in rich countries. They have pointed out that it is biological immaturity rather than childhood that is a universal feature of human groups. To overcome the problems of assuming that children are the same throughout the world, we also need to take into consideration the different cultural contexts of children growing up in developing countries (see Chapter 12). Childhood is a social construction because of the specific ways in which very young children become socialised in different societies. In this framework, a comparative, cultural analysis enables us to identify a variety of different childhoods in a wide range of contexts.

Poor children

What are the experiences of today's children throughout the world? Children account for 40 per cent of the world's population, the largest generation of children in history (White, 2001). Worldwide, poverty is a major factor in malnourishment and child mortality. Throughout the developing world, one out of four children under the age of five – about 146 million children – is underweight (UNICEF, 2006a). Lack of access to clean water leads to a high death rate among children under five years of age. By 2025 there will still be 5 million deaths among children under 5; 97 per cent of them in the developing world and most of them due to infectious diseases such as pneumonia and diarrhoea, or malnutrition (WHO, 2007).

Let us now turn to the national context. What is the level of poverty experienced by children today in British society? In the British context, children living in poverty are defined as those living in families with below 60 per cent of the average income, after housing costs are considered. From 1979 to 1997, the number of children in poverty tripled – one child in three was defined as living in poverty, and Britain had the highest proportion of children in poverty of all European countries (Bradbury and Jantti, 1999). As a consequence,

New Labour made the eradication of child poverty a strategic goal, with a commitment to halve child poverty by 2010 and eradicate it within 20 years. A cornerstone of New Labour's policy to tackle child poverty and social inclusion is the Sure Start Programme, which aims to improve the life chances of children before and after birth, offering services such as family support and advice on parenting. These initiatives have had some success: in the Green Paper, *Every Child Matters* (DfES, 2003a), the government claimed that there were 500,000 fewer children living in households with relatively low income than in 1997.

Although levels of poverty are beginning to decline and some individuals or families may benefit, 'solutions' to the problems of poverty offered by government programmes and services are 'illusory' – they are partial solutions to a problem rooted in wider economic conditions. As Ball (2008, p53) comments:

> *Exclusion is constructed and addressed as primarily a social problem of community and family inadequacies rather than a problem of structural inequality.*

Structural inequalities are continually being reproduced in our society – the poverty experienced by young children can only be ameliorated by government social policies. Ultimately, it will only be eradicated by changing social structures (Petrie, 2003). When we look at some of the groups of children who are living in the poorest social circumstances, it is clear that they are born into particular environments. It appears that child poverty is still heavily concentrated in certain types of household, and in particular regions of the country. For example, London has the highest proportion of children living in poverty: in spring 2006, 26 per cent of all London's children lived in households with no adult in work. This is the highest of any of the English regions and well above the UK average of 16 per cent (ONS, 2009).

Children in families

When I started my degree in social sciences at a college near Glasgow, a major topic for discussion on a first-year course was how we could explain the emergence of the nuclear family from extended family networks. As students, we studied a well-known text by Young and Willmott (1957) on changing family patterns in Britain. Their study highlighted the weakening of kinship networks as young members of the family moved from working-class communities in Bethnal Green in East London to housing estates in Greenleigh in outer London. The caring arrangements of the extended family were threatened by change as the nuclear family became more dominant:

> *In a three-generation family the burden of caring for the young as well, though bound to fall primarily on the mothers, can be lightened by being shared with the grandmothers. The three generations complement each other. Once prise out two of them, and the wives are left without the help of grandmothers, the old without the comfort of children and grandchildren.*

(Young and Willmott, 1957, p197)

The above quotation is highly representative of the way in which children have been 'fused' with their parents into an 'ideal' family unit. Only passing references are made to children:

they are subsumed under the concepts of family and socialisation. One of the important consequences of this marginalisation is that children have rarely been asked to speak about their family lives: it is assumed that their interests and identities are integrated within a single family unit. But family relationships have significantly changed in the last 40 years. The ideal image of the nuclear family, consisting of a white, heterosexual co-residential married couple with their children who are economically supported by a husband, no longer fits with the rich diversity of ways in which family members live their lives. In the twenty-first century, there is no longer one dominant family form that could provide a model for all others. Family structures are changing through divorce, separations or re-partnering, and evolving in relation to employment patterns, shifting power balances between men and women, and increasing acceptance of choices in sexual orientation. In 2009, there were about 13.1 million dependent children in the UK, 63% of whom lived in married couple families but the number of these children fell by 1.0 million between 1998 and 2008.

In contrast, the number of dependent children living with cohabiting couples and lone parents both increased, by 0.6 and 0.1 million respectively. The proportion of dependent children living with cohabiting couples rose from 8 per cent to 13 per cent, and the proportion of dependent children living in lone parent families rose from 22 per cent to 23 per cent. These changes were driven by changes in family formation and separation, as well as an increase in the proportion of births outside marriage (ONS, 2009b).

These changes to family structures have encouraged the development of a new way of thinking, one that studies 'children in their families', rather than 'families with children'. Children's perspectives are now taken seriously by researchers, who are exploring what children value about family life, how they negotiate family rules, roles and relationships, and how they engage with their parents, siblings and wider kin. A research project by Smart et al. (2001) explored children's perspectives on the issue of being listened to and participating in family decision-making by carrying out in-depth, conversational interviews with children living under post-divorce/separation arrangements. One aspect of this research examined whether children aspired to participation in decision-making or to making more autonomous choices, and in what circumstances arrangements could be open to renegotiation according to the changing needs of family members. James and his parents, for example, used trial and error to determine what kind of co-parenting arrangement would work best:

> *James (9): I thought I'd probably like to spend a bit more time at each house, so I said, 'can I spend a week [instead]?' We talked about it and thought, well, a week is a long time, but ... then we decided we'd try it and if it didn't work we'd go back to before ... We tried it ... just as a test ... and thought about it and then we went back for a few weeks ... and then we decided it might be a good idea.*

(Neale, 2002, p462)

The evidence of the importance that children attach to family life, and the significance of family relationships for their well-being and sense of identity, is now increasingly being taken into account by researchers and professionals working with children. In today's society, children are no longer invisible, without a voice, but are actively engaged in negotiating their own relationships.

Children in schools

An important starting point for understanding children's opportunities for learning in different settings is to briefly sketch the historical processes which shaped the emergence of schools as a dominant institution in children's lives. This historical context can help us to understand contemporary developments in early childhood education by making us more aware that schooling and the curriculum are shaped by powerful adults who make decisions about the ways children are taught and about how they will spend much of their time.

In the nineteenth and early twentieth centuries, the central place of work in children's lives was changed by child labour legislation and compulsory education. According to Hendrick (1997), the campaign to prevent young children from working in the factories was one of the first steps in the construction of a universal childhood.

This removal of children from the workforce started with the Factory Acts of the 1830s and 1840s, continuing in the latter half of the nineteenth century with the introduction of the Elementary Education Act of 1870, which established a requirement to provide universal elementary education. A state-funded education service was promoted by policy-makers as a way to relieve poverty and to prevent the spread of civil unrest and crime that was perceived by the middle and upper classes to be developing as a result of the large numbers of children roaming the streets in inner cities (Petrie, 2003). Once these children entered school, local authority officials and Victorian governments in the latter part of the nineteenth century became increasingly concerned that the children were unable to 'concentrate' and attend to lessons, due to undernourishment and infectious diseases. Concerns for children's health and fears that the next generation would not provide 'fit' soldiers for war (see Chapter 4) eventually led to the introduction of free school meals, medical inspections and treatments. A graphic example of this link between schooling and the military is the following excerpt from an interview with a pupil who was growing up in a Foundling Hospital during the first part of the twentieth century:

> We were young soldiers in the making, not that we realised it then ... we used to march up to our places. Stop opposite our plate and our mug. Wait for the next thing [bang of the gavel], turn smartly in, bring our hands together in supplication. Next thing was another clap and then we would say grace. Stay in this position till another [bang], and then smartly to the side again, you see ... you get over your seat and then sit down. Wait for the next go [bang] and then you could eat.

> (Frederick, 87, quoted in Oliver, 2003, p53)

Alongside this concern for fitness and obedience was the government expectation that investment in children would lead to the development of a disciplined and skilled work-force – scripture, reading, writing and arithmetic were instilled through rote learning. Children were required to write in a 'fair hand', often by copying poems from the established canon of English literature or from morally uplifting tracts. They had to learn the discipline of parsing sentences in order to learn the syntax of the English language, and had exercises in the comprehension and paraphrasing of high-status texts. It is interesting to compare this emphasis on pupil discipline and the three Rs with contemporary government policy on education and schooling and to ask ourselves whether our children are under less pressure to perform and conform than a previous generation of children. In the 1990s there were a number of important government initiatives in primary education: implementation of a National Curriculum; national tests in Key Stages 1 and 2 when children are seven and ten; frequent inspection by Ofsted and competition between schools. Testing has once again become common and overt – on spellings, times-tables, arithmetic and the 'facts' of history and geography.

There is growing research evidence to suggest that the introduction of national assessment tests across the key stages of the National Curriculum is creating stress and anxiety among pupils and contributing to a drop in their self-esteem. A recent influential report by the Cambridge Primary Review argued that there are methodological problems with some of the test procedures and data:

> *The narrow focus of SATs, which treat literacy and numeracy as proxies for the whole of primary education, should be replaced by a system which reports on children's attainment in all areas of their education, with minimal disruption and greater use of teacher assessment.*

> (Cambridge Primary Review, 2009)

As a result of this emphasis on an early introduction to print and numbers, young children are beginning to disengage from schooling. The following excerpt is taken from a competition that *The Guardian* hosted, asking children about the school they would like (Burke and Grosvenor, 2003, p74):

> *… The school I'd like could do more sensory things, more hands on, more touchy/feely. Everyone has loads of senses. We can feel with different parts of our body, we can see, hear, taste, smell. How many senses does the national curriculum focus on? Sometimes I find life in the classroom boring and sometimes the pace is too fast and I switch off. Well, who wouldn't – day in, day out, literacy hour, numeracy hour, registration. How about smelling hour, tactile hour, music hour and physical activity hour.*

> Hugh, 6 (with help from his Mum), Wellington

Moss and Petrie (2002) have argued for an alternative way of thinking about young children, a move from children's services to children's spaces. This concept of a children's space does not just imply a physical space, in terms of a particular setting or environment for different groups of children, but a social space where meanings are kept open for adults and children, a place for wonder and amazement, curiosity and fun. In this alternative view of childhood, children's learning is based on mutuality and reciprocity – children are partners in the co-construction of knowledge with adults and other children.

So far we have explored some of the issues that face young children as they are growing up in British society. To understand these changes, we should use sensitive tools of inquiry to listen to children's concerns and worries. But we also need to explain some of the important historical processes that led to this growing concern about contemporary childhood and the way in which adults' concepts of childhood inform the important conceptual distinction between 'adulthood' and 'childhood'.

Preamble: memories

Time it was, and what a time it was, it was

A time of innocence, a time of confidences

Long ago, it must be, I have a photograph

Preserve your memories, they're all that's left you

(Lyrics from Paul Simon and Arthur Garfunkel, 'Bookends Theme')

In what ways do adults' concepts of childhood influence our relationships with children? How do our childhood memories of the past affect the way we 'think', behave, and work with adults and children? Our memories of having been a child remain a central part of who we think we are and who we think we once were. But they are elusive and cannot be read as direct evidence of what we were like as a child. The child we think we remember may be constructed as much from more recent influences, films or books, as from recollections from years ago. Drawing on images from photograph albums or from family stories that we were told when we were growing up we try, as adults, to reconstruct or imagine what our childhood was like, or what we would have liked it to have been. At the personal level we frequently look to our own childhoods as a measure by which comparisons between past and present might be made. Yet very often memories of this period in our lives can become imbued with nostalgia or, where too painful to recall, they are shaped by our adult understanding of acceptable norms of childhood and childhood experiences. What can sometimes result is a conflict between our understanding of the concept of childhood as an idealised time of innocence and protection, and our more individual memories of personal unhappiness (Davidoff et al., 1999).

When, for example, I turn to my own childhood, I initially think of a wonderful time for play and adventure with close friends. But then I stop. I was about four and playing on my bicycle with my best friend Kenneth when he said he could no longer play with me because I was different. I did not understand what he was saying, so I asked what he meant. He told me I was Jewish. I ran home crying, telling my Mum and Dad what had happened. They reassured me that being Jewish was not terrible – I was beginning to learn what it felt like to be different.

Romantic aspects of childhood

Jean-Jacques Rousseau was one of the most important thinkers of the eighteenth century, offering a radical, alternative vision of childhood. He criticised the Christian doctrine of original sin, arguing that children are born innocent. Although Rousseau did not believe that children were virtuous in the first 12 years of their life, he advocated a form of 'negative education' that would shelter them from adult vices. As innocents, children should be left to respond to nature and be protected from the risks and prejudices of social institutions. Emile, his ideal boy, was not to learn to read until after he was 12: he must be free to roam outdoors in loose clothing, learning by his own interests and experience in a natural environment. Only in adolescence would Emile be allowed to learn to read and write and to master a craft.

The important part played by the concept of 'Nature' in Rousseau's thought is sometimes seen as a precursor to the more radical romanticism of the late eighteenth century. However, the dissemination of his fame and ideas should also be understood in relation to the highly detailed rules that regulated the lives of people in his society. We can interpret Rousseau's natural child of innocence as a response to the advancing urban development of French society – the idealisation of nature was used by members of court-aristocratic circles as a counterpoint to the constraints of royal rule and suppression of feeling in court life (see Elias, 2006). As more and more people moved into cities and towns, the child became a symbol that could be used to represent innocence and the 'Nature' that had been lost in adults' estrangement from the countryside.

The concept of the child as 'natural', 'pure' and 'innocent' functioned as a basis for the late eighteenth- and early nineteenth-century Romantic poets' vision of childhood. The early Romantics – Blake, Wordsworth and Goethe – drew attention to the ideal of childhood as an unmediated source of experience within each individual. Their idea of an interior self with a personal history suggested that we all retain an aspect of our individual pasts in our psyches. For Wordsworth, innocence was deeply rooted in the 'natural' world: the child is a part of his own childhood as remembered by an adult looking back in time. Central to this concept of the child is a sense of oneness between his body and the world that surrounded him in childhood:

> *Oh! Many a time have I, a five years Child,*
>
> *A naked Boy, in one delightful Rill,*
>
> *A little Mill-race sever'd from his stream,*
>
> *Made one long bathing of a summer's day,*
>
> *Bask'd in the sun, and plunged, and bask'd again,*
>
> *Alternate all a summer's day*
>
> (Wordsworth, 'The Prelude', 1, pp291–300, first published 1805; in Ford, 1982)

Gittins (1998) offers an important interpretation of Wordsworth's poem, one that is crucial for understanding the concept of the 'inner child'. The 'inner child' remains within the adult as the repository of feeling and joyousness. She argues that it is not just the child's joy in nature and his own body that is apparent here, but an image of the past seen from the adults' perspective, a drawing on the past from the adult's perspective of childhood. The child is a remembered child, reinterpreted by the adult in an idealised process – he is not only reminiscing about himself as a boy, but making generalisations about childhood innocence and the 'nature' of childhood itself. For adults, this remembered knowledge of the child survived in memory. Memory was central for Wordsworth in relation to his feelings about the loss of childhood:

> *… I cannot paint*
>
> *What then I was …*
>
> *That time is past*

And all its aching joys are no more,

And all its dizzy raptures

(Wordsworth, 'Tintern Abbey', lines 75–6 and 83–5, first published 1798; in Ford, 1982)

According to Gittins (1998), loss, informed by melancholic yearning, is the main theme of this poem. This was the beginning of a trend towards interiorisation, in which adults were more and more looking inwards, as well as backwards in time, to their own personal child-hood. Steedman (1995) has traced this concept of 'interiority of the child' in the nineteenth century. She examines the various representations of Mignon, the homeless orphan (origi-nally portrayed by Goethe, the great German writer, in *Wilhelm Meister*) who was uprooted by the adults training her to be an acrobat. Throughout the nineteenth century, this mythical image was a crucial source for intensive adult longing and desire – images of the remembered and imagined child were woven together in a quest to rescue the lost child.

This idea of rescuing unfortunate children from factories or brothels developed in nineteenth-century England, where there was an expansion of philanthropy as well as an increasing state interest in children's well-being. In 1881, Lord Shaftesbury, a British philanthropist, was asked by a Liverpool clergyman to introduce a bill into Parliament to prevent parental cruelty to chil-dren. At first he refused, arguing that the matter was 'of so private, internal and domestic a character as to be beyond the reach of legislation' (quoted in Hendrick, 1997, p45), but he later supported the bill. In 1889 the Prevention of Cruelty to and Protection of Children Act was passed. Ill treatment and the neglect of children became illegal, and a new offence of causing suffering to children was created.

Religious and medical moralities

In marked contrast to the natural goodness of the 'romantic child' were the traditional beliefs held by members of the Evangelical Movement. Despite their relatively small number, they were very influential through their prolific writings about child-rearing practices. Their beliefs dominated both the advisory literature available to parents and children's own reading for nearly two centuries (Newson and Newson, 1974). During the eighteenth and nineteenth centuries a severe view of childhood emerges, one where socialisation is seen as a battleground where the wills of stubborn children have to be broken, but for their own good. For the Evangelicals, the prospect of heaven and the threat of hell were major sources of motivation in their attempts to 'form the minds' of their own children. Each child enters the world as a wilful material force, is impish and harbours a potential for evil that can be mobilised if adults allow them to stray from the righteous path that God has provided.

'Break the will, if you would not damn the child' (Wesley, 1872) expressed the ever-present fear of damnation, in an age when most families would have lost at least one child. James Janeway, a Puritan minister, famous for his influential 'Token for children' (1830), first published in 1672 and reprinted well into the middle of the nineteenth cen-tury, makes the connection between dying and hell quite explicit:

Are you willing to go to hell, to be burned with the devil and his angels? ... O! Hell is a terrible place ... Did you ever hear of a little child that died ... and if other children die, why you may be sick and die? ... How do you know but that you may be the next child that may die? ... Now tell me, my pretty dear child, what will you do?

(quoted in Newson and Newson, 1974, p57)

From Janeway onwards, the pious and happy deaths of good little boys and girls are compared with the terrible deaths of irreligious children who were assumed to have passed straight to the eternal fire of hell. Children's deaths are continuously described and lingered over in children's books of the eighteenth and nineteenth centuries. For example, the *Child's Companion* of 1829, a well-illustrated little volume of poems and stories, contains 13 deathbed scenes, together with one discourse on death and two poems inspired by gazing on children's graves. In a society in which death is such a familiar occurrence and an authoritarian God has unlimited powers to decide who will be rewarded through Heaven or punished by Hell, children need to be prepared as carefully for death as for life. In the painting 'Childhood' (1896) by Charles Sims, a group of angelic children dressed in flowing white are acting out the funeral of a doll.

Miller (1987) sees strict aphorisms on child-rearing such as 'spare the rod and spoil the child' or 'you have to be cruel to be kind' as part of a wider discourse on *poisonous pedagogy*. Poisonous pedagogy is the process by which adults rationalise their own needs and re-enact the humiliation they experienced in childhood. This rationalisation disguises their own negative feelings and experiences, becoming part of a set of common-sense beliefs about what is good for children and informing the larger debate on childcare and education. Phillips (2006, p106) also points to the way that childhood can become the touchstone for the insanity of the human condition:

The ways in which we conceive of children, our obsession with child development and with so-called 'parenting skills' has become a code for our forlorn attempt to find a sanity for ourselves. If children are not, in our terms, actually mad, they have been burdened with the fears adults harbour for their own sanity.

An evangelical concern to eradicate fears about 'the devil in the child' has important links with the medical-hygienist movement which dominated the 1920s and 1930s in Britain (Newson and Newson, 1974). Scientific mothercraft offered parents the hope that babies could be successfully reared provided that medical advice was faithfully followed: the vengeful God of Heaven and Hell was replaced by science, an equally authoritarian expert. A good example of this authoritarian advice was the *Mothercraft Manual* written by Liddiard (1928). Although this was not a government publication, it was extremely important before the Second World War, and even more significantly became the main vehicle for the principles of Sir Truby King (1937) and his Mothercraft Training Society. Babies needed to conform to adult expectations – in a sense, their wishes were suspect because they could conceal dangerous impulses or a rebellious determination to dominate the mother. Truby King (1937) believed that when mothers were in constant control, a 'good' baby was reared:

The mother who 'can't be so cruel' as to wake her sleeping baby if he happens to be asleep at the appointed feeding-time, fails to realise that a few such wakings would be all she would have to resort to ... The establishment of perfect regularity of habits, initiated by 'feeding and sleeping by the clock', is the ultimate foundation of all-round obedience.

(quoted in Newson and Newson, 1974, pp60–1)

Moralities of 'natural' development and 'natural' needs

A major shift in child management was developed under the influence of psychoanalysts like Susan Isaacs. In her book *The Nursery Years* (1932) she advised parents to observe children in 'natural' play because it was an important part of their development, and recommended that mothers take a more tolerant attitude towards prohibited practices, like thumb-sucking and masturbation. In a similar vein, the publication of Margaret Ribble's very influential book *The Rights of Infants* (1943) represented a humanitarian response to earlier and harsher infant-feeding regimes. There was a growing acceptance that babies' desires were legitimate: babies and children needed not only their mothers' presence, but also the rocking, cuddling and lap play that had previously been forbidden. To deprive babies of the 'natural' expression of maternal warmth could prevent the development of their social relationships and personalities. Ribble (1943, p100) insisted on the need for the correct guidance of mothers, and the necessity of separate spheres for both parents: 'Two parents who have achieved maturity and happiness in their respective biological roles are the native right of every child.'

By the 1940s and 1950s the influence of psychoanalytic theories, especially the work of Donald Winnicott and John Bowlby, was changing the advice given to mothers. This was now more closely focused on the nature of the relationship between mother and child, and their need for close contact. In his theory of attachment, Bowlby (1969) argues that every newborn baby arrives in the world with an innate tendency to remain close to his or her primary caregiver. For him, attachment is a system of regulation geared to producing a dynamic equilibrium between mother and child: children can be emotionally or psychologically damaged by even minimal separation from their mothers. Theories of maternal deprivation also helped to support the growth of the child welfare movement. This movement had its origins in the war years as a result of the concern of Medical Officers of Health about the physical and emotional deprivation experienced by children in day nurseries and the effects of evacuation.

Waves of informalisation

If we now turn to today's society, we can see that the continuation of this trend to offer parents more informal advice can be explained by a longer trend, by waves of informalisation that have occurred from the twentieth century onwards. According to Elias (1998), this trend represents a period of movement from an authoritarian to a more egalitarian parent–child relationship where there is a loosening of barriers of authority in relations between children and adults.

In his essay 'The Civilising of Parents,' (Elias, 1998) Elias argued that during the late-twentieth century, the parent-child relationship had lost some of its hierarchical character, with children being given more autonomy and a greater degree of decision making. He also maintained that this had occurred in the context of a 'tightening of the prohibition of the use of physical violence in family life,' which 'applies not only to the relations between adults and children within the family', but also 'to the relations between adults and children in general, particularly to those of teachers and children at school' (p207).

This has had the effect of eliciting a high degree of self-restraint from adults in their relations with children and also of encouraging similar patterns of behaviour in children. In more equal and affective relationships, parents appeal more compellingly to affection and reflection, teaching their children to direct themselves more according to their own conscience, rather than simply to obey the external constraints of adults (Wouters, 2007).

Newson and Newson (1974) refer to this new trend as 'fun morality' in which the fundamental need of parents is to be happy in parenthood. The advice given to parents has now changed from the strictly authoritarian to the friendly, more persuasive approach: whereas in the 1930s, mothers were given solemn warnings about what would happen to them if they failed to enforce the rules, they are now given continual reassurances about what might possibly result from some mistaken actions. Benjamin Spock (1946, p54) is the supreme example of the friendly, conversational approach – paternalistic enough to give confidence and reassurance, but willing to talk to the mother on equal terms.

> *Every baby needs to be smiled at, talked to, played with, fondled gently and lovingly....*
> *Be natural and comfortable and enjoy your baby.*

Significantly, a similar change has occurred in the balance of power in the relations between men and women, as women have become an integral part of the workforce. Men are now expected to become more involved with the care and education of their children, and parents are under pressure to renounce violence as a means of disciplining their children.

Children at work

Child labour is a subject that still provokes fierce debate and discussion, whether it concerns the exploitation of children in the developed world or the employment of children for a newspaper round. These debates are based upon what is harmful to a working child's development and what the nature of intervention should be, given a range of different social and economic circumstances. When we look at the history of child labour, it is difficult to avoid the influence of our own adult experiences of living and working in a modern world. It is tempting for us to ask at what age children started work, as if it were the same as starting school today, or whether they were employed or unemployed in the same way as adults (Heywood, 2001). The climbing boy suffocating up a chimney or the little mill hand working to the relentless pace of a machine have become common representations of the Industrial Revolution.

But a more useful way of looking at these representations is to examine the way that street children were portrayed and legislated for from the 1830s onwards. In mid-Victorian society, between 1800 and 1900, children were highly visible on the streets, because they represented such a high proportion of the population: from the line of sight established by adults, children running, playing, crouched in the gutter, dancing, begging and importuning, are noticeable. According to Cunningham (1991), there were three 'overlapping discourses' concerning street children in the period from 1840 to 1870. First, there were religious attempts to rescue these children and restore them to 'order' through voluntary efforts like the Ragged Schools. Mary Carpenter (1807–77), for example, was a philanthropist who was very active in the movement for the reformation of neglected children. She advocated a kind and loving approach, one where children would be seen as different and requiring special treatment. Second, there were more 'professional' attempts to deal with the problem of juvenile delinquency. Third, there were journalists, writers and social commentators who wrote about and represented such children to various audiences.

One important social commentator was Henry Mayhew who, in December 1850, visited the greengrocers' markets of London as part of his *Morning Chronicle* series on 'Labour and the poor'. During this month, he met and interviewed the Little Watercress Girl, an eight year old who defined herself as a worker. She told Mayhew of her life at home with her mother, her brother and two sisters, and her mother's common-law husband, a scissor-grinder by trade. When Mayhew described her narrative, he placed it within a framework of anonymity and ignorance, yet he took from her a detailed account of family organisation, both at the economic and domestic level. Mayhew's attempts to present the children as utterly strange, remote, filthy beyond belief and products of impoverished home circumstances produced quite different evidence (Steedman, 1995). His adult conceptions of the 'lost' child distorted his interpretation of her own words to such an extent that he underestimated her ability to explain her social and economic conditions.

As children were increasingly being seen by adults as closer to 'nature', their relationship to work began to be questioned. Because children were considered to be innately innocent, special and vulnerable, it was felt that they should be sheltered from the adult world. Working-class families were criticised by the Evangelicals in terms of the 'order of nature': 'In the order of nature parents, and particularly fathers, would labour for the support of their young children' (Cunningham, 1991, p83).

The distinctive 'nature' of childhood meant that children were fundamentally different from adults – child labour in factories was distorting the order of both 'nature' and England. As children were coming to be seen as precious and valuable, they needed to be protected from the harsh world of labour. Adults therefore tried to rescue individual children from the more extreme forms of child labour, such as chimney-sweeping and prostitution, and at the same time, they campaigned for state legislation that would give children protection. For example, journalist WT Stead's campaign against child prostitution in the 1880s was characterised by moralistic and highly sensationalist stories of young girls. He proved how easy it was to buy children for sexual purposes by purchasing a 14-year-old girl from her mother and publicising how he had bought and then rescued her. He argued that children should be allowed to remain innocent of adult knowledge in order to develop as individuals through freedom and joy, play and education.

Education legislation from the late 1870s onwards had a profound effect on the regulation of child labour and the lives of working-class children. By the end of the twentieth century, by which time free and compulsory universal primary education was established, children were being controlled and watched not just by the growing army of child rescue organisations, but also by officials such as the school nurse. Through its legal authority and daily inspection by school attendance officers, schooling was able to impose a vision of regularity and normality on its pupils and their parents. Obedience, punctuality and deference became cardinal virtues in all schools. No longer able to sell their labour, children were taken by schools from a 'state of ignorance' to a disciplined form of behaviour that reinforced dependence and vulnerability.

These changes had important financial consequences for the lives of children: they would become much more dependent on adults and sheltered from the adult world – children became economically 'worthless', but emotionally 'priceless' (Zelizer, 1985). However, this urge to rescue and protect working-class children can also be seen as a result of fear. Children who lived and worked in the streets were regarded as 'out of control' or 'wild' because they had no adult supervision and were not directly dependent on adult protection and surveillance.

Conclusion

In this chapter, I have looked at some of the rapid changes in institutional structures which are pressurising today's children to grow up too fast – to learn to read and write at too early an age, and to be involved in difficult decisions in increasingly complex family arrangements. I have argued that it is important to look beneath these contemporary changes in order to explain how adults have developed powerful concepts of childhood which define the ways in which we think about children. I have highlighted the concept of 'nature' by tracing the different versions of childhood that have emerged, especially since Rousseau. The 'innocent' version of childhood that needed to be protected from the corruption of adult society, represented by his Emile, was later developed by writers and poets in literary representations of a lost childhood, one that could uncover the deeper, more intuitive parts of ourselves concealed under the armour of adulthood.

This 'inner childhood' became a very important touchstone for later scientific and moralistic developments in child-rearing practices, because it retained the division between the 'good and 'bad' child. If children were 'naturally' good, then parents would have to develop skills to meet their needs and educate them. But if they were 'naturally' bad or sinful, then according to the Evangelicals children risked being damned forever. I discussed these changing views about how parents ought to bring up their children by focusing on the shifts that occurred from a more authoritarian view of parenting that concentrates on the needs of parents to control their offspring, to a more relaxed view where scientific theories advocated the importance of responding to babies' requirements, to today, where there has been a gradual erosion of power imbalances in relationships between men, women and children.

But is childhood just a series of adult constructions? According to Stainton Rogers and Stainton Rogers (1992), our concepts of the child are created by language and narrative: factual information on children is just as much a story as the more obvious narrative of Peter Pan. Gittins' (1998, p45) response is crucial here. She asks: but who is telling the story? Why is it being told? And how are certain stories used to determine opportunities for some children, but not others?

There is the problem of forgetting real children and the centrality of power relations. But we can go one step further and suggest that even those researchers who wish to study children's own views and perspectives have lost sight of real children. This is especially troubling given that they seem to be aware of the problem. For example, James et al. (1998, p28) state that, 'Social constructionism does run the risk of abandoning the embodied material child'. How can this happen? The answer may stem from their model.

These influential sociologists of childhood have placed at the centre of their analysis a concept of interaction that is dependent on an individual child who 'interacts' and 'negotiates' with adults and children:

> *This interaction concept, too, owes its central position in present-day thinking to the perspective of adults who have lost sight of their own and other people's development from a child, who proceed in their reflections about human beings as if they had all been born as adults, and who see themselves from within their armour as single individuals interacting with other adults equally armoured.*

(Elias, 1969, p143)

The human individual is regarded as a *homo clausus* – a closed box, a 'completely self-reliant adult, forming no relationships and standing quite alone' (Elias, 1978, p118). Elias's response to this problem of the closed individual is to introduce the concept of figuration, a 'structure of mutually oriented and dependent people' (Elias, 2000, pp481–482). In his version of a relational sociology, human beings are embedded in figurations, interdependent webs that are always changing and developing. An important implication is that we need to move beyond an exclusive focus on the immediate present, the experiences of being a child today – instead we need to understand childhood and adulthood as related concepts with deep historical roots. Across generations, in the course of humanity's development, we are all connected.

ACTIVITY 1

Reflecting upon the memories of your own childhood, account for some of the major influences in your development as an adult. In what ways have these influenced your current view of childhood and children? Sharing these views with another person, can you notice any similarities in your stories about your childhood? And can you explain any differences?

FURTHER READING

Corsaro, W (2005) *The Sociology of Childhood*. 2nd edition. London: Pine Forge Press.

A good introduction to how sociological perspectives on childhood can be used to explain the complexity of children's lives.

The following books are also very helpful introductions to the historical and social construction of childhood:

Cunningham, H (2006) *The Invention of Childhood*. London: BBC.

Hendrick, H (1997) *Children, Childhood and English Society*, 1880–1990. Cambridge: Cambridge University Press.

Kehily, MJ (2008) *An Introduction to Childhood Studies*. 2nd Edition Buckingham: Open University Press.

12 Children's well-being in the developing world

Rebecca Carter Dillon and Valerie Huggins

Introduction

Perhaps the greatest barrier to our development as reflective professionals is allowing our thinking to be constricted and shaped by beliefs, assumptions and taken-for-granted practice narrowly based upon our own personal and social experience (Paige-Smith and Craft, 2008). By exploring the complex and challenging issues around childhood and well-being in the developing world, we may be able to take a more balanced and critically reflective view of education, care and child well-being in the UK. For example, if we can appreciate the grinding poverty in which an estimated 1.4 billion of the world population live (World Bank, 2008) we can both gain a critical perspective upon our comparatively affluent lifestyle, and relate more sympathetically and intelligently to the needs of the significant number of poor people within our own communities.

We need to consider the experiences of children in developing countries and to recognise indigenous peoples' understanding of childhood (Kostelny, 2006). In the United Nations Convention on the Rights of the Child (UNCRC), childhood is taken to extend to the age of 18 (UN, 1989) but in many cultures this is far from the case, and the roles and responsibilities that children take on also vary, sometimes because of their gender. Indeed, we cannot even assume that our taken-for-granted ideas about child development and well-being will necessarily apply to other regions of the world, based as they are on literature and research with an overwhelmingly Western perspective (Penn, 2005).

For instance, our basic notion of the child is as an individual, as exemplified in the English Early Years Foundation Stage framework (DCSF, 2008b), whereas in many cultures much more emphasis is given to children's roles as part of their family and community (Gottlieb, 2004; Penn, 2008; Penn, 2010). Being aware of such differences can give us a better understanding of childhood and enable us to appreciate the diversity of children's experiences within our own communities (Brooker, 2005). We also need to acknowledge that there are still huge inequalities between developed and developing countries. In 2000, the countries of the developed world agreed a set of eight targets, termed the Millennium Development Goals (MDGs); which aimed to address some of these inequalities by the year 2015 (UN, 2008, UNDP, 2010). In 2010 it is clear that, although progress has been made, none of the targets have yet been met (Penn, 2010a).

In this chapter we will consider interrelated issues affecting children in the developing world, looking at livelihoods, health, conflict, and education, as well as examining the roles of Non-Governmental Organisations (NGOs) and the State in supporting children's well-being.

Economic well-being and sustainable livelihoods

It is useful to consider the problems of the developing world not just in purely economic terms, as problems of 'poor' people living in 'poor' countries with limited financial resources, but more broadly in terms of the opportunities and choices that people have to earn an income, reduce their vulnerability, recover from shocks, and enhance their life chances in a sustainable way. A child's well-being is very much affected by the assets that their family has, the political, social and environmental context in which they are growing up, and the strategies their families and communities can employ to achieve sustainable livelihoods. The UK's Department for International Development (DfID) and other key governmental and charitable development agencies therefore take a so-called 'livelihoods approach', which is very much about putting people at the centre of any poverty-reduction initiatives, and making any intervention context-specific (DfID, 1999).

This approach considers that the key assets needed for a family to prosper are human capital, natural capital, physical capital, financial capital and social capital (DfID, 1999). Human capital refers to the level of education, skills, and knowledge that people have, and how healthy they are. It is extremely important that there is investment in children's human capital in terms of ensuring they are well educated and have immunisations, for example, if they are to do well in life. Families may have to make difficult choices about whether their child will work, in order to contribute to the family finances, rather than attend school. Children living in rural areas often contribute towards their families' livelihoods by engaging in herding cattle or helping on the family farm, whereas in urban areas children may be more likely to hawk goods or work in factories. The work that children engage in may further deplete their human capital if it is exploitative or dangerous, such as working with heavy machinery. The United Nations Children's Fund (UNICEF) estimate that more than 120 million children worldwide are engaged in hazardous work and girls in particular are at risk of being sent out to work rather than to school (UNICEF, 2006b, p15).

Natural capital is the natural environment – assets such as unpolluted air and water and productive farming land that families rely on for food. Physical capital is the enabling infrastructure such as transport, good housing, sanitation systems and affordable, reliable energy supplies (for example electricity), all important for people in accessing employment, education and other opportunities. Access to information via good communication systems is also crucial, especially in ensuring that people can make well-informed decisions about how best to respond to challenges and take up opportunities. In the UK we do not have to worry about serious threats to our natural or physical capital; on the whole we are not susceptible to natural disasters such as devastating floods or earthquakes. These unfortunately tend to inflict most damage in countries where the infrastructure is not able to withstand the shock, as was seen in the recent earthquake in Haiti where the collapse of poor quality buildings killed a great many people (DEC, 2010).

Financial capital may include stocks such as cash, or liquid assets such as livestock or jewellery, which can be sold when times are hard. The poorest people struggle to build up even tiny amounts of financial capital; this limits their ability to set up small businesses or take other steps to improve their livelihoods. Access to credit is therefore very important, and credit unions and small loan institutions such as the pro-poor Grameen Bank in Bangladesh can make a huge amount of difference to people such as impoverished women who are traditionally unable to access credit (Grameen Bank, 2010). A regular income from paid work or financial support from the government is also very important, but the safety net of a system of welfare benefits that we enjoy in the UK is on the whole not available in developing countries, due to budget constraints. Many families in the developing world rely on remittances – financial support from friends or relatives living and working far away; once people are educated and are aware of opportunities available elsewhere in the world, the understandable temptation is to migrate to the economic stability of a developed country in order to support one's family financially.

Social capital is the glue that binds communities together; it is the sources of support on which people can draw when times are hard, the networks, trust and reciprocal arrangements around childcare, for example, and the social structures and norms that dictate how people are treated within a given society. Some social structures make and keep certain sections of society poor, such as the caste system or social systems which deny education and employment opportunities to women.

These different assets are interdependent, and in different communities there will be different strengths and challenges; for example social capital may be very strong in some poorer communities, but financial capital may be very limited. In particular, we can see how levels of human capital influence all other areas; people who are well educated can make better decisions about managing their natural environment or finances, and about keeping themselves and their children healthy.

Disadvantaged communities must therefore be enabled to build up and make the best use of their assets, and any external intervention needs to be appreciative of the local context. For example, when food aid is brought into famine-stricken areas to preserve life, humanitarian agencies need to be conscious of the risk of undermining the local economy, in particular local food producers, and of encouraging dependency. Ultimately solutions must lie in working with communities to enable them to develop workable and sustainable livelihood strategies, thereby improving economic well-being, and the ability to provide children with happy and productive lives.

Children's health and nutrition

The human capital of many children in the developing world remains a deep concern, in stark contrast to that of the majority of children in more developed countries. For instance, despite the aim of MDG 1 to eradicate extreme hunger and poverty, this is still a reality for millions of children (FAO, 2009). In 2006 the number of children who were malnourished and underweight exceeded 140 million (UN, 2008), while in the developed world we are concerned about childhood obesity and unhealthy diets. A crucial aspect of improving human capital must be to help communities and families to feed themselves better, whether by enhancing their capacity to produce food, or by improving their financial capital through opportunities for regular employment or for developing small scale businesses.

In developed countries, we take our access to plentiful clean water and effective sanitation for granted. However, almost half of the world's population face a scarcity of water, and one billion people do not have access to safe drinking water (UN, 2008). Poor sanitation facilities, such as no access to basic toilets, which is a major factor in contributing to water-borne diseases such as cholera and infant diarrhoea, affects one person in four. Any proposal to construct major sanitation networks like those of the developed world is totally impracticable even in the medium term. Instead effective support must be in terms of small scale community projects, such as improved wells, which can be constructed and maintained by the local people themselves.

The well-being of children is substantially affected by the parenting that they receive and maternal health in particular has an impact upon this. In the developing world patterns of child rearing are a significant factor. In many regions women experience large numbers of pregnancies; for example in Zambia there are 5.1 births per woman compared with just 1.31 in Italy (CIA, 2009). Multiple pregnancies, together with frequent stillbirths and deaths in infancy put severe strain on mothers' physical and emotional health and increase their susceptibility to other widespread illnesses such as malaria and HIV/AIDS. Death in childbirth also remains common in the absence of obstetric and gynaecological health care services.

However, a woman's status as a child bearer may be highly significant in terms of social capital. Where life is uncertain, livelihoods precarious and where there is no welfare support for the elderly, having as many children as possible is one of the few strategies that offer a family hope for the future. There are also advantages for the children from having a support network of siblings who, in many communities, play an important part in childcare. Thus, even where contraception is available, affordable and not proscribed by cultural or religious beliefs, efforts to control population may meet with considerable resistance.

Another key issue is that of breastfeeding (Lucas et al., 2008). Where bottle feeding is dangerous because of problems with sterilisation and contaminated water supplies, early and exclusive breastfeeding is vital to infant health. It has the potential to prevent 12–15 per cent of deaths of children under five in the developing world and many organisations, such as UNICEF, actively promote it (UNICEF, 2008). However, many companies in the developed world actively market formula milk to the developing world, advertising it as being more beneficial to the children.

A particular impact upon the well-being of children in the developing world is that of HIV/AIDS, especially in Sub-Saharan Africa. In 2004, in Botswana, a relatively affluent and developed African nation, 23.9 per cent of people aged 15–49 were HIV positive and 95,000 children were orphaned through AIDS (UNICEF, 2004). Children and their grandparents now constitute a majority of some communities in Sub-Saharan Africa and even more children are likely to have lost at least one close relative. The impact upon such communities in terms of human, financial and social capital is yet to be fully appreciated; the emotional cost is immeasurable.

All these issues are compounded by the fact that many regions in the developing world lack an adequate medical infrastructure and even when medical treatment is available access to it can be difficult – unthinkable in countries where a variety of medical treatment is a short trip or a phone call away. Arguably, it is unrealistic to attempt to remedy this by introducing the high-tech solutions of the developed world. Instead we may need to develop affordable, sustainable, low-tech strategies to improve the situation, such as bicycle ambulances rather than cars or helicopters (Practical Action, 2010). Lucas et al. (2008) argue powerfully that as the family is the front-line care system for children, strategies should focus on household- and community-based interventions. Local health-care services should be provided wherever possible, e.g. many separate health centres in townships or slum areas rather than one large hospital in the city. In terms of enhancing human capital, cost-effective medical solutions may involve the limiting of sophisticated, developed world approaches in favour of models that will reach far more people – paramedics instead of doctors, local people trained in very basic health care and the use of traditional healers within the community alongside more modern medical resources and personnel (Gottlieb, 2004).

A final concern in terms of human capital is that damaging and lethal conditions, which have largely been eliminated from the developed world, are still prevalent in less affluent countries. In 2008, 164,000 children died of measles, 95 per cent of them in low income countries with weak health infrastructures (WHO, 2009). However solutions can be simple and relatively inexpensive; it costs less than £1 to immunise a child against measles. There are already treatments for HIV/AIDS which could have a huge impact if the money and the will were available. But despite all these difficulties, steady progress is being made towards the MDGs and an important milestone was reached in 2006. For the first time, the number of children worldwide dying before their fifth birthday fell below 10 million – to 9.7 million – compared with an estimated 20 million infant deaths in 1960 (UNICEF, 2007b).

Children and conflict

Armed conflict in the twenty-first century differs from our historic understanding of wars which were fought for political reasons by soldiers, usually men in uniform, against soldiers from another nation state. Modern conflicts often involve men, women and children, both as combatants and victims. Disputes are frequently within rather than between countries, and may be fought for a combination of economic, social, religious and criminal reasons (Singer, 2006). For example, during the conflict in the West Darfur region of the Sudan, which has continued since the 1970s, worsening periods of drought have intensified competition between different tribal groups for natural resources, such as water and grazing pastures, which they rely on for their livelihoods (Jaspars and O'Callaghan, 2008). When communities are in dispute over land and are violently attacked and displaced, even killed, children are inevitably affected.

There are a number of internationally agreed protocols for the protection of children in situations of armed conflict, including the 1949 Geneva Convention and the 1989 Convention on the Rights of the Child (UNICEF, 2006a). However, in many countries, especially in the developing world, children continue to be adversely affected by violence. It is estimated that 1.5 billion under-18s, two thirds of the world's children, live in war-torn countries (UNICEF, 2007b, p48), and up to two million have been killed during armed conflict in the past decade (SOS Children's Villages, 2009). Exposure to conflict is therefore a reality for a great many children and when considering issues of child well-being it is important to consider the impact this experience has on children, both in the immediate and in the longer term.

Conflict impacts negatively on children in many ways. It seriously undermines the achievement of the MDGs and depletes human capital by increasing child mortality rates and incidences of injury and ill-health. Conflict disrupts school attendance and affects livelihoods by reducing household incomes as families flee fighting, leaving jobs and possessions behind. Displacement due to fighting increases the likelihood of children contracting diseases such as cholera and malaria, as families are forced into tempo-rary housing or refugee camps with little or no provision of sanitation facilities. Conflict increases incidences of bereavement and other loss which puts children under serious emotional strain. It also impacts on the efforts that governments and other agencies make to provide adequate services for children and their families; the resulting damage to a region's physical capital and infrastructure such as roads, schools and hospitals, hinders the provision of the support that children need to achieve their potential and to stay safe.

When families are vulnerable, conflict increases their vulnerability; for example, sub-sistence farmers who are reliant on their crops to feed their family are at risk of severe malnutrition, even starvation, if conflict forces them to flee their land. Again, this depletes families' assets and their ability to sustain their livelihoods. The displacement of families can lead to separation, with children in particular then in increased danger of being inad-equately protected from harm, or even co-opted into the violence. The conflict against the Government in Northern Uganda, led by the Lord's Resistance Army (LRA), has been raging since the late 1980s and has seen an estimated 10,000 children forced, through abduction and intimidation, into becoming child soldiers (SOS Children's Villages, 2009). The long-term effects on such children, who have often been forced to commit atroci-ties, and on the communities who are subject to LRA attacks, is difficult to appreciate fully. When children are coerced into such damaging roles, the post-conflict rehabilita-tion of communities is made all the more difficult. How can families recover and trust one another again? Violent conflict depletes social capital, destroying the social networks and sources of support that poor families in particular rely on for survival.

Children are often framed by the media and humanitarian agencies purely as victims in conflict situations, often in phrases such as 'women and children'. These simplify a com-plex situation by using language and imagery that makes the most sense to most people, for example, stereotypical visions of mother and child, helpless and unequivocally non-participants in the conflict. Paradoxically, this may pose additional dangers to male children. For example in 1995, during the war in Bosnia, Serbian forces separated and massacred an estimated 8,000 boys and men in Srebrenica on the grounds that males were poten-tial combatants, and so legitimate targets (Gendercide, 2010). They sought to justify their definition by allowing humanitarian agencies access to women and younger children whom they constructed as 'innocents'. Thus, use of terms such as 'women and children' as syn-onymous with 'civilian', whilst male children are seen as potential or actual combatants, provides yet another challenge for agencies and communities trying to protect children from the effects of conflict. The issues around conflict and child well-being are therefore extremely complex and must be considered differently in each and every context, yet we must recognise that as victims, witnesses, even perpetrators of atrocities, children in war-torn countries are too often robbed of their right to a safe and happy childhood (UN, 1989).

Education

The availability of educational opportunities is a key element in acquiring human capital. Pearce (2009) argues that education, literacy and lifelong learning are the key drivers of development and education is seen by millions of families in the developing world as the only way out of poverty, mirroring a similar pattern in the developed world in the nineteenth century. Yet in some parts of West Africa, for example, more than 40 per cent of people over 15 are still unable to read and write. This shortage of educated adults may be a key barrier to a country's political, social and economic progress and there are huge challenges for some regions in terms of creating a healthy, well-educated workforce, no longer reliant on sub-sistence farming, which can be wealth-generating in the modern globalised economy and thereby provide health, education and other services for a growing population.

Significant progress has been made during the last decade towards MDG 2, to achieve universal primary education, particularly in Sub Saharan Africa and Asia (UN, 2008). However, further progress will not be straightforward. Firstly, there are huge problems to overcome in terms of resourcing education. The continuing increase in the birth rate in some countries, coupled with improving survival rates and better health, mean that there is enormous demand for school places, for example in Ethiopia, where 46.1 per cent of the population are under 14 years old (CIA, 2009). Provision of school buildings, renewal of resources and staffing all require an ongoing stream of funding which many governments find difficult to sustain. Pearce (2009) notes that spending reforms driven by the International Monetary Fund (IMF) and World Bank have actually led to a cut in the teacher workforce in some West African countries. Throughout the developing world, children are often taught in very large classes in mixed age groups, in broken-down class-rooms or outdoors, and with minimal resources.

Secondly, though observers from developed countries often comment on the powerful motivation of children in the developing world to access educational opportunities, cul-tural attitudes and practices may be a barrier. Within some communities, there may be ignorance about what is possible, linked to fatalism arising from despair, poverty, poor nutrition or religious beliefs. A clear example is that there may be reluctance to allow girls to attend school, because they are needed for childcare and other household duties, because education is seen as unnecessary for girls who will marry and raise children, or because of fears that they will be vulnerable to attack or abduction on their journey to and from school, a reality in areas of Ethiopia, for example. However, given limited resources, educating girls can be argued to be a priority since it can lead to huge capital increase in terms of family health and earning power. Educating women may be as impor-tant for the developing world as the emancipation of women was for the developed world in the twentieth century.

Thirdly, financial factors can restrict children's access to education. Even where it is 'free', parents may need to provide uniform, pencils and notebooks which they may not be able to afford for all or even some of their children. There are also difficulties in providing edu-cation in remote rural areas; not least because teachers who have trained in large towns or cities may be reluctant to go back to remote villages, where pay and conditions and lifestyle are almost certainly inferior and hugely less than they could enjoy abroad, where they can earn enough to be able to send money back to support their families.

How then to move forward? As with health, there is a real danger that governments may misguidedly look to impose developed world 'solutions', backed by western finance, which although well-intentioned may be inappropriate or unsustainable in the long term. A good example is the provision of plasma TVs for all Ethiopian government secondary schools (Bitew, 2008). Similarly models of education and developmentally appropriate practice grounded in the developed world and shaped by its historical and political context are unlikely to be relevant or successful (Brooker, 2005; Penn, 2008). Education needs to be community based, emerging from the developing needs of a community, and supported from within the community. It could be argued that this is also the case in the UK.

However the rapid spread of modern technology through the developing world (Hankin, 2009) may offer support with this and begin to overcome some of the resource difficulties. In particular the growth of wireless technology, linked to the spread of mobile phone use, offers to leapfrog the financial constraints of installing landlines and may afford even remote communities the opportunity to connect to worldwide resources without the costs of sustaining libraries. But all this depends on the ability at individual, local and national level to accumulate sufficient financial capital to support such developments.

Role of NGOs and the state

The well-being of children in the developing world is affected by macro, meso and micro level economic and political factors. At the macro level international institutions such as the World Bank and the European Union have an extremely powerful role in providing aid funding and loans to governments in the developing world, coordinating humanitarian responses to crises, and influencing (even controlling) world trade protocols. The financial and technical support that they provide to developing countries is often conditional on implementation of reforms and improvements to financial systems and governance which they dictate. However the debate continues over the effectiveness of the top-down imposition of a western model of free-market democracy upon the developing world. Increasingly, there is an argument that trade agreements often disadvantage poorer nations, and that loans serve only to lock them into debts that they can never repay.

Western governments' fulfilment of funding commitments to developing countries is a contentious issue, with many wealthy nations failing to meet internationally agreed targets. In 2000 the United Nations Development Programme (UNDP) asked the world's richest nations to give 0.7 per cent of their GDP in development aid (UN, 2008) in order to achieve the MDGs. Caught in the spotlight of high profile events like the 2005 G8 Summit, which was accompanied by a groundswell of public concern to *make poverty history* (Make Poverty History, 2005), a coalition of world leaders made this pledge to increase aid spending but by 2005 only Norway, Sweden, the Netherlands and Denmark had met the agreed target (Penn, 2005, p35).

At the meso, or government level, it is important to appreciate that each nation has its own set of strengths and challenges with regard to governance, infrastructure, natural and man-made resources and so on, and education, health and welfare services, which are particularly important for safeguarding the well-being of children, therefore differ in scope and quality from one country to the next. Some countries, such as Tanzania and Zambia, have been proactive in prioritising the needs of children by making primary education free for all, and have seen improved attendance and retention rates as a result (UN, 2008). However, Non Governmental Organisations (NGOs) are often particularly active in providing education, care and welfare services in the most disadvantaged communities.

NGOs make up the so-called third or voluntary sector between the public and private sectors. NGOs are usually charities, working for philanthropic rather than profit-making or political ends. They often take up issues and deliver services that governments are unwilling or unable to tackle, and can be seen either as indicative of the failure of states to provide adequately for ordinary people, or as a positive demonstration of humankind's commitment to helping those who are less fortunate. UK based NGOs such as OXFAM, Save the Children and Action Aid are very active in providing welfare services in the developing world, either directly or through a partner organisation based in the community that they want to support. They also take on a valuable campaigning role, seeking to improve the life chances of disadvantaged communities by challenging the structures and practices that make and keep countries poor. NGOs are not necessarily large, influential organisations, but may be local single-issue organisations working on a very small scale, or with a particular community. As issues are context-specific, by definition, the sector is extremely diverse.

NGOs are funded by a range of donors, including public donations, but may also be contracted by governments to provide services. They therefore have a number of lines of accountability to balance and they work hard to promote the work they do in a way that will generate continued support. There is competition between NGOs for funding, but there are also examples of collaboration such as the creation in 1963 of the Disaster Emergency Committee (DEC) which has seen key International NGOs including the British Red Cross, Christian Aid and World Vision come together to coordinate a response to disasters such as the 2004 Asian Tsunami and 2010 earthquake in Haiti (DEC, 2010).

The micro or local level work that NGOs take on in developing countries is extremely important in building the capacity of communities – enabling people to help themselves. They are able to bring additional resources into a community, to invest in local people's skills and knowledge, and to run projects that seek to enhance well-being. It is now acknowledged that real positive change can only be achieved by working with communities in a participatory way – poor communities should not just be recipients of aid monies but become active agents in identifying and working towards solutions to their problems. This principle also guides the provision of community-based services such as Sure Start in the UK.

The old model of well-meaning westerners going out to the developing world to help is being increasingly replaced by local people being employed or trained to take on the design, implementation and maintenance of community development projects themselves. A key word is 'sustainability', the aim being that any improvements should continue beyond the time span of a particular project. It is argued that an NGO can be said to have achieved its aims when it is no longer needed and can disband. However, many governments in the developing world are not in a position, financially or in terms of expertise, to take over the work of NGOs, and need them to help to continue to prioritise the needs of children, the key to any country's future.

Conclusion

By considering the range of issues affecting communities in the developing world, we can begin to appreciate the scale of the challenge involved in improving life chances for the millions of children worldwide who continue to live in poverty, especially given the current global economic climate and the ongoing presence of conflict and natural disasters. Understanding the interrelated and complex nature of the problems that families face in terms of sustaining livelihoods, educating their children and keeping them healthy and safe, reminds us that in order to be successful any interventions need to be people-centred and context-specific. Working with families, and children in particular, does not lend itself to a top-down 'one-size-fits-all' approach, but needs to be sensitive to innovative and different ways of identifying and implementing solutions. This principle can also be applied to the approach international institutions, governments and NGOs should take in helping the developing world to help itself.

The UNCRC sees children as having universally-applicable rights to an adequate standard of living, protection from harm and opportunities to participate fully in society (UN, 1989), yet we can see that the efforts to fulfil the aims of this convention and meet the targets set out in the MDGs still have a long way to go. Having a well-informed, critical understanding of key global issues makes us more aware of provision here in the UK, the things we take for granted, and also of the continuing inequality in our own society. For practitioners interested in the care and education of young children, having an eye on the global context enables us to appreciate how far we have come in the UK, and also to acknowledge how much there still is to do.

ACTIVITY *1*

Over the next month, look through newspapers and magazines for articles on children in the developing world. What are the key messages that come across? Which messages do not?

ACTIVITY *2*

Research non-governmental organisations working in the developing world. Choose one, and find out what its aims are, how it raises finance, what kind of projects it supports and how it involves local communities.

ACTIVITY *3*

Organise a group to discuss the issues raised in the section on Conflict.

Some potential questions:

- *Are child soldiers victims or criminals? What might be some of the challenges involved in rehabilitating them into their communities?*

- *Why might civil conflicts, for example between different communities within the same country, be particularly difficult to resolve?*

- *Can the MDGs be achieved in war-torn countries? Which might be particularly difficult to achieve?*

Garcia, M, Pence, A and Evans, JL (Eds) (2008) *Africa's Future, Africa's Challenge: Early Childhood Care and Development in Sub-Saharan Africa.* Washington: The World Bank.

This collection of articles gives an in-depth perspective on children's lives in sub-Saharan Africa, one of the most fascinating and significant areas of the developing world.

Penn, H (2005) *Unequal Childhoods: Young Children's Lives in Poor Countries,* London and New York: Routledge.

This book uses case studies from four different countries to illustrate the diversity of children's experiences, challenging Western assumptions about families and childhood.

Smidt, S (2006) *The Developing Child in the 21st Century: A Global Perspective on Child Development.* London and New York: Routledge.

This book offers a fascinating insight into how ideas about childhood have changed over time and place.

13 The research, policy and practice triangle in early childhood education and care

Verity Campbell-Barr

Introduction

The interplay between research, policy and practice can take many forms, from the simple linear relationship where research informs policy and policy informs practice, to a more complex relationship where research, policy and practice can all inform one another and question one another. It is perhaps unsurprising that it is the more complex and questioning relationship that I want to focus on. To explore this relationship, I will begin with an overview of what is meant by social policy within the field of early childhood studies. Whilst looking at policy developments I will consider how research has interacted with the policy process before moving on to consider the implications of national policy for practice. Early Childhood Education and Care (ECEC) is a broad term that covers many different areas, but I will be focussing on the provision of free early years education for three and four year olds, the relationship between childcare and parental employment and the professionalisation of the workforce as examples. By looking at these examples, I will demonstrate how research policy and practice interact with one another in both harmonious and contentious ways.

What is social policy?

The term social policy can take on different meanings depending on the context in which it is used, for example social policy the academic subject and social policy the process (see Dean, 2005). Even within social policy the process there is the policy making process at national, regional, local and practitioner levels and also the policy implementation process. For the purpose of this chapter, I will be focusing on the national policymaking process. Therefore, social policy is a statement of intention for social intervention that is designed to promote the well-being of citizens. Policies are developed to improve the life chances and social relations of society (Alcock, 2004).

The formation of policy is a gradual (and messy) process.

> *At its most basic level the policy process has been described as a 'black box' into which are entered 'inputs' and from which emerge 'outcomes'.*

Alcock et al., 2004, p58

At the simplest level, a policy represents a course of action that will allow those in power to define what they see as the well-being of society (their political purpose) and how they aim to achieve this (Forman and Baldwin, 2007). Policy will normally develop by identifying a social problem and then finding a solution (that can be implemented) for it. However, there are a number of 'inputs' that will inform what are identified as social problems and what are the possible solutions, making the process of developing the 'outcomes' complex (and long winded).

To develop the initial idea of a social policy, a social 'problem' has to be identified, this can be as a result of research, lobby groups, the media, parliament or those working on behalf of parliament (civil servants), but often it will be a combination of these (each claiming to represent the views of the public). Having acknowledged a social problem, possible solutions will be identified and again this can involve research, lobby groups, parliament or those working on behalf of parliament. The possible solution will then be consulted on. Those consulted can include the general public and/or experts in the field and opposing political parties. The consultation process may involve several stages and could involve the commissioning of research as well (as I will discuss when we come on to evaluation research). The solutions will also be debated by parliament before the judiciary (judges, courts and tribunals) pass any new legislation (see Figure 13.1). However, this presents a very simplified version of policy formation, as it assumes that all policy formation starts from a blank slate and this is rarely the case. Rather, an existing policy will be identified and the process outlined above will be followed to amend this policy to address the problem.

Policy developments can be in relation to all members of society, but often they will focus on a specific section of society, such as families or children, and even within these groups, they will focus on sub-populations, such as lone parents or children living in poverty. Although a policy might be targeted towards a specific sub-population, the aim will always be improving the well-being of the whole of society.

Policy developments inevitably have implications for the way in which we live our lives. Looking at children, government has made numerous decisions that impact on the lives of children, such as that they should be educated, but they should not work (Piper, 2008). Child based policy developments impact on how lives are lived by representing children as a project, something that needs to be controlled, regulated and surveyed to ensure that they fit in with the social order. Such policy developments contribute to a definition of what is deemed an appropriate childhood (see Chapter 12). Thus, policy becomes involved in the social construction of childhood (and adulthood, family life, etc). For example, education policy imposes spatial and temporal constraints on children by stipulating when and where education takes place. Curriculum guidance also imposes a series of rules around what are deemed appropriate activities for children. Education policy, therefore, becomes involved in the institutionalisation of childhood, having direct implications for the ways in which children live their lives (see Moss and Petrie, 2002).

Where the outcomes of the policy are clear and relate to the group named in the policy (for example children), they are direct outcomes, but there will also be secondary and indirect outcomes for other members of society. Continuing with the example of education policy, the direct outcomes are that children become more educated (albeit in a particular form of education as defined by the state), but the secondary outcomes will include the social and economic gains of a more educated population that can compete in the global knowledge economy. Indirect outcomes include that parental time can be freed up (whilst the children are at school) enabling them to enter employment, furthering the possible economic gains.

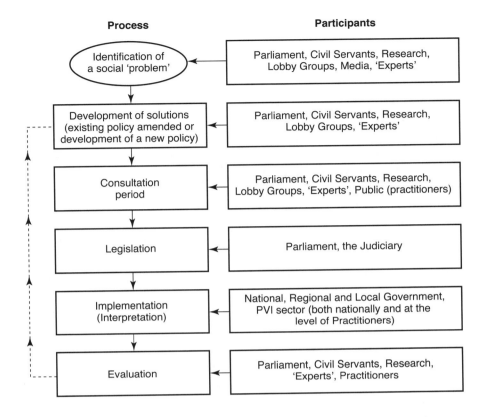

Figure 13.1 The development of policy

Equally, policies that are for other groups of society will have implications for children. The more obvious examples of where this occurs are in relation to *family* policy developments. For example, there have been numerous policy developments aimed at getting lone parents who are out of work and on Income Support back into employment. In 2007 the Green Paper *In Work Better Off: Next steps to full employment* (DWP, 2008) laid out plans which meant that from October 2010 lone parents would lose Income Support once their youngest child reached the age of seven, meaning that they would be forced to seek employment (there are some exceptions, such as where a child has severe disabilities). Although working part-time (such as during school hours) is advocated in the Green Paper, there are nonetheless implications for children; such as that they may have to attend childcare or be cared for outside of their immediate family.

When we look at policy that is presented as being for children, we must always consider whether children are the true focus or whether there are secondary and indirect outcomes and, if so, which of these outcomes is the most important in the minds of policymakers. Therefore, when you look at policy, you should ask:

● who is the policy for?

● does it have implications for any other social group,?

● what are the expected initial outcomes of the policy?

● and what are the possible wider effects of the policy?

Early childhood education and care policy

For many years children were largely invisible in policy, being referred to in relation to the family rather than having policy developments targeted at them in their own right (Daniel and Ivatts, 1998). Education offers an exception to this invisibility, but only in relation to school age education, not early years education and childcare (such as out of school clubs). Prior to the 1980s there was a lack of national political interest in ECEC. Although some local authorities had begun to develop their own ECEC policies, the geographical coverage was patchy and often it was only children deemed 'in-need' who were targeted (see Randall, 2000). Nationally, ECEC was regarded as a private, family matter with the state only intervening with policy developments in extreme circumstances, such as in cases of child neglect. In 1988 the government maintained that parents were primarily responsible for the care of their children (OECD, 2000). When ECEC policies began to emerge, they had their roots in a truly child centred starting point: promoting child development and well-being. However, such aims have arguably been hijacked by the secondary and indirect interests of the family, economics and wider society, such as parental employment, which I will discuss later.

Following the signing of the United Nations Convention on the Rights of the Child by the UK in 1990 (later ratified in 1991 coming into force in 1992), the then Conservative government took some tentative steps towards developing ECEC policy. For example, The Out of School Childcare Initiative (which ran from 1993–6) and the 1994 Childcare Disregard (an in-work benefit that helped low-income families to pay for childcare for children under the age of 11), were both introduced. These policy developments signalled a shift in thinking, recognising that ECEC might offer benefits for society as a whole and no longer seeing it as something that was just a private matter for families.

The election of New Labour in 1997 resulted in a plethora of ECEC policies. Building on previous limited policy developments around ECEC and (as will be discussed further) emerging research and debates, New Labour developed a number of initiatives that arguably had children and ECEC at their centre. Key to these developments were the development of the Children and Young People's Unit (including the appointment of a Minister for Children) and the introduction of the National Childcare Strategy, including ring-fenced funding to support the expansion of ECEC provision, a tax credit system to help parents to pay for childcare and a number of initiatives to develop the quality of ECEC (see for example DfEE, 1998a; DfES, 2003; HM Treasury, 2004).

The Labour government's policy focus on ECEC presented a shift in political thinking that saw children as the direct objects of policy development and not just the secondary beneficiaries of family policy:

> *This centre-staging of children in social policy represents a significant shift in British politics and culture away from a society which has traditionally preferred to leave the responsibility of children's care outside of school to their parents.*

> (Williams, 2004, p407)

Why invest in early childhood education and care?

The interest in developing policies targeted directly at ECEC was the result of a number of factors: research that resulted in greater knowledge about child development; research on the cost benefits of ECEC for national economies; research on the role of childcare in supporting family employment; feminism (more specifically changes in understandings of women's roles and motherhood); equality agendas (such as ensuring mothers had equality of access to the labour market and addressing child poverty); changes in family structures; the position of the economy and pressure from lobby groups (Randall, 2000). In acknowledging the influence of each of these factors, we can begin to see how policy develops within the social and political context. As shown in Figure 13.1 it is not just government officials and their aides who develop policy, rather policy develops in response to social changes and social pressures.

Maternal employment

Prior to the National Childcare Strategy, there had been a growth in the number of women working and this, and other changes in family structure, had contributed to a rise in the use of childcare. McDowell et al. (2006, p144) summarise census data that demonstrates the rise in numbers of women working, stating that by the 'close [of the 1990s] just over half of all mothers of pre-school children, for example, were in the labour market compared to 27 per cent twenty-five years earlier'. However, this change was not experienced equally among all groups of mothers, as even now the proportion of lone parents in paid employment (55 per cent) is lower than that of mothers with partners (71 per cent) (Self and Zealey, 2007). Even within these employment statistics there is considerable variation in proportions of full-time and part-time employment.

Despite the rise in maternal employment and the subsequent rise in demand for childcare, policy (prior to the National Childcare Strategy) had relied on market forces to respond to the increase in demand (Land and Lewis, 1998), while leaving families to decide whether to use childcare. However, the National Childcare Strategy demonstrated that ECEC had a role to play within the wider social policy system. The Green Paper: *Meeting the Childcare Challenge* (DfEE, 1998a) argued that if more childcare was available, more women would enter employment. In particular, by identifying the variation in employment rates amongst mothers, *Meeting the Childcare Challenge* identified how the provision of childcare could contribute to the equality agenda by ensuring equality of access to the labour market for mothers. While the evidence for this claim is not referenced in the document (policy documents seldom acknowledge the sources of their information), it echoes Bertram and Pascal's (1999) finding that four out of five mothers said they would work if appropriate childcare was available.

Child outcomes

Research also emerged that demonstrated the benefits of ECEC for children. *Meeting the Childcare Challenge* (DfEE, 1998a, section 1.4) states that ECEC can enhance both 'social and intellectual development'. Again there is no referencing within the document, but international research supports this claim. For example, in the UK Osborn and Millbank (1987) found evidence that children who received some form of preschool education showed better cognitive functioning. In the United States, the Perry Pre-School Project (Schweinhart et al., 1993) found that even at age 27 the long term benefits of attending the High/Scope preschool programme included reductions in school dropout rates, drug use, teenage pregnancy, welfare dependency and crime, whilst the Head Start programme (also in the States) demonstrated improvements in cognitive development (see Melhuish, 2004 for a more thorough discussion on the international evidence of the benefits of ECEC).

However, we do have to be cautious when we look at the evidence. Firstly we need to consider the context of the research, as often specific social groups have been targeted (as was the case in the Perry Pre-school Project which targeted particularly deprived families) and there are questions as to whether the findings are then applicable to all sectors of society. Secondly, can a study that has taken place in the US be relevant in the UK context? Thirdly, we need to be aware that the sample sizes of the projects are very variable and where they are small (for example the Perry Pre-school Project only had 123 participants) the extent to which the findings are generalisable may be limited.

In addition to examining methodological issues, we also need to ensure that we have fully understood the findings and the complex nature of any benefits of ECEC. For example, the effects of childcare on birth to three-year-old children are mixed, with some studies demonstrating negative effects (Melhuish, 2004). More recent studies, such as EPPE (Effective Provision of Pre-school Education), have also shown that there are a number of variables that need to be considered when looking at the benefits of ECEC. For example the quality of the care provided and the socio-economic status of the children's families act as important variables that affect the extent to which positive outcomes are achieved (see Sylva et al., 2004). In addition, it is important to distinguish between studies of outcomes of early years education and of outcomes of childcare, as there can be a tendency to assume that the findings from research on one form of provision can be applied to the other.

Economics

Whilst the developmental benefits for children may suggest that ECEC policy is targeted at them, there are a number of indirect benefits that suggest that economic considerations are the main drivers for ECEC policy. Financially, ECEC can reduce social stratification and can equalise life chances (see Lloyd, 2008), representing a twofold economic benefit of ECEC: firstly, children who become more educated will benefit themselves and the economy by being able to make a greater contribution to the knowledge economy of the future; secondly, the provision of ECEC enables mothers to return to paid work. Increased employment rates have the obvious national economic benefits of more people paying taxes and fewer people being on benefits. Thus, a policy that appears to be driven by the interests of children can actually have much wider outcomes.

In identifying that ECEC policy has outcomes for children, secondary outcomes such as enabling maternal employment and indirect outcomes for the economy, we can see how ECEC policy affects the social well-being of all citizens. However, we are also now aware that how policy is presented and 'sold' to the public may mask the full extent of the outcomes. This is why we always need to consider the questions laid out at the end of the section: What is Social Policy? In considering these questions we can begin to get a picture of what the drivers for policy development may be.

Policy can also be informed by theory. The future economic benefits of ECEC policy can be modelled by Human Capital Theory, which is based on the principle that an investment in knowledge, skills and values will result in an economic return for society (see Penn, 2010b, for further discussion).

> *Investment in human capital is at the heart of strategies in OECD [Organisation for Economic Co-operation and Development] countries to promote economic prosperity, fuller employment, and social cohesion. Individuals, organisations and nations increasingly recognise that high levels of knowledge, skills and competence are essential to their future security and success.*

> OECD, 1998, p7

When government policymakers invest in the future they are gambling on what they see as the greatest potential risks (Piper, 2008). However, when deciding what to invest in, the government also has to make a number of assumptions, such as what knowledge the future workforce will need and how many jobs will be available to employ growing numbers of highly skilled people.

Policies intended to deliver economic gains are based on the assumption that people will make rational choices. Rational choice theory assumes that parents' decisions about childcare will be motivated by a desire to maximise their financial income. However, there are a number of emotional factors in the decision to use childcare, such as attitudes to where is the best place for the care of the child (including staying at home with the mother), the quality of available, affordable care, levels of trust and confidence in childcare providers, attitudes towards what makes a good mother and the mother's own career aspirations (for example see Hoggart et al., 2006; Duncan, 2003).

Hakim (2000) developed preference theory, as an alternative to rational choice theory, maintaining that decisions to enter employment are based on individual preferences. However, the decision to use childcare and enter employment is not a simple matter of preference because it is constrained by the realities of the labour market and the availability of childcare. For example, studies have demonstrated that a lack of atypical hours childcare (care that is before 8am and after 6pm) can prevent mothers from taking such jobs as may be available (see, for example, Bell and La Valle, 2005; Statham and Mooney, 2003). Childcare also needs to be accessible, but whilst the number of childcare places has increased many Childcare Sufficiency Assessments have demonstrated that new places are not always in the same locations as new demand (OPM, 2008). Thus policy objectives can be constrained by both practical and emotional factors.

The interplay of research and policy

The example of maternal employment that I have used above has already begun to demonstrate how research can inform policy developments, but we must be cautious as the relationship between research and policy is extremely complex. This relationship can take one of two forms:

1 Social policy research can monitor, evaluate (and suggest changes to) existing policy;

2 Research can uncover findings that suggest a need for new policies or for changes to existing ones (see Alcock, 2004).

Evaluation research, which can range from quick literature reviews to extensive field research (Forman and Baldwin, 2007), looks at how policy is implemented, why it is implemented and whether it should be implemented at all. An essential question that is typically asked is whether the intervention (such as the policy initiative) has achieved the anticipated goals (Bryman, 2004). The connection between research and policy in evaluation research is relatively linear, but it might not always be transparent. For example, the research may be closely connected with the development of policy, but the relationship may not be politically neutral and objective. When we look at evaluation research we must be conscious of who is funding it. For example, New Labour endorsed evidence-based policy and commissioned research to explore its own policies, raising two important questions:

• Whilst those who undertake the research may seek to be objective, the government is funding them, so can they be truly impartial?

• Will the government publish findings that do not support their political convictions?

Where research uncovers findings that have implications for policy, the relationship between policy and research is less clear. It can take time for research, such as that which demonstrated the benefits of ECEC, to result in policy changes (see Randall, 2000). Yet it is more than this, research findings are only likely to be acted on where they fit the political ideology of the policymakers (Alcock, 2004). New Labour, within its policy developments, advocated a work-first focus, based on a desire to reduce poverty and to promote social equality (see Brewer et al., 2002). The provision of childcare, as we have already seen, fits in with this work-first ethic. In addition, the 'commitment' to promoting maternal employment was intended to reduce poverty by increasing families' opportunities to generate an income. Social equality was addressed not only by the attempt to reduce poverty, but also by the concern to equalise life chances by enabling all children to benefit from ECEC.

Having acknowledged that policymakers will favour research that fits their political ideology, we must be alert to the possibility that they may be tempted to manipulate research findings. Thus, whilst evaluation research may appear to offer a 'bottom up' approach, in that it listens to the views of practitioners, there are limits to this. Research that does not support policy developments is likely to be ignored, only to regain favour when policy takes a different direction.

The interplay of practice and policy

Implementing national policy can involve a number of stakeholders including national government (government departments such as the Department for Children, Schools and Families), regional government (such as Government Office Southwest), local government and private, voluntary and independent organisations (such as The Preschool Learning Alliance) and practitioners (day nurseries and childminders). Thus, whilst there are national policies, they will in fact operate at a number of levels: national, regional, local and practitioner. At each level there is a process of interpretation and implementation (see Figure 13.1) that can result in subsequent policy developments, such as local authority policy and a setting's policy. Here I will focus on practitioners and the relationship between national policy and practice.

The numerous policy developments in ECEC since the launch of the National Childcare Strategy have had a number of implications for practitioners. In each ECEC setting it is practitioners who have to implement policy and to find ways of coping with the changes and pressures that this entails (Alcock, 2004). To consider the interplay of policy and practice I will be focussing on the theme of economics, as well as looking at the professionalisation agenda.

Economics

Whilst the economic interests of the country, families and children have been considered in ECEC initiatives, those of practitioners have been ignored. For example, there are a number of economic issues for providers who are delivering free early years education for three and four year olds. First, it is important to note that the National Childcare Strategy was designed to deliver a national free entitlement of early years education via a mixed market approach. The Government did not set out to establish state run early years education settings, rather they opted for a mix of private, voluntary, independent (PVI) and maintained settings (Campbell-Barr, 2009a). Funding to expand the provision of early years education favoured the PVI sector and, as a result, the number of PVI places increased at a far greater rate than maintained (state) settings (see Stokes and Wilkinson, 2007). This represents an interesting stance for policy as the government is committed to making early years education available to all families by funding, monitoring and ultimately controlling provision, but not by delivering the service directly in the same way that they do with other forms of education. Whilst this may look like a lack of true commitment to early years education, it also means that the government is reliant on others to provide a state entitlement. This makes the implementation of the policy vulnerable in that there is an assumption that providers will deliver early years education as the government intends and that sufficient places will be available. In practice, however, this may depend on them remaining profitable and committed to the provision of early years education.

To ensure that settings provide early years education in line with government policies, Ofsted (Office for Standards in Education) now inspects all ECEC settings in England (with equivalent bodies in the devolved administrations). However, it is clear that there is both interpretation and playfulness in the implementation of policy in ECEC. How do we know this? Because all settings are different, as is evident from how they all implement the minimum standards differently. The implementation of policy into practice reflects a process of micro policy development. By micro policy development I am referring to the 'black box' of inputs and outputs that I mentioned earlier. At the micro level, the input will be the policy, but practitioners will interpret policy initiatives in different ways (the development of solutions) resulting in different outcomes. They will also reflect on their own practice to further develop it (a kind of internal consultation). To an extent, this helps practitioners to develop a sense of ownership of the policy developments: making a strange policy familiar and appropriate for a particular setting. In 'playing' with the implementation of policy a degree of flexibility can be introduced when policy is not always in the interest of practitioners. Also, this process of interpreting policies will enable practice to continue to develop as providers will (in theory) reflect on their practice (making the familiar strange) and continue to try new things. Allowing room for this playfulness is important as it helps to ensure that policy is not too restricting. However, the degree of 'play' in any policy will vary, with some having more scope for interpretation than others.

However, this playfulness also poses a problem: Can we be sure that practitioners interpret policies with the best interests of children in mind? It raises the question of who knows more (or perhaps even best) about meeting the needs of children – policymakers or professionals and parents? We have already seen that policy developments are driven by political ideologies and that policies 'for' children may not always be concerned primarily with meeting the needs of children, so how much scope should practitioners be given to interpret or even challenge policy?

To ensure that sufficient numbers of settings remain open to deliver policy objectives they must be economically viable. Settings inevitably close for a number of reasons, but sustainability has always posed a threat to ECEC settings (see Campbell-Barr, 2009b). If we look in more detail at just the level of funding that providers receive for delivering the free early years education places for three and four year olds, the rate of funding is insufficient to cover operating costs (NDNA, 2006), with some settings even making a loss (Clemens et al., 2006). The funding could be insufficient to support quality and the mixed market may not be the most appropriate form of delivery (Sylva and Pugh, 2005).

The rate of funding for delivering a policy initiative, such as early years education, leaves less scope for 'play' than other aspects of policy. However, this does not mean that practitioners have to be passive in the development and implementation of policy. For example, the Single Funding Formula required local authorities to conduct research into the true cost of providing early years education in their areas, and to come up with a single formula that would determine the rate of funding that providers would receive for delivering early years education (DCSF, 2009c). In essence the idea was for a transparent approach to funding that would not favour any particular sector. However, practitioners campaigned against the implementation of the Single Funding Formula by raising concerns about the quality of the research and questioning whether the Formula really was 'fair', particularly for the maintained sector, which stood to lose financially. Subsequently, a decision was taken to delay the implementation of the Single Funding Formula by a year whilst further work was done to look at the issues raised (DCSF, 2009d).

The relationship between research, policy and practice is based on social negotiations. Practitioners are not passive in the triangle (as seen in the example of early years education funding). Whilst the government will have its own political ideologies, both researchers and practitioners can have their say and influence the direction of policy developments. Even once policy has been rolled out, this does not mean that practitioners have to stop questioning it, rather they can explore ways of responding to it: Making the familiar strange, and they can seek to develop ownership of it: Making the strange familiar. Equally, in considering micro policy at the level of settings, managers may have their own ideologies, but staff and parents can have their influence and say as well.

Qualifications

Within the National Childcare Strategy there have been a number of policies that have looked at the skill level of the workforce (DfES, 2003; DCSF, 2007b). This focus has been prompted by the growth in evidence showing that better qualified staff will improve the quality of provision (PriceWaterhouseCoopers, 2006; Sylva and Pugh, 2005; Sylva et al., 2004; Barnes, 2001), thus contributing to the government's aim of improving outcomes for all young children and reducing inequalities between them (DfES, 2006c). However, there is a fear that ECEC could become more exclusive, as the drive for higher qualifications restricts entrants to the workforce and reduces opportunities for those with lower level qualifications (Moss, 2000) and there are also questions around whether those in the sector want to undertake further training (Callendar, 2000; Penn, 2000). The training requirements that are now required have been imposed on those working in ECEC with little engagement with those concerned (Osgood, 2006; McGillivray, 2008; Miller, 2008). In particular, those who work in ECEC have not been consulted on the nature of the skills needed for this work. Nor is there a consideration of how professionalisation sits with historical constructions of the ECEC sector as requiring (gendered) attributes such as being maternal, kind, warm, sensitive and liking children (McGillivray, 2008).

The professionalisation agenda demonstrates that policy may not always reflect the values and judgements of those working in the sector or the implications of the policy for those who are expected to deliver it. However, the drive for professionalisation is centred on child well-being (high quality staff lead to high quality settings, which in turn provide better experiences and outcomes for children), so what does this mean for the relationships between research, policy and practice? It suggests that, at times, evidence from research should outweigh the views of practitioners. However, I am not advocating that the views of practitioners should be ignored. Rather, this highlights the need for practitioners to take an active role in both research and policy development to ensure, for example, that a shared understanding of professionalisation can be negotiated, rather than imposed.

In addition, the developments around the professionalisation of the ECEC workforce demonstrate the fluid nature of policy. In an ideal world policymakers would be able to start from a blank slate, but instead they are involved in a process of political and social interaction where they must make adjustments to existing policies to suit the political ideology of the party in power (Alcock, 2004). Even where a political party has introduced policies, they will adjust them (as they see how they are applied in practice) to ensure that they continue to meet their political objectives. Given the fluid nature of policy development, and the role of social interaction in this process, practitioners must be involved in this interaction if their perspective is to be heard. All practitioners should take opportunities to engage in consultations when policy proposals are being developed (for example green papers) in order to express their views and opinions on matters that will impact on them (see Activity 1).

The fluid nature of policy can leave providers in a position where they feel they are constantly struggling to 'keep-up' with the latest developments. Being actively involved in the social interactions around policy developments can help to reduce this. One way to be involved is to engage in research. The continual changing of policy is often due to a realisation that existing practices will not result in the intended policy outcome. Here we see how research can have implications for practice – as research reveals new evidence to inform policies or uncovers problems in how they are implemented, the policies can be adjusted to encourage changes in practice.

Equally, at a micro-policy level, settings need to recognise the social interactions that take place to inform their own policy development and implementation. The micro policy process reflects the national one in that there are both inputs and outputs. Key inputs will be national and regional policy directives, but the notion of 'playing' with a policy in practice means that providers can interpret policy in relation to the context of their setting in order to generate their desired outputs. How much they can play will vary between policies, but teams in settings can strive to generate a sense of ownership over policy developments. In playing with policy in practice, practitioners can be involved in their own research, reflecting on practice and engaging with the views of parents and children to further develop their practice. The micro policy level is a good model for the national one. However, whilst practitioners are in a position to interact with parents and children every day that their setting is open, at the national policy level the social interaction is more artificial and formal. Although the policy process includes opportunities for interaction (such as research and consultation) practitioners have to ensure that they are actively involved if national policy is to reflect the level of social interaction that takes place at the micro level.

The research, policy and practice triangle

The relationship between research, policy and practice is complex and dynamic. Each can inform and shape the others, whether by providing support or challenges. Although (at the national policy level) the government has the power to create policies, it may not always be the most powerful contributor to the research, policy and practice triangle. Both researchers and practitioners can provide evidence that can inform policy. Figure 13.2 represents the interaction between research, policy and practice and shows that the development and implementation of policy will involve social interactions between all of these.

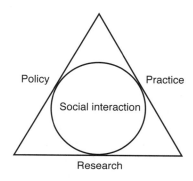

Figure 13.2 *The research, policy and practice triangle*

However, we always have to be mindful of the political ideologies of the party seeking to introduce any policy, as unwelcome evidence from research or practice may have been ignored. Whilst policymakers seek to promote social well-being, different political parties will have varying views on how best to achieve this. Thus the importance attached to each side of the triangle can vary.

The methods by which social well-being is to be achieved may not be in harmony with the needs of practitioners. In particular, we have seen that there are a number of economic tensions, such as insufficient funding for providing early years education and the assumption that financial gain is the only motivation for mothers returning to work. What is evident is that despite a professed focus on social well-being, economic factors frequently override this. Although policies may be in the name of children, we must always consider whether children are their true focus. As we have seen, ECEC policy may focus on improving children's well-being, but it also has economic impacts on families and society.

The social policy objective of achieving social well-being is actually more complex than this, as social well-being must be balanced with economic well-being. Further, the social and economic well-being at a national level has to be balanced against the social and economic well-being of children, parents and practitioners. Thus, the inputs for the development of policy are numerous and go far beyond just research and practice. However, although we can recognise that the policy process is a balancing act, I would suggest that the balance is now tipped in favour of the economic well-being of the nation resulting in the economic and social well-being of children, parents and practitioners being secondary outcomes in the policy process.

ACTIVITY *1*

Visit the DCSF's website and look at their consultation pages (www.dcsf.gov.uk/consultations/).

In a small group find a consultation that you feel is relevant. Discuss the consultation and develop a group response and submit it – remember, you have expert knowledge in Early Childhood Studies and can contribute to the debates taking place!

FURTHER READING

Lloyd, E (2008) The interface between childcare, family support and child poverty strategies under New Labour: tensions and contradictions, *Social Policy and Society*, 7 (4): 479–494

This article picks up on how New Labour sought to improve mothers' employment rates, child outcomes (particularly educational ones) and child poverty, but that in doing so there were tensions in the delivery of the National Childcare Strategy. In particular, the article questions the use of the mixed market in the National Childcare Strategy.

Randall, V (2000) *The Politics of Child Daycare in Britain*, Oxford, Oxford University Press. Chapter One: Introducing Childcare: Questions and Themes

I would love everyone to read the whole of Randall's book, but failing this, the first chapter provides a really good overview of the history of politics around childcare. The chapter looks at what prompted the rise in interest in ECEC in the post-war period, considering feminism, the character of Britain's political system, beliefs around the role of the state and the state/society relationship.

175

Part 5

Researching practice: developing critical engagement

14 In praise of reflective practice

Caroline Leeson

Introduction

An early years practitioner is helping children get changed for a gym session in the hall. She helps them get out of their everyday clothes, coping with zips and buttons and into shorts, t-shirts and plimsolls. Afterwards, a colleague points out that she helped the boys far more than the girls and actively encouraged the girls to manage themselves. Both practitioners pause to think about what that means, why it might be, what was in her mind, what messages she was giving to the children and whether they had noticed. They decide to observe their own behaviour and that of other colleagues over the next few days and try to understand what was going on and what the implications were.

Reflective practice, or the importance of thinking over one's actions past and present and identifying the lessons learnt for future action, should be a crucial aspect of professional work and lifelong learning. The practitioners in the above example will learn far more about their behaviour, their underlying values and the impact on the children from reflecting on their own practice than from anything they read in a book. This will then help them in future practice to be more confident, more responsive and ultimately more creative in their work, leading in its turn to a positive influence on the world around them.

Donald Schön (1983) suggests that one's ability to reflect on action and thereby engage in a personal journey of lifelong learning is a defining characteristic of professional practice, arguing that a model of education where students receive input as one would fill a glass and are then sent into situations where that knowledge is expected to simply spill forth, is not good practice and will lead to ineffective work. Rather, we should be encouraging the creation of opportunities to link theory to practice, to understand one's actions and the impact of those actions and thereby to develop enhanced knowledge and skills that can be taken into subsequent situations.

Recent initiatives (NCSL, 2004; CWDC, 2007; DCSF, 2008a) seek to promote the use of reflective practice, but there is still a preference, in the workplace, to have fact based, routine responses to situations (Lam et al., 2007) that can lead to greater anxiety and uncertainty on behalf of the practitioner (Ruch, 2002; Attard, 2008) and a poor experience for families (Saltiel, 2003).

In this chapter, I will argue that reflective practice should be regarded as an integral part of developing competent professionals in early years care and education. I will look at different models of reflection offered by theorists and explore how reflective skills may be taught, encouraged, achieved and maintained. In attempting to make sense of this area, I ask several questions – what is reflective practice, why should we engage in it, how do we actually do it, who can help with the process and what are the obstacles and opportunities that it offers us? I offer the reader my own reflective voyage around these issues and hope to persuade many to become such practitioners themselves.

What is reflective practice?

Reflective practice is taking the opportunity to think about the work that we are doing, either as we are doing it or after we have done it, attempting to draw the lessons we can learn from it in terms of how that work has impacted upon us and others and how it made, or makes, us feel about ourselves.

Reflecting *in* action (whilst doing something) and *on* action (following the action), both terms coming from the work of Schön (1983), are critical skills that offer the opportunity to develop insight and understanding, especially in those professions that have a substantial impact upon the lives of others such as social work, teaching and health care. It is my opinion that, unless we engage in this process, the work we do has the potential to be ill-informed and possibly dangerous as we perpetuate actions and decisions that no longer have relevance, simply because that is the way it has always been done and no one questions it.

The scenario comes to mind of the nursery which offered children plastic building bricks that had been disinfected in boiling water and thereby lost their shape and ability to click together. The fact that the bricks were thereby rendered useless escaped the attention of the staff and the practice continued over several years, with the practitioners expressing surprise that the children did not play with them. A practitioner who takes time to notice what is going on and thinks about the implications would have seen and questioned the practice and maybe used an alternative way of ensuring the bricks were clean!

Similarly, within my own field of child protection, a past colleague showed herself to be extremely keen to remove a child from an abusive household before she had fully engaged with the parent, establishing what might be done to remedy the situation. When encouraged to reflect on her actions, it became apparent that her own abusive background had allowed her to over-identify with the child and fail to see the many positive signs that demonstrated the family would benefit from active help rather than removal. Very often, decisions made to remove a child from a dangerous situation have an underlying corporate anxiety about failing to protect rather than anything to do with the best interests of the child. A reflective practitioner can begin to attempt to make these decisions openly and honestly, questioning the influence of personal prejudice, social policy or current trend and examining the issue objectively and sensitively.

> *A major challenge for these students is the integration of theoretical knowledge with practical experience so that their practice is ethically grounded and skilled enough to respond to the complex demands which society places on them.*
>
> (Dempsey et al., 2001, p631–632)

This integration of knowledge and practice, using the theories available to us, is a crucial aspect of reflective practice. Research has shown (Eraut, 1994; Ruch, 2002; Saltiel, 2003) that practitioners do not always see theory as related to real experience. Instead, theory is regarded as a sideshow; it is interesting, but not applicable to the situations that they work in and therefore feels remote and unusable.

Schön (1983) talks about technical rationality, where knowledge is divorced from experience, where values underpinning practice are never questioned and may not even be identified, leaving the practitioner unaware of how the context they work in, both locally and nationally, liberates or constrains the decisions and actions they take.

Frequently the way reflective skills are taught fails to fully integrate the intellectual meaning of the experience with personal feelings and intuition, leaving people feeling that all they have engaged in is 'navel gazing', a pointless activity, of little use to their daily lives (Newton, 2004). Reflective practice should promote the use of theory when reflecting on experiences, events and situations, thereby encouraging a deeper understanding of the impact of one's work on self as well as others. Schön would argue that reflection enables one to develop one's own theory that is then articulated and explored with others in order to become mutual understanding. It is up to tutors in the first instance and workplace supervisors in the second to encourage and promote the development of the necessary skills and create an ethos of reflective practice that ensures sensitive and effective actions are taken and that risk is accepted as a necessary step in becoming self-aware.

Reflection is, therefore, not just thinking about what you do. Ghaye and Ghaye (1998) define it as practice with principle: 'Being professionally self critical without being destructive and overly negative' (p3).

It is all too easy to become over-critical, to denigrate one's own actions and doubt one's practice. We should be very careful that we do not do this as it is personally damaging and is often given as the reason why people do not reflect, preferring the less dangerous route of working by the book, on automatic pilot, working in our comfort zone, thereby becoming mindless practitioners.

Reflective practice should encourage practitioners to 'feel' their work, an approach which appears to run counter to the current, dominating belief that we should concentrate on and value hard facts rather than soft intuition. Reflective practice demands that we go beyond simple observation (Brown and Rutter, 2008), challenging perceived wisdom, attempting to identify both the rational and the irrational and thereby moving to a place of understanding; an acknowledgement that every experience and every relationship is unique and therefore worthy of reflection and note, rather than just another aspect of our working life. Reflective practice encourages us to find the creativity within uncertainty (Attard, 2008), allowing us to be alive to possibilities and to remain sensitive to the events and people around us (Mason, 2002).

Why should we engage in reflective practice?

When considering why we should engage, I think it is important that we should discuss what it means to be professional; to make professional decisions and how our work might be improved or developed through becoming reflective. Within the early years field, a professional is, increasingly, seen as someone in a position of power or authority over others in the way they think, make decisions and act upon those decisions in their work with children and their families (Leeson, 2009). Practitioners engaged in working with young children and their families have a powerful impact on the lives of those they care for and this should be recognised. Each practitioner's personal attributes, attitudes and methods of engaging will, together, inform the people they work with about their self-worth and how they in their turn should engage with others. In other words, by treating children and their parents/carers as unique and valued individuals, they will be encouraged to develop strong resilience and self-esteem which will have a powerful impact on their lives and the lives of those they come into contact with.

By virtue of their job role, practitioners are often seen as experts in childcare and education and therefore a valuable source of knowledge and information on how to bring up children and conduct oneself (Devereux and Miller, 2003). In education, the manner in which children are taught will determine their eventual educational outcome, the strength of their self-esteem and their ongoing engagement with the world around them.

In the field of early years the demands and expectations are similar; practitioners have a responsibility to enhance and maximise the potential of the children in their care using the Early Years Foundation Stage Framework (DCSF, 2008a) to assist. However, the EYFS has been used in some settings as a book of instruction with little regard to the learning and social needs of the children in their care which has led to poor practice and a lack of opportunity for the children. Reflective practice could considerably assist the practitioners in this situation, enabling a process of mediating and adapting the statutory framework to permit innovative and creative practice to proliferate, thereby improving the quality of learning and the emotional content that they and the children experience (Pollard, 2002). Professionals working in early years settings have considerable power derived from the legislation they work under. For example, under the Children Act 1989, social workers have the power to remove children (section 44); and the right to intervene in the way members of a family seek to conduct themselves (section 47). This power should come with a clear expectation that practitioners are reflective, able to think through the implications of decisions and actions, asking fundamental questions about assumptions, knowledge and power (Lam et al., 2007). The social work taskforce (DCSF, 2009e, electronic source), charged with the responsibility to identify major improvements in social work has emphasised the importance of reflection for effective practice and recommends high quality supervision to support the reflective process.

Gould and Taylor (1996) identified compelling reasons for professionals to engage in reflective practice:

- to reduce uncertainty in practice;

- to enable competent transference of knowledge and skills between situations;

- to generate creative as opposed to programmed responses to the demands of the families we are working with.

By engaging with our work in these ways we can begin to meet the requirements of our respective disciplines and remain alive to possibilities in our practice.

In order to make professional judgements, defined by Eraut (1994) as 'the interpretive use of knowledge' which 'recognises that it also involves practical wisdom, a sense of purpose, appropriateness and feasibility' (Horwath and Thurlow, 2004, p9), it is vital to use systematic processes of collecting information that show the steps taken to analyse and subsequently act. Engaging in reflective practice whilst collecting the necessary information for assessment allows for a thorough evaluation to take place that recognises the essential thinking and emotional processes and begins to identify the appropriate actions to take (Brown and Rutter, 2008), thereby helping practitioners to make open and honest professional judgements that further the needs and requirements of those they work with. It also means that decisions and actions are made from an informed position, using the theory, knowledge and understanding available to us (Attard, 2008).

As the demand increases for early years practitioners to be in the front line in improving the life chances for young children and their families (DfES 2003, DCSF, 2008a; Stone, 2008) reflective practice would appear to be highly relevant and of great importance and attempts have been made to acknowledge the central position of reflection in effective practice. The National Professional Qualification in Integrated Centre Leadership (NCSL, 2004) uses reflective journals as an integral part of the programme, helping students to engage and using mentors to facilitate deeper reflection. The new Early Years Professional Status (CWDC, 2007) also regards reflective practice as key, identifying it as one of the thirty-nine standards practitioners have to evidence in order to achieve.

Thus, I would argue that reflective practice should be available to all, a cultural mode of working that all engage in and are encouraged to adopt. It should not be regarded as a 'bolt on' or optional extra, it should be a conscious act, a way of being and therefore standard practice, examining the apparently routine and everyday, noticing new subtleties and making fresh connections for others and ourselves (Mason, 2002). If practitioners engage in reflective practice in this way, I would argue that the benefits are legion; a greater understanding of self and our own motivations; a chance to resolve past conflicts; to develop new skills, knowledge and understanding in the workplace and to begin to question why we do things in the way we do them. Thus, reflecting on practice:

> ....*validates knowledge created from subjective experience inherent in human interaction.*

> (Davis, 1985 in Gould and Taylor, 1996, p51)

There are also considerable benefits for those who practitioners come into contact with: other professionals; children; parents and colleagues. Decisions and actions taken are considered, creative and recognise the relationship and interaction with each person as a unique experience with a unique individual:

> ..*dealing with both the cognitive and the emotional understanding of the client, valuing both as informative to the process.*

> (Gould and Taylor, 1996, p59)

In order for reflective practice to happen effectively, one has to adopt a model or structure that gives a meaning to the process and that guides practitioners.

How do we do it?

One of the difficulties of engaging in reflective practice is the myriad of possible models available for developing the skills, which may lead to a confused attempt to identify the best.

Several writers on reflective practice identify cyclical models with stages frequently described as: having an experience; reflecting on this experience; taking learning from that reflection; and using it to inform future practice (Lewin, 1946; Kolb, 1984; Gibbs, 1988). These stages are worked through systematically with equal importance given to each. These early models of 'experiential learning' (a term developed by Kolb) have frequently been criticised as failing to emphasise the importance of reflection in stage two and also that all the steps identified do not always fit with the ways in which people think (Pickles, 2003) or perform.

Seidel's model (1996, in Dempsey et al., 2001) has similar stages, defined as looking backwards, looking inwards, looking outwards and looking forwards. However, this model appears to promote deeper introspection and thought by asking highly personal and intimate questions. This model has certainly been used to great effect on social work training courses (Dempsey et al., 2001), helping to improve the confidence and skills of many practitioners. Seeking to address these criticisms, further models have been developed that encourage ever deeper reflection. For example, Mezirow (1981) identifies seven hierarchical levels of reflection; he regards the first four as 'consciousness' and the final three as 'critical consciousness' as the practitioner moves into a greater awareness of the situation, event or circumstance under scrutiny, allowing 'perspective transformation' to take place. Similarly, Pollard (2002) list seven characteristics of reflective practice that gradually become more introspective, thereby encouraging deeper and more enriching understanding to take place.

For me, the model that offers the greatest potential is that developed by Ghaye and Ghaye (1998) where they give excellent opportunities for reflection at different levels enabling practitioners to improve and deepen their knowledge, skills and understanding as they become more proficient. Their model sees reflection as a spiral of action, thought and understanding, rather than a closed circle, allowing for moving backwards and revisiting steps and for development from one cycle on to another, similar in action to Dewey's (1933). I especially value their emphasis on placing any reflection within an organisational context, identifying how the workplace or society a practitioner operates within affects their actions and values and has the potential to exert power and influence over them. The underlying premise of Ghaye and Ghaye's model is that at all times, practice is a value-laden occupation and that effective, reflective practitioners should make clear links between their values and their practice. In the example at the top of the chapter for instance, the actions taken by the practitioner could have many underpinning values, including, for example, her understanding of the respective positions of men and women in society.

Ghaye and Ghaye suggest various stages of reflection:

- Descriptive – an account of the incident under scrutiny;

- Perceptive – making links between the description and our own feelings;

- Receptive – allowing ourselves to be open to different perspectives on the incident described;

- Interactive – creating links between learning and any future action; and

- Critical – where we begin to question accepted practice in a creative and constructive manner, developing new theory and ways of working for ourselves and for others.

By reflecting in these ways, an individual is enabled to develop in far more intrinsic ways than with other, more closed, models that could be seen as suggesting that once one has extracted all the learning from an experience, that experience can be forgotten about and one can move on to the next. As a tutor, I can see a danger in students compartmentalising their learning, failing to make links for themselves between the apparently different actions they take and thereby failing to develop a keen sense of their own identity.

How do we actually do this in practice?

We have already seen the difficulties of practitioners not always appreciating the relevance of the activity and of the failure to create a culture of reflection in and on action. I have identified a potentially useful model, but how do we actually do it? First of all we should acknowledge that reflection is not easy, the answers do not emerge instantly and one may exist in a state of uncertainty that is difficult to endure, especially when working in a culture that promotes certainty and precision (Attard, 2007). Thus, we have to create an ethos in which reflective practice can flourish; a culture of trust, of working together, in order for people to feel safe about opening up and examining their practice. Reflective practice requires a culture that holds the intrinsic value of each individual and promotes the belief that everyone has something worthwhile to say. Within a college or university, it could be argued, one should expect to find such a context which promotes reflection and the necessary risk taking involved. If we wish to promote the creation and development of lifelong reflective practitioners, we have to ensure that the workplace continues this process and scrutinises its environs carefully to ensure that people feel safe enough to share and investigate their practice. In a research project funded by ESRC, Ruch investigated what made a successful reflective workplace (2003):

> The potential for reflective practice is greater in work contexts which afford containing, reflective spaces in which practitioners have the opportunity to think, feel and talk about their work. Team structures and practices and team managers are identified as pivotal in determining the existence and effectiveness of these reflective, containing spaces.

> (Ruch, 2003)

So time, space and the value placed on the activity are all important. Secondly, we should think about the practical strategies available to us. One strategy is to write things down, engaging in an internal dialogue (Tsang, 2007) that allows one to think about actions for oneself, and then to share those thoughts and analyses with others both on paper and verbally, offering one's experience to an individual or a group to be unpacked and investigated (Stefani et al., 2000; Dempsey et al., 2001; Gould and Taylor, 1996; Boud et al., 1985; Schön, 2003; Attard, 2008). Reflective journals are a popular choice for engagement in internal dialogue, where practitioners are encouraged to write down the general and particular experiences they have had throughout their day, reflecting on their emotional and intellectual impact (NCSL, 2004) before sharing their thoughts and emotions with others.

Storytelling is advocated by McDrury and Alterio (2000). This involves students engaging with each other telling a narrative and exploring with colleagues what learning and understanding has taken place. McDrury and Alterio identify eight different storytelling methods and feel that an informal setting, where there is only one listener and the story is spontaneous, that is, not prepared and probably appearing as if out of nowhere, offers the most learning and a sense of catharsis for the narrator. In a tutorial, a student related an experience where she had been involved with a child playing with a marble run. Other children had come to join in, moving in and out of the action, demanding different things of themselves, the toy and the student. As she talked, her face began to light up as she identified where she had taken a back seat, where she had seen genuine co-operation between the children and where they had solved a problem on their own and taught her something. By the end of the tutorial, I had a student before me, filled with awe at what she had learnt from a seemingly innocuous encounter and excitement at what she could now understand about her role in children's lives.

> One listener can provide undivided attention to the story and is more likely to focus on the affective domain. This pathway may also provide greater freedom for the teller to express unedited ideas, concerns and feelings.

(McDrury and Alterio, 2000, p66)

Another possible tool is critical incident analysis (Chambers et al., 2003; McBrien, 2007) where students work on their own, reflecting on a specific event, thinking about what has happened and how they feel about it. They might also take the opportunity to share their thoughts with others to deepen their own understanding through discussion.

Statements of relevance have developed as an alternative way of encouraging reflection. Students are encouraged to think about any learning event they have participated in and write down not only what they have learnt, but also how they may use that learning in the future (Bourner et al., 2002). This work can then be shared with others for greater learning and understanding to take place. Statements of relevance are not simply descriptions and evaluations of the learning event, they are accounts that investigate feelings, current knowledge and procedures, and seem to coincide with the critical reflective stage of Ghaye and Ghaye's model. Finally, reflection can be encouraged through the use of sculpting, a family therapy technique (Anderson, 1987), by using popular film to provoke thought (Tan, 2006) or through creative activities such as poetry or collage (Newton, 2004) or sculpture and art (Hughes, 2009). What is evident in all of these strategies is the need for communication, discourse, a *'reflective conversation'* (Schön, 1983; Kolb, 1984) that offers practitioners the opportunity to explore different perspectives, to become aware of the multitude of voices in each situation and to articulate the core values of respect, justice and equality (Tsang, 2007).

Who can help?

It would appear that we need other, like-minded people involved. We can only reflect so far on our own, we need the opportunity to co-reflect, to think about what we are looking at, to challenge our assumptions and prejudices and encourage each other to look at the things we are avoiding because they tell us things about ourselves we would rather not face. Reflective practice is, potentially, a risky business and many are reluctant to engage – we are taking the time to challenge ourselves, demand answers from ourselves and look critically at parts of ourselves that we take for granted. Dewey (1933, p151) sums up this dilemma:

One can think reflectively only when one is willing to endure suspense and to undergo the trouble of searching. To many persons, both suspense of judgement and intellectual search are disagreeable, they want them to be ended as soon as possible. They cultivate an over positive and dogmatic habit of mind, or feel, perhaps, that a condition of doubt will be regarded as evidence of mental inferiority. We must be willing to sustain and protract that state of doubt which is the stimulus to thorough enquiry.

Ruch (2002) talks about a state of confusion and anxiety that often prevents practitioners from taking these risky steps in analysis and reflection. She cites Papell (1996, p203):

Social work learners must perceive the human situation which they confront in their practice and recognise that their perceptions are filtered through their own thinking and knowing processes, through their own emotions and feelings processes and through the way they themselves integrate and regulate their own doing and behaving. Knowing the self is more than knowing how one feels. It is knowing how one thinks and acts.

This raises considerable anxiety around the amount of personal exposure that may be required. Lindon and Lindon (2000) explores how much personal risk is attached to different levels of communication and sees personal, peak experiences as the most risky of all. There is a danger that people will be less than honest if they perceive a risk that they are not prepared to take or that there are considerable demands placed on them to cope with uncertainty or to deal with grey areas. Those are the moments that are the best opportunities for reflection, giving chance for self-knowledge as well as reconsidering decision-making, interventions and actions taken (Gould and Taylor, 1996; Newton, 2004; Attard, 2008).

A supervisor or tutor who promotes and encourages this risk taking can also be helpful. Hobbs (1992) suggests that an effective supervisor or tutor – should:

- be able to give away control;

- be able to negotiate structure;

- allow mistakes;

- be able to cope with becoming redundant as the group or individual develops their own way of working.

Any techniques used in the classroom to assist the learning of reflective practice should be directed at the student's constructions rather than those in the tutors' head or on their agenda (Boud et al., 1985). This is a challenge to the best of us; who can resist evangelising our own viewpoint and allow students and practitioners to develop their own theory and to question ours? It is hard to permit 'mistakes' and allow the agenda to apparently slip away from your control. Indeed, Pearson and Smith (in Boud et al., 1985) argue that we are natural reflectors and it is often educated out of us as one teacher with many pupils means there is no time or space to reflect. Schön (1983) feels that this is nevertheless what must happen; the balance of power must shift in a learning community of reflective practitioners away from the teacher (or employer) towards the students themselves, as they pursue meaning and challenge accepted practice and thought. He talks about a 'practicum'; a group-learning environment where high levels of anxiety are acknowledged, allowed and supported:

> *A practicum is a setting designed for the task of learning practice. In a context, which approximates a practice world, students learn by doing, although their doing falls short of real world work…it is a virtual world relatively free of the pressures, distractions and risks of the real one, to which, nevertheless, it refers. It stands in an intermediary space between the practice world, the 'lay' world of ordinary life and the esoteric world of the academy.*

(Schön, 1983, p37, cited in Dempsey et al., 2001, p634)

This enabling environment may be easy to establish in a university or college, but what about in the workplace? It has been argued that a colleague or a group of colleagues should be identified to assist with reflective practice. The current call for improved supervision for social work practitioners (DCSF, 2009e) is to be welcomed as an acceptance that reflection cannot and should not be left to the individual, that engagement in a reflective process with a supportive 'other', whoever that might be, allows for greater quality, deeper understanding and thereby enhanced decision making. Knight (cited in Boud et al., 1985) talks about people being paired together and forming a 'buddy' system to talk about their ongoing practice. This close relationship has the advantage of promoting greater honesty, although it could be criticised as having the potential of collusion and thereby perpetuating dangerous attitudes, if there are no opportunities to check with others the things that are being talked about.

> *Meaningful, reflective conversations can sustain and nourish us. They can raise individual and collective consciousness. Above all else they involve a discussion of values. This is at the heart of the improvement process.*

(Ghaye and Ghaye, 1998, p122)

Smith and Halton (1993, cited in Gould and Taylor, 1996) talk about the use of a critical friend in much the same way, encouraging the reflector to look beyond the superficial and think about their feelings and deeper learning. Their research showed that far more reflection occurred through the use of a critical friend than through any other medium, including interaction with other members of staff.

Mentoring, formally recognising a role for an important 'other' to assist in reflection, as identified above, is increasingly acknowledged as an important component of successful reflective practice (NCSL, 2004; Fowler and Robins, 2006; Pemberton, 2006). Reflection within a mutually supportive mentoring relationship could be dynamic and an essentially individualistic, creative way of learning for both parties;

> *Critical skills of reflection are crucial to all workers in the field of early years, as the importance of insight and understanding will shape and form not only immediate practice, but potentially the lives of children in our care and their families. Our role as effective mentors, supporting and teaching reflective practitioners, is vital to the ongoing maintenance and development of quality provision in our early years settings.*

(Fowler and Robins, 2006, p44)

What are the obstacles?

But there are problems and obstacles to overcome in order for this to happen, not least of which is the current climate of anxiety about the dangers of taking risks, the risks inherent in being creative in response to need within a culture that regards expertise as the ability to assess a situation quickly and put into action a plan to rescue, sustain or modify almost instantaneously (Fook, 1997; Saltiel, 2003), rather than one in which reflection is valued as a tool to enable more considered decisions to be made. Taking social work as an example, research by Ruch (2003) identifies:

> *A steady increase in risk averse bureaucratic responses to the uncertainty, ambiguity and risk inherent in childcare social work.*

There is a danger of failing to really look in depth and work on issues, within our practice and ourselves, and move forward. Beck argues that we need to ensure that our reflective practice means 'critical appraisal and change' as opposed to reflexivity, which he feels allows practitioners to deny that which is challenging to the ways in which we normally perceive the world, our workplace norms and culture (Beck, 1996 in Scourfield and Welsh, 2003, p403).

There is also the problem that reflective practice is not taken seriously enough, with:

> *a real danger of reflective learning becoming a populist bandwagon which legitimates the abandonment of academic rigour.*

> (Gould and Taylor, 1996, p74)

Again, the danger of being perceived as navel gazing is great and practitioners need to establish a clear argument for the importance of reflection and to ensure that it is given the priority it deserves (Newton, 2004). Students and tutors and practitioners and managers need to see reflective learning and practice as an opportunity to put academic theory into context, rather than a soft option that allows people to talk about their work in unstructured, incoherent ways. This is no easy task in a world that seems to value convergent knowledge (fact gathering) as opposed to divergent knowledge (more creative and experiential), seeing this as difficult to judge in terms of quality and relevance. We need to ask the question of whether tutors and managers can do what Hobbs requires of them as identified above, to let go and allow the development of the individual rather than the creation of dogma. Pemberton (2006) examines the value of the mentoring role in facilitating this process, finding people who were initially reluctant and anxious, who subsequently flourish, developing confidence and competence within their roles, taking risks, being brave and challenging preconceived ideas and ideologies;

> *The potential involved in dialogue between mentor and participant can be far reaching for participants, other leaders, teams, upon children, families, and communities.*

> (Pemberton, 2006, p35)

Stefani et al. (2000) identify the obstacles to reflective practice that are inherent in college cultures that encourage students to focus on getting good marks rather than on developing their own learning goals, taking risks, failing at certain tasks and re-learning rather than rote learning. We need to carefully look at all our procedures and routines to ensure we promote rather than discourage.

The opportunities reflective practice offers us

I would argue that reflective practice offers many opportunities for practitioners that render the obstacles worth overcoming. There is the rich quality that deep learning adds to our practice (Boud et al., 1985; Whalley, 2006) offering us the opportunity to develop more creative answers to difficulties (Gould and Taylor, 1986; Attard, 2008), enhancing our problem-solving skills and moving us into a world that sees individual needs and can devise individual solutions to meet them:

> *Reflective learning only has value if its effect is to deepen the complexity of practice; rather than rejecting the sphere of the intellect, the reflective paradigm actually requires an engagement with some of the particularly difficult debates within social theory.*

(Gould and Taylor, 1986, p74)

Accomplished reflectors can begin to challenge political and philosophical aspects of procedures and policies (Moffatt, in Gould and Taylor, 1986) and attempt to shape future policy and practice.

As reflectors, we are offered an opportunity to know ourselves and study our motivations, needs, hopes and aspirations, leading us to explore the deeper depths of our innermost being and bring them into the light for systematic observation and thought, allowing us to become rounded and grounded individuals, thoughtful, engaged practitioners and true advocates for those with whom we work (Tsang, 2007).

There is the opportunity to widen our scope; current literature and research on involving children (Lancaster 2003; Broadhead, 2004) has already begun a dialogue on the value of engaging children in reflecting on their own experiences and actions, helping them, their families and the practitioners around them to develop a unique insight into their world, a skill that will be invaluable throughout their lives. As we begin to take seriously the rights of young children, we should value their ability to reflect upon their thoughts and actions.

We have a window of opportunity at present, the current political climate and its spotlight on childhood offers us the chance to develop early years communities where practitioners from different disciplines can come together and reflect on the work they do, both separately and together, towards a theory of good practice that all can relate to. Government Departments have sought to encourage and promote the developments of reflective skills in practice (SCIE, 2003; CWDC, 2006; DCSF, 2008a).

For the final word, I turn to Attard (2008, p315)

> *If I thought I knew it all, I would not search for new understandings, but realising deficiencies in my own understandings makes me strive to better observe and better understand.*

1. *Write a descriptive account of an incident or event from your practice.*

2. *Highlight and link your feelings during the incident.*

3. *Consider the view of anyone else involved in the incident/event. This may be a colleague, parent or child.*

4. *Rewrite the incident from the perspective of the other person.*

5. *Ask yourself – What? Why? How?*

6. *Create links between what you have learnt from this incident/event and what you could do in the future.*

7. *These links should be recorded as Action Plan Points for the future.*

8. *Are there any concerns with established practice that you would like to address in your action plan?*

Then answer these questions.

- *Why is a reflection on your effectiveness important?*

- *How has this task affected your confidence and self-esteem?*

FURTHER READING

Ghaye A and Ghaye K (1998) *Teaching and Learning through Critical Reflective Practice*. Trowbridge: David Fulton.

For a full discussion on one of the most influential models of reflection.

Robins A (2006) *Mentoring in the Early Years*. London: Sage.

This book looks at reflection within the early years community and provides useful pointers for further development of reflective practice in the workplace.

Mason J (2002) *Researching Your Own Practice: the Discipline of Noticing*. London: Routledge Falmer.

An inspiring read giving many techniques and urging us to use a skill we already have, but take for granted; noticing what is happening around us.

15 Research projects in early childhood studies: students' active explorations of children's worlds

Jenny Willan

Introduction

Early childhood practitioners are frequently required to make important professional judgements on behalf of the children in their care. The judgements may be about a particular child's needs, or a course of action in the child's best interests, or about the best provision for children in a setting. Good professional judgements rely in large part on the systematic collection and recording of information and the thoughtful sifting of evidence from wider reading. This chapter sets out to introduce you to the process of research which you will need both as a student and as a professional practitioner in your chosen field within early childhood.

What do we mean by research?

The word 'research' has a daunting ring about it. It conjures up images of white-coated scientists and learned professors earnestly discussing esoteric topics in impenetrable language. But we are all researchers. We all gather information and make observations and build theories as part of our day-to-day interactions in our jobs, in our families and in our social lives. It is a necessary part of living. It is part of a process of constructing the world view that helps us to operate on a daily basis.

The distinction between everyday research and the research we need in our professional lives is one of degree. For instance, we might note that a child in our care is hostile with his peers and destructive of his environment. If we know him well, we may know that there has been a recent bereavement in the family and we would take this into account in assessing how best to interact with him. But if the behaviour was a complete puzzle, we might want to investigate further to see what might be causing it. We might suspect bullying perhaps, or disaffection with school, or a parental attachment problem, or abuse, or perhaps a hearing impairment or a learning disability that is making him frustrated and confused. In a situation like this, we would need to be more systematic in our approach in order to get at the root cause of the difficulty. We would need to ask questions, make observations and gather evidence to build a picture that best accounted for his behaviour. This is the kind of research this chapter is concerned with.

Research approaches and perspectives

There is no set recipe covering the techniques and procedures of research. There are many ways of investigating a topic and the type of research you choose to do will depend on the topic you want to pursue. Research seeks to throw light on an issue, sometimes to improve practice, sometimes to clarify thought. Early childhood research seeks for evidence to inform understanding and practice with young children. According to Stenhouse (1975, p142), research is 'systematic inquiry made public'. However, although all research is systematic, the degree to which it is made public will vary. Children engaged in discovering something new are researchers – they are systematic in their approach but they may only make their findings public in the sense of sharing their discoveries with a parent or another child. Students engaged in research projects may limit their audience to colleagues or tutors. Practitioners may produce research but only distribute it among the people or children in their workplace.

Research is sometimes described as 'conceptual' or 'empirical' but most research is a mixture of both. Broadly, *conceptual* researchers consider a puzzling phenomenon and try to *think* their way to a solution, perhaps involving others in a dialogue to test out the strength of their explanations. Socrates employed this method to analyse the great questions of his day and Rousseau used the method in building his theory of education in his book *Emile*. Purely conceptual research depends on the experience, imagination and intellectual vigour of a single person or a small group of people who meet to exchange ideas.

Empirical researchers operate differently. They collect evidence and then develop it into a theory. Empirical researchers may *start* with a concept, an idea, but they base their theories and recommendations on an analysis of real-world data. But just like conceptual researchers, they need to collaborate and talk things over with others to refute or confirm the reliability of their theories. Perhaps the most familiar empirical researcher in early childhood studies is Piaget. His explanations of the way in which young children actively construct their world according to their stage of maturation has had a lasting impact on our understanding of how children learn (Gardner et al., 1996). Over the past half century, his studies have been replicated (repeated) and sometimes disputed by other empirical researchers who have gathered further evidence to support or contest his earlier explanations. This is part of the empirical process: slowly and gradually we build up more and more evidence to refine and strengthen our understanding of what is going on around us. The process continues until the weight of evidence pushes us into a new way of thinking or a 'paradigm shift' (Kuhn, 1970).

Theory and research

What is the relationship between theory and research? At a conference, a friend of mine was expanding on her research when a member of the audience asked, 'What is your research paradigm?' My friend was momentarily nonplussed. What the questioner wanted to know was what theoretical stance the researcher was adopting towards her research. Newburn (2007, p931) suggests there are two contrasting approaches to research – the *hypothetico-deductive* approach and the *grounded* approach. Don't be put off by the jargon! *Hypothetico-deductive* theory was what underpinned the kind of research Piaget did on children's learning – he generated a theory or hypothesis, made his observations and then deduced from the evidence whether his theory was correct or *verified*. The problem with this approach is that it is narrowly focused on individuals and the constraints of a hypothesis restrict the researcher to a very narrow field of enquiry. A further problem is that the need for verification makes it tempting to concentrate on the quantifiable data at the expense of contextual data – this hypothetico-deductive approach led Piaget to overstate his case about 'ages for stages' in his early research. *Grounded* theory, on the other hand, underpins the kind of research done by Stanley Cohen (1972) in his book *Folk Devils and Moral Panics: The creation of the Mods and Rockers* where he famously examined the relationship between young people's actual behaviour and its subsequent reporting by the media. Cohen systematically collected a wealth of data and then subjected it to analysis and categorisation in order to construct a theory that would explain the relationships between 'reality' and the reporting of that reality. There are problems with this approach too – firstly the researcher and the data are never really neutral – we already adopt a particular position when we decide what sort of data to collect. A second problem when collecting context specific data is that it is then difficult to generalise from the study to other situations. This grounded approach tends to favour qualitative, contextual data over quantifiable data and this makes it difficult to verify. Perhaps the most satisfying research takes the best from both approaches, hypothetico-deductive and grounded, combining and adapting different styles of gathering and analysing data in imaginative ways so that your research becomes a synthesis of both.

Many research projects in early childhood are empirical. The empirical approach to research is to gather evidence in a systematic way. This evidence or data is used to build up a model (or picture) of what researchers and researched understand about the topic under investigation. Empirical researchers try to take account of their own 'perspective' – the beliefs and assumptions that underpin the way they set about looking for evidence. For example, in attempting to explain the hostile and destructive child mentioned earlier, a psychologist, a medical practitioner, a teacher or a social worker would all approach their explanation or interpretation according to their particular professional theories and values. By comparing the evidence each systematically gathered, we might be able to decide if the child was bullied, suffering an attachment dysfunction, hearing impaired, learning disabled or abused, or a combination of any of these. If the tests for evidence were applied by other professional individuals, the interpretation would be similar. Of course, some research seeks to overthrow a shared interpretation, perhaps to bring about a change in thinking or practice, and here the researcher needs to marshall evidence in the same systematic way to counter prevailing points of view.

This brief introduction shows how empirical research combines theory and practice in order to improve understanding. The more evidence we gather, the more reflective we are, the more we discuss our theories with our colleagues, the better we can serve the children in our care. Research is a process which is never finished; it is always open to modification through reflection and discussion with others – in early childhood work, a willingness to learn through collaboration with children and colleagues can help to clarify our growing understanding of issues. Research is a state of mind, a way of staying curious about the world and the people in it – it is not over once the report is written.

So how do we go about doing a research project?

Finding a topic

The first step is to identify a problem, a puzzle, a conundrum, something that sits uneasily in your understanding. For instance, you may have a feeling of vague anxiety about all the government money being pumped into early years when at your own preschool you see vast amounts of effort expended on jumble sales to raise a few pounds for a new climbing frame. Or you might have a worry about your own child who has not yet reached a particular developmental milestone – late talking perhaps, or mastery of the skill of riding a bicycle, or successfully making friends. It may be the rise of a new orthodoxy that bothers you – increased educational testing for young children, the removal of children from families where abuse is suspected, the adoption of 'no cuddling' policies in childcare settings for fear of litigation under child protection laws, the suitability of inclusion programmes for young children with special needs. Wherever there is disquiet, there is an issue for research.

Reading around the topic

Once you have identified an area that you would like to investigate, the next step is to find out what other people have said about it. You might start by talking to friends and colleagues, watching TV programmes, listening to radio coverage, reading newspapers and magazines. Or you might go straight to the internet or the library bookshelves and journals. You will gradually build a portfolio of ideas and opinions and information, a list of sources, a list of names and organisations that have something to say on the topic. You will know who tends to take which position in a debate, who the key thinkers and researchers are, who are the mavericks and iconoclasts. Through your reading and discussion you will gradually refine your own viewpoint until you have reached the stage where you can formulate a research question.

Coming up with the research question

This is the point at which you ask yourself what exactly it is that you want to find out. What is the question you want to investigate? Is the question manageable? Can you collect evidence about it? Can you find out enough in the time available? Do you have the contacts, the money, a suitable group or individual that could help answer your question? Does the question lend itself to empirical study? Can you collect data on it in a live setting? Are you being realistic about your limitations? For instance, if you live in a rural village in England, it would be very difficult to design an empirical study to evaluate the relative merits of Sure Start, Reggio Emilia and Te Whariki. However, if you were an Italian speaker with contacts in New Zealand, you might manage, via email and internet, to gather teachers' views of childhood or education from practitioners in each system that you could then compare with local teachers' views. Be as ambitious as you like but be aware that you need to find a match between your skills and your aspirations, your resources and the time available.

Reaching your target group

Opportunity might be the constraining factor in choosing your target group for a small-scale research project. Ask yourself which group of people will provide you with the most useful information. Can you access them easily? Do you need to write a letter of introduction requesting permission from someone in authority to approach the group? Can you find a mutually convenient date to meet? If you are going to include children in your data gathering, do you need to know term and holiday dates?

Risk assessment and health and safety issues

Now do a quick mental risk assessment. If you embark on this investigation, does it carry any risks or threats to your proposed target group, the subjects of your study? Will you be putting yourself at any personal risk? Are there any issues such as being alone with a participant? What about health and safety? Does the investigation leave you open to litigation? For example, would you need special insurance cover if you wanted to conduct research into children's ability to manage themselves in a challenging environment? Once you have satisfied yourself that you have covered all the wider risks, you can begin to think about the detail.

Ethics

As your research questions crystallise and you identify the people you want to study, you will need to think about the ethical issues involved in human research. At all points you need to act with integrity. You will already have considered this in broad terms when you thought about a risk assessment and considered aspects of health and safety. Now and throughout the study, you need to think about the detail – your research project should be an ethical process at every stage. There may be issues of access to your research group, issues of confidentiality and of your own accountability that may arise at any point during the investigation. It is your duty as a researcher to take responsibility for the well-being of the people who take part in your research – they are the collaborators in your research enterprise, not the objects of your study. You also need to remember that all participants in your research are bound by the same rules of confidentiality as you are.

There are published guidelines spelling out the issues researchers need to consider, to ensure that the subjects in a study are protected (e.g. British Psychological Society (1997) Code of conduct, ethical principles and guidelines). The following list of points should help to keep you on track. You should:

- provide a clear statement of the purpose of your research;
- obtain the informed consent of all participants;
- ensure that you are not deceiving or misleading participants;
- offer a debriefing after the study;
- allow participants to withdraw at any stage if they wish;

- guarantee appropriate confidentiality of information gathered in the course of the study;

- protect participants from physical and mental harm;

- observe without infringing privacy during your research;

- give advice to participants if results show up information that might cause harm if withheld;

- be accountable for the fairness and accuracy of your written report;

- be aware of the cultural sensitivities of the participants.

All the participants in your study should have a written copy of the ethical guidelines relating to your particular research, spelling out their rights and your guarantees, before they embark on the study. You should keep a copy for your own research report and include it as an appendix to your study.

Reviewing the literature

As you work on your research you will begin to identify specific areas of concern. As your focus becomes clearer you will need to do a systematic review of the literature relating specifically to your topic. Start with recently written articles and books and check the list of references for the most frequently cited articles and try to read as many of them as you can. Reading the literature is an interactive process involving both your own ideas and those of the writers you are reading. List the strands of thinking represented by the various writers you discover. Critically review the research; as you read, keep asking questions about what you are reading – is it fact, is it opinion, is it merely assertion? Monitor your own response – what do you tend to agree with? What strikes you as odd, unreasonable or challenging? As you study, talk with colleagues and tutors, debate the issues, share ideas, discuss concepts, co-operate over difficulties, refining and clarifying your understanding as you go. To keep you on track and to give you ideas about approaches to your own investigation, keep a list of points, such as:

- Is this study empirical?

- How did the researchers arrive at the research question(s)?

- Were the ethical issues of the research addressed?

- How did they investigate the questions? Can I summarise their approach?

- Why did they do it this way?

- What did the participants in the study have to do in order to provide information?

- How did the researchers justify their methods?

- How did they represent their data?

- How did they interpret what they found?

- Were there any aspects I wanted more information on or were there questions raised that they didn't answer?

- How valid is it (i.e. did it measure what it set out to measure)?

- How reliable is it (i.e. would it yield a similar result if it was repeated under similar circumstances)?

- What perspectives (paradigm, mindset, assumptions) underlie the study?

- If I was asked to investigate the same questions, would I follow the pattern of this piece of research?

- Could lessons learned from this approach inform my own investigation?

A useful way to keep track of what you are reading is to use Endnote, or a similar referencing software, which follows the conventions of the Harvard citation system and guides you through recording the information you need to build a bibliography. This is essential. There is nothing more frustrating than to copy down a relevant quote without the reference and finding, when you come to write up, that the book you used has been borrowed by someone else! If you don't want to use referencing software, use a card index or notebook. But be systematic and always write the whole reference down. Look at the references in this and other books for examples of what information you will need for your references – and don't forget to note the page number for direct quotations.

As you read, you may want to refine the focus of your investigation, so that it concentrates on a particular aspect of the research question you first thought of – this isn't a change of mind, it is a focusing of mind, a familiar part of the process of research. Keep talking to your colleagues, bounce ideas off them; you will find they have a lot to offer, things that might not have occurred to you.

Research approaches

Your path will largely be determined by the topic you want to investigate but it will also depend on how you see the world yourself. The kind of empirical research that has been done in the social sciences over the past century has been subject to various fashions and political influences. Sometimes scientific experiments have been in vogue, sometimes surveys of large populations, sometimes case studies with 'neutral' observers, sometimes case studies with participant observers. More recently, case studies rooted in action research (where practitioners study and develop the effectiveness of their own practice) have been popular. Currently, in early years there is a concern with children's rights issues and many case studies involve listening to children's own voices. Whatever approach you use, the key point is that you should choose an approach that is fit for your purpose. An essential point about doing empirical research is that it needs to be systematic. Any data you collect will only be as good as the research design that produced it. Whichever methods you choose for your research, you must plan meticulously and keep careful records.

Look at your topic and ask how best you can gather evidence to address its concerns. Let the topic lead your design. You can gather evidence through both qualitative and quantitative approaches. The methods associated with each approach are different but most investigations involve both.

The qualitative approach

Qualitative data are produced when you gather information in a continuous form – interviews, observations, video, reflective diaries, written accounts, focus group transcripts, audio recordings, language analyses, document analyses. Qualitative data are bulky and difficult to manage. The data can be reduced to a manageable size by summarising and generalising, by coding and clustering, by searching for underlying patterns. The reliability depends on the integrity of the researcher to honestly represent the ideas that form the core of the data collected. Generally, qualitative research is illustrated by *verbatim* quotations or detailed descriptions of occurrences as they were recorded in the field and gives the reader a sense of the authentic voice of the children and adults involved.

The quantitative approach

Quantitative data are produced when you reduce information – for example, from checklists, question responses, coded observations, scores, test results – to a numerical form. Reducing data into a quantitative form may not be the most appropriate for a small-scale study – there is a danger of generalising from small numbers. Numbers and statistics are notoriously slippery, especially when the sample being studied is small. Patterns can only be found in large samples – think of comparing the average height of three people against the average height of 1000 people. However, you may well be using some quantitative data, either from your literature review or in your own study. You need to look at the figures with a critical eye. In particular, you need to distinguish between correlation (a link between two or more factors) and *causation* (one factor affecting another) – many things can be linked or correlated by chance without being in any way causally related. You need to look carefully at the figures and ask what it means to say something is 'statistically significant'. For example, we might find that Key Stage 1 maths results in a school show that boys are lagging behind girls. Could it be explained by random chance or is there a strong relationship between one factor and another? Is the relationship between boys and maths, or is it between the particular cohort of boys in that class and their ability to do maths? Would the result be different with another year group?

Many small-scale empirical investigations are necessarily qualitative in nature because they are often limited to individual case studies, but they may have some quantitative elements and you will almost certainly come across quantitative data during your reading around your topic, so you need to be aware of both elements.

Collecting data

There are many ways of collecting data. You may even want to invent your own. One student observed three-year-olds spontaneously interviewing one another with a hairbrush that doubled as a microphone. The results were fascinating and prompted her into thinking of ways of using children as researchers rather than as subjects of research. The following selection of methods is not exhaustive but is intended to give you a flavour of what is possible.

You will probably choose a single case study or limited study of a few cases for comparison, rather than a larger survey for your research. These may involve a particular individual, a group, an event or perhaps an institution. Whichever you choose, you will need to design a method of collecting qualitative and/or quantitative evidence that will give you the best information to fit your purpose. Below is a selection of some common methods for collecting data – you may want to use one or several methods in your own study. For more detailed information on each method you might like to consult one of the many books devoted to research design, some of which are included in the further reading section at the end of this chapter.

Observation

You may want to do observations as part of your data gathering – for example, to study a physical setting, or a group, or an individual, or an event. You need to think about how you will position yourself to do your observation, both physically and metaphorically, depending on how involved you want to be with what you are observing. There are degrees of participation in observational approaches – at one end of the scale is the detached observer behind a two-way mirror, at the other end is the participant observer making covert notes or recordings alongside the people being studied. You may want to be somewhere in between. Generally, the tools for observation are pencil and paper, supplemented by observation schedules, audio recordings, video or photography (see Chapter 5, 'Observing children', for more details about observational methods). The box below shows some of the observational methods you might use.

Narrative observation – this is a naturalistic record taken *in situ*, using everyday language, picking out points that seem particularly salient at the time.

Focused observation – this is targeted on a particular child or children. It might entail making detailed notes of everything that happens in a short burst of time – perhaps five minutes. You could use this to focus on a particular child at regular intervals over time, to record changes in behaviour or development.

Timed observations – you might make notes on an activity, a particular child, or a group, timing your observations according to a predetermined interval. Or you might make detailed notes on how much time is actually spent on an activity or piece of behaviour, recording who, what, where, when and how.

Incident observation – you might choose to record the frequency with which a particular event or behaviour occurs and make detailed notes of each occurrence.

Observations are a useful source of information for many situations but they don't let the researcher get below the surface to probe the motives and understandings of the participants themselves. For this, some of the other methods are more suitable.

Questionnaires

Questionnaires are easy to send out and difficult to get back! They are also difficult to get right. If you are sure that a questionnaire will answer your purposes better than any other method, you will need to think very hard about the questions and you will need to try them out on several people before you use them for real.

There are some common pitfalls in writing questions for questionnaires. The following list might help you avoid some of them.

Ambiguity – where respondents don't know exactly what you mean. For example, 'How many places do you have at your nursery?' The nursery may have 25 places in the morning, 25 in the afternoon, and different children attending full- or part-time throughout the week. Do you want to know about full-time and part-time places or full-time equivalents? Or do you want to know how many different children attend each week?

Loose wording – where you don't know exactly what you mean. For example, 'Are the recent government policies on young children helpful?' Helpful for whom? Which policies do you mean?

Insensitivity – where you fail to take account of your respondents' possible circumstances. For example, asking of someone over 50 'Would you agree that the quality of the workforce is improving as more young people with better qualifications join?'

Double questions – where you expect people to answer both halves of the question in the same way. For example, 'Are you a regular visitor to nurseries and reception classes?' They could be a visitor to only one of these.

Hypothetical questions – where you ask an 'if' question and only elicit a meaningless answer. For example, 'If you had a child in your class suffering from separation anxiety, what would you do?' They might do any one of a hundred things, depending on the child.

Leading questions – where you imply within the question which answer you expect to get. Sometimes these questions contain assumptions – where you think you know all the possible answers but in reality you don't. For example, 'Do you agree or disagree with the proposition that teenage mothers are irresponsible?' Some may be, others may not. Sometimes they contain presumptions – where you think that there is only one way of looking at something but there are many. For example, 'How far do you think poor results in your school are due to the number of children from single parent households?' There may be no connection at all.

Overlapping categories – where you offer overlapping alternatives that can be misinterpreted. For example, 'How many children do you look after aged 0–2, aged 2–5, aged 5–8?' A child aged two and a half could go into either of the first two categories.

(adapted from Bell, 1999, pp121–5)

There are many ways of asking questions in a questionnaire; you will have come across them many times and probably never given a thought to how they were constructed. The answers you get will depend partly on the wording you use but also on the way you frame the question. As you write your questions, try to imagine the sort of answers you might get and how you will deal with the information they elicit.

You could ask an *open-ended question*, such as 'How do you feel about the present management structure?', and then group your responses under headings. You could ask people to tick items in a list of alternatives, such as 'Which of the following apply to you?', and then summarise the number of responses in a chart or graph. You could provide a list of categories, such as 'Tick one of the following to show which best describes your job – Professional, Managerial, Skilled, Semi-skilled, Manual'. You may want respondents to indicate a rank order of preference, such as 'Put the following in order of importance ...', or to use a *rating scale* such as 'On a five-point scale, rate how useful you found the management training session on child protection'. Both rank order and rating scale questions express mathematical relationships and require careful use. As you write your questions, try them out on colleagues so that you cover as many eventualities as you can to iron out any difficulties in the design. Most importantly, ensure that your final draft questionnaire gets a thorough tryout before you use it for real. You will be surprised how differently people can read the same straightforward question!

Interviews

You may decide that questionnaires are too limiting and that an interview or series of interviews would serve your purpose better. Interviews depend for their success on achieving a rapport between interviewer and interviewee – quick-fire questions without any personal dimension are unlikely to yield any more than a postal questionnaire would. Face-to-face interviews are usually more successful at getting people talking than telephone interviews. A comfortable seat, a cup of tea, some small talk, all help to put you and your interviewee at ease – if you are doing an interview by telephone these will have to be metaphorical. But remember, interviews are time-consuming to conduct and even more time-consuming to analyse, so allow yourself plenty of leeway. An interview requires much the same thoughtful preparation as a questionnaire but unlike a questionnaire it has the advantage of allowing the interviewer to ask for further clarification, or to pursue an interesting line of thought, or to probe into motives and feelings. However, interviews are open to data 'corruption' through mishearing, misunderstanding, questioner bias, or a too cosy or too hostile relationship between interviewer and interviewee – so think carefully about every part of the process.

There are several ways to conduct your interview.

- *Structured interviews* are really verbally administered questionnaires, useful for collecting specific information which can be quickly categorised but not at all useful for probing.

- *Semi-structured interviews* are based on written questions or topics for discussion. They allow for a good deal of exploration but minimise the risk of straying away from the central purpose of the investigation. The interviewer can note down responses briefly and write up fuller notes immediately after the interview. It is useful to make an audio recording of the interview to check against your field notes. Transcribing is a slow process and it may be better only to transcribe verbatim those parts of the recording that illustrate the argument most succinctly and those parts that do not fit your expectations.

- *Unstructured interviews* are not usually scripted and generally lead to wide-ranging discussion, much like a conversation. They are rather difficult to control but are very good if you want to analyse people's perspectives to try to find out what they consider to be the important aspects of the topic under discussion. They can also be useful as preparatory interviews when you are trying to get a sense of the area you want to investigate.

At the end of each question or topic during semi-structured and non-structured interviews, it is a good idea to check with your interviewee that you have correctly identified the main gist of the argument. You should keep all your field notes and recordings to check the reliability of your interpretations – as long as they are anonymous, or you have permission from participants, you can include them in your appendices.

Focus groups

A focus group is rather like a group interview except that the researcher takes on the role of participant observer instead of the disinterested interviewer. The researcher controls the broad topic while the participants are free to exchange opinions, reactions and experiences within the group discussion. This technique is very useful for exploratory research at the beginning of a project because participants may well raise issues that you have not yet considered. However, the discussion may be difficult to control, particularly if there is one senior or dominant member who may steer the topic in a particular way and impose an artificial consensus on the whole group. Ideally you would record the discussion and also take notes during it (preferably using an assistant). Brief notes about body language, expression, tone of voice, feelings and attitudes will help flesh out the speech you have recorded.

You will need to think carefully about the validity of your data – for example, how representative was your sample, how much did the group dynamics affect the discussion? Your analysis should focus on shared views and on dissenting views. The dissenting views are often the most rewarding because they mark out the limits of consensus and lead you to new and emergent themes in the topic under discussion. Many of the caveats listed under the section on interviews apply to focus groups too.

Documentary evidence

Documents can be anything from film, radio, emails, pictures, government policies, minutes of a meeting, letters, diaries, even inscriptions on gravestones. They can cast light on present practice or through historical research show how the preoccupations of the past have shaped emergent thinking in the present. Documentary evidence comes in two forms – primary and secondary. Primary sources generally relate directly and contemporaneously to the event being studied, while secondary sources are further removed. For you, doing your small-scale research project, the documents you are most likely to use are primary sources that flag up a contradiction for you. They could be contemporaneous accounts – of punishment, perhaps, in an investigation into views on smacking, or government policies on the Early Years Foundation Stage in a study of reading, or children's drawings, letters and diaries in an investigation into the experience of hospitalisation.

If you use documentary evidence, you should ensure its authenticity by providing full details of its source. For example, if you asked someone to write about their early childhood experience of being evacuated during the Second World War, you would need to record their name (or initials) and the date of their account. If you make inferences from the documents, you should back up your statements with evidence from the text and ensure, as far as you can, that your reading of the meaning is consistent with the tone of the whole. For instance, you may believe that evacuation was probably a 'damaging' experience for the children involved. Your interviewee might have recounted one unhappy memory in an otherwise positive account – but you would not be justified in concluding from this one memory that evacuation had been a negative experience. The main danger, in using documentary (or any) evidence, is to select only those parts which best support your argument and to ignore the rest.

Logs and reflective diaries

Logs and reflective diaries are mainly used as a data source in action research studies where practitioners want to observe the effect of changes in their work practices or to follow their own development or learning curve over a period of time. An action research log or reflective diary follows a cyclical path of initial observation, a plan of campaign to effect a change in behaviour or practice, implementation of the plan, reflection on the outcome of the action, modification of the plan in the light of reflection, implementation, and so on. You might use it in helping a mother deal with 'the terrible twos', for example. You might discuss her reaction to her child's problematic behaviour and suggest an alternative approach. You would then note the effect of the new approach and reflect alongside her whether the new approach was having the desired effect or whether further modification was needed. Your log or reflective diary provides a record of the evolution of your thinking as you work through a process towards a deeper understanding.

Stories

Stories, both written and oral, can be particularly useful in early years research. Understanding how a child (or adult) represents his or her version of reality through the stories they tell can give us an insight into the way they think. There are several ways of using stories in research. You could look at the stories themselves – for instance, if you wanted to investigate what sort of choices adults make on children's behalf when they select books for them. You could look at children's relationships to the stories they choose – for example, you could investigate the fairy tales particular children ask for most often and relate their choice to their current concerns. You could look at the way people tell stories about their own experiences – for example, you could compare and contrast different people's versions of an event. Or you could ask a group of teachers to describe a 'challenging' child and relate their stories to constructs of childhood. You could even investigate the ways in which your own investigation is a form of storytelling! You might ask yourself how you make a 'story' out of your research, or how you tell yourself the story of your research experience. Using stories in your investigation involves you in thinking about intention and interpretation, about meaning systems, about the dynamics of an unfolding narrative and about the nature of 'truth' and 'reality'.

Analysing and interpreting data

As you collect your data – your questionnaires, your interviews, field notes, tape transcripts, video material, children's work, accounts or stories – try to see what is emerging. Your purpose at this stage is to discover patterns in the data. Patterns depend for their authenticity on your integrity as a witness to your data – it is your duty to be truthful. Be systematic. Make your data more manageable by using grids for questionnaire responses, highlighter pens for transcripts, line numbering for interview data, time indications for video and audio, charts to map the ebb and flow of dialogue. It is worth spending time on this at the outset, to find a system that works best for you. You may want to use a software package such as SPSS for quantative data or NU* dist for qualitative data. Begin your analysis by looking at surface features – sample size, number of responses, frequencies of response, common concerns, patterns of behaviour, different points of view – and move on to an evaluation of the relative importance of those. Your interpretation will rest on your understanding of the underlying patterns revealed through your analysis.

Use the following checklist to analyse and interpret your findings.

Sample size – How many people did you ask to take part?

Achieved sample – How many people actually took part?

Response rates – How many people answered each question?

Patterns – What are the most frequent and least frequent features?

Similarities and differences – Are there any differences or similarities? Are they related to any variables relevant to your research question – age, gender, ethnicity, attitude, likes and dislikes?

Clusters – Can you usefully group things together under a category? For instance, in interviews with childminders about smacking, you might want to cluster responses under headings such as 'child-centred', 'authoritarian', *'laissez-faire'*.

Themes – Are there common or contrasting themes running through the data?

Data that don't fit – Are there maverick responses? Remember, negative data are still data and worthy of comment because what is not there, or doesn't fit, can be revealing.

Dominant perspectives – Is there any evidence to show that your respondents subscribe to particular views that might account for their responses? Are there any counter-examples to help define the limits of your developing theory?

Testing propositions – Can you test the strength of evidence for your proposition/hypothesis/research question by collecting quotes, or examples or figures that illustrate or fail to illustrate it? (Remember your job is to provide a fair summary of your findings, not to sell your proposition or to talk it up to confirm it).

Checking your interpretations – Can you check your interpretations with other viewpoints? (Social scientists test evidence through triangulation* – interrogating it from at least two viewpoints or through multiple techniques of investigation – see page 72).

Small-scale research studies are unlikely to produce conclusions that can be applied more widely to society at large; the purpose is more often to cast light on a quite specific situation or event or child or relationship. Students producing quantitative data in their investigations are sometimes tempted to make grand claims for their research with liberal sprinklings of percentages and pie charts to show their findings. By all means present your data in the form of a table or graph, but be very clear that the numbers involved are small and the effects you are describing are specific to your study. The best way to check that your analysis is sound and your interpretation fair, is to collaborate with other people – the people who were involved in your investigation and/or colleagues. Ask them to help you check the strength and accuracy of the evidence on which you base your arguments and conclusions, by reading it through and discussing it with you.

Writing up

Writing up can be fun; it is very satisfying to bring all that work and information neatly together in a tidy binding. But it can also be lonely and demoralising. Keep talking to friends and colleagues, understand that you will be your own fiercest critic, share your anxieties with other people who know how hard it is to write reports and take plenty of breaks!

Honesty is the key to writing a decent research report – honesty with the participants, honesty with the data and honesty with yourself. Don't worry if you haven't added to the store of human knowledge – it is more important that you acted with integrity and wrote up your report with due regard for the difficulties and rewards that you encountered on the way. Lots of research is inconclusive and many published research reports end with the words 'more research is needed...'. As long as you have collected your evidence fairly and thoroughly and considered the strengths and weaknesses of your methods and conclusions, you should have nothing to fear. However, you must avoid at all costs the two major crimes of research: fabricating evidence and plagiarising the words of others. Fabricating evidence means making up data or making claims that do not stand up to scrutiny. Plagiarising means using other people's ideas or words without acknowledging the source, whether that source is a book or the internet or any other medium. Both these misdemeanours can, and do, result in failed degrees and ruined reputations.

There are many different ways to write up your research. Your choice of model will depend on the kind of investigation you carry out and your intended audience. To give you an idea of the relative proportions of a report, you might like to look at the following guidance we give to undergraduates on our early childhood studies course.

Title page – a title to capture the spirit of your research question; author; date.

Acknowledgements – a courtesy page to thank all the participants and the other people who have given you support during the project.

Abstract – a one-page summary of your research topic, your methods, the data collected and the main findings.

Contents – main section headings with page numbers.

Introduction – 500–1000 words explaining what sparked your interest in your investigation and what each section of your report will cover.

Literature review – 1000–2000 words describing the main arguments around the topic.

Methodology and methods – 1000–2000 words explaining *why* you chose the methodological approach and what are the strengths and limitations of your methods in exploring your research question (some people include their questionnaires/interview schedules, etc., here; other people prefer to put them in an appendix).

Findings – as many words as it takes to present the results of your investigations. This may include charts and summaries of questionnaire responses, observations, interviews, documentary evidence, logs, reflective diaries, stories.

Discussion/analysis – 2000–3000 words explaining what your findings show and how they relate to previous studies.

Conclusions – 500–1000 words showing the implications of your study for further thinking and the recommendations you would make in the light of your findings.

References – an alphabetical list of all (and only) those sources referred to in your research.

Appendices – these should be numbered and should include your ethics protocol, permissions, any letters sent out to participants, raw scores and results, transcripts, copies of questionnaires or interview schedules, documentary evidence, logs, reflective diaries, stories.

Conclusion

Research is central to studying and working in early childhood – not only for adults but for children too. Children are also researchers, continually putting forward and testing theories as they build up a view of the world and their place in it. As students and practitioners, we need to keep this link between theory and practice alive in adulthood so that we can continue to develop our own understanding. As adults we can learn from investigating how things work in our own practice and relating our observations to the theories through which we operate. We can also learn through investigating the perspectives of those we work with – children's perspectives are just as worthy of investigation as those of the adults who work with them. Reflecting on people's behaviour, children's or adults', can inform understanding and improve practice and it is important that we make time to cultivate a habit of research and investigation as part of our thinking and working. This chapter has outlined some of the ways to do this.

Becoming a researcher and developing evidence-based practice is not just a question of a once-and-for-all training; it is about developing a research mindset. It is about an orientation towards continuing learning, a belief that every opportunity brings with it fresh opportunities for learning something new or understanding something differently. Research flourishes in an atmosphere of open inquiry where there is a will to share understanding and examine practice. It flourishes where there is a commitment to hearing and considering the views of everyone – children, colleagues, parents and students – in an honest spirit of open collaboration. If we fail to investigate our practice and interrogate our theories, we are in danger of simply perpetuating an uncritical repetition of doing things the way they have always been done.

ACTIVITY *1*

Choose a published research article which interests you and which describes an empirical piece of research.

Five key journals you might like to use are:

Early Years, An International Journal of Research and Development. *Abingdon: Routledge.*

The European Early Childhood Education Research Journal. *Worcester: European Early Childhood Education Research Association.*

International Journal of Early Childhood. *Dublin: World Organisation for Early Childhood Education (OMEP).*

International Journal of Early Years Education. *Abingdon: Routledge.*

Children and Society. *Chichester, Sussex: John Wiley.*

Look at the section 'Reviewing the literature' in this chapter. Use the bullet points to help you read and analyse the journal article you have chosen.

FURTHER READING

Bell, J (1999) Doing your research project: a guide for first-time researchers in education and social science. 3rd edition. Buckingham: Open University Press.

This is an old favourite for students new to research – easy to find a second hand copy.

Mac Naughton, G, Rolfe, SA and Siraj-Blatchford, I (eds) (2001) Doing early childhood research: international perspectives on theory and practice. Buckingham: Open University Press.

This is a challenging book which uncovers the debates and dilemmas underlying the apparently straightforward exercise of finding out about a particular topic.

Roberts-Holmes, G (2005) *Doing your early years research project: a step-by-step guide*. London: Paul Chapman.

Several students have recommended this book as very useful and readable.

Robson, C (2002) Real world research: a resource for social scientists and practitioner-researchers. 2nd edition. Oxford: Blackwell.

This is a very thorough general book on research methods and approaches.

16 Action research

Ulrike Hohmann and Karen Wickett

Introduction

The trademark of a popular version of action research is a clear focus on one particular aspect of practice, initially contained in one location, for example a nursery. Individual practitioners identify a problem or an area where improvements can be made, introduce changes to their practice, reflect on subsequent observations and discuss these with their colleagues (for example, Mac Naughton and Hughes, 2009; GTC, 2003; Nind, 2003; Burgess-Macey and Rose ,1997).

The term action research originates in the social experiments in natural settings designed by Kurt Lewin in the 1940s. As part of this work Lewin developed the model of action research as a spiral of steps that repeats cycles of planning, action, observation and evaluation. In this respect action research is reminiscent of Kolb's (1984) experiential learning or Dewey's (1938) experiential education and Piaget's theory of cognitive development which represents children as weaving between assimilation and accommodation as they make sense of the world. However, a number of other influences can be traced, for example from liberationist thought, pragmatism, and feminism (Cohen et al., 2007; Reason and McArdle, 2004). For some, action research offers an answer to Marx's appeal to change the world. We will return to this aspect of action research later.

The family of action research approaches that emphasise changing professional practice (Mac Naughton and Hughes, 2009), has been recognised as being especially useful in education, health care (Koch and Kralik, 2006) and organisational research. Many research methodology books contain chapters or sections on action research (Coles and McGrath, 2010; Mukherji and Albon, 2010; Punch, 2009; Cohen et al., 2007; Roberts-Holmes, 2005) and new books which focus exclusively on action research are published every year (for example, Koshy, 2010; Mac Naughton and Hughes, 2009; Altrichter et al., 2006; McNiff and Whitehead, 2006; Taylor et al., 2006). Despite the frequent use of subtitles such as 'a step by step guide', there is general agreement that action research is not so much a methodology as an orientation to inquiry.

> [A]ction research is a participatory, democratic process concerned with developing practical knowing in the pursuit of worthwhile human purposes, grounded in a participatory worldview .... It seeks to bring together action and reflection, theory and practice, in participation with others, in the pursuit of practical solutions to issues of pressing concern to people, and more generally the flourishing of individual persons and their communities.

(Reason and Bradbury, 2001, p1)

Three interdependent strategies of action research

To achieve these aims action researchers use three interdependent strategies. The first-person research practice level relies on the ability of an individual to inquire into his or her practice and to act purposefully, being aware of and interested in the effects of these actions on the outside world. The second-person action research/practice level addresses questions of collaboration and cooperation in small groups of practitioners/researchers who share an interest in particular areas in which change should take place. This level of inquiry is most amenable to the emergence of cycles or spirals of action and reflection by a small group of cooperating peers. Third-person research/practice develops broader networks and draws together a number of inquiries (Reason and McArdle, 2004).

Adding to the description of the persons involved in action and research is a discussion of the kind of research that is possible by using this approach. Action research can be of a technical nature, undertaken by practitioners under the watchful eye of an academic researcher, of a practical nature, when the practitioner takes on a more proactive role to improve his or her own practice. It may also take on a more emancipatory nature, linked to political action, striving for collaborative learning, allowing people to understand themselves as agents, connecting the micro and the macro by conceptualising this kind of research as a form of social action and social movement which aims to change the social world for the better (Kemmis, 1993).

In this chapter we explore how action research can enable those working in the field of early childhood studies to strengthen the integration of theory and their practice. Sometimes integration of theory and practice is described as praxis which refers to tacit knowledge, things we can do without having to be aware of every decision along the way. Action research can help practitioners to raise their knowledge and practice into the light of conscious examination so that new forms of praxis can be developed. Everything we do is informed by theories, even if we are not aware of them. Every time people act or decide not to act they also adjust their theories of the world. Sometimes unsettling experiences motivate us to talk with colleagues or read up on a topic or they may change our understanding and judgement of a particular explanatory model.

Denscombe (2007) summarises the common features of action research as follows: action research is practical; it introduces change; it is a cyclical process and it relies on participation. In the following section we will explain these characteristics, relate them to particular forms of action research and explore their strengths and weaknesses. We will illustrate each section with reference to the relevant features of one example of action research (Wickett, 2006) which took place in a day nursery which is part of a children's centre. Karen Wickett's role, as children's centre teacher, was to oversee and support the development of teaching and learning within the setting.

Action research is practical

Practical: It is aiming at dealing with real-world problems and issues, typically at work and in organizational settings.

(Denscombe, 2007, p123)

Practitioners in early years settings and academics appreciate the fact that action research addresses issues that are of real concern to people, or in other words that it is a form of living inquiry (Wicks et al., 2008). However, a preference for action research can also imply disillusion with theoretical thinking and this form of research may also be attractive to those who are cynical about the value of theoretical or academic forms of inquiry. Ideally, however, decisions about research questions and about actions to be taken will emerge out of collaboration between practitioners and those who engage with early childhood issues at more theoretical levels. Some researchers argue that questions should initially be identified by practitioners (for example Somekh, 2003). There may, however, be questions that practitioners are unlikely to ask, because they fail to see a problematic side to particular practices, because there is a concern about highlighting less than perfect practice or to avoid exposing latent conflict (Elliott, 1991). Another threat to the idea of linking knowledge to practice, leading to empowering praxis, is the temptation to concentrate on raising standards, or on demands for evidence based practice (Campbell et al., 2004). It is useful to look closely at the motivation to engage in action research, who formulates research questions, the wider context of a setting and how willingly participants move on from their initial ideas. It may reveal that other interests than improving practice for the sake of children, their families and practitioners are prominent. These difficulties have led to criticism of the partisan nature of action research.

Some of these problems can be avoided if action research is informed by theoretical understanding and academic insights. For example, deconstructing contemporary perceptions of childhood can lead to a better understanding of existing practice and may help to explain strong feelings about the best ways of educating and caring for young children. If children are seen as weak and dependent on very close relationships with a very small number of significant adults – one interpretation of Bowlby's (1953) work on attachment – then the implementation of key person systems in Children's Centres is understandable. However, armed with other ways of understanding children's ability to thrive in different contexts it is possible to develop models of learning and spending time together that are less focused on trying to emulate the mother and child relationship (Dahlberg et al., 1999).

Karen's research: the context

Children have a right to a place, as do teachers and parents. All of us have a right to spend our days in school, surrounded by places and spaces that enhance our lives, support our growth and hold us in respectful ways.

(Cadwell, 2003, p117)

Although my role was to develop the teaching and learning I perceived it as more than just developing systems for planning and assessment for children's learning and development. I aspired to develop the children's centre as a learning community (Whalley, 2006), so I wanted us to establish an ethos and culture of learning. Within this community of learners it would be recognised that all participants, children and adults alike, were learners. Therefore I embarked on an MA to model learning and to show that although I was a teacher there was still much I had to learn. It was a requirement of the MA to undertake a piece of research. As well as being the researcher leading this study I was also the children's centre teacher.

During 2005, the year before the research question was identified, the practitioners within the nursery spent a day reflecting and considering the beliefs about children and their families which underpinned the team's principles. This day resulted in the team agreeing their guiding principles for the setting. One of our principles was 'we recognise that all adults and children are capable learners who can use the opportunities provided to develop their own learning' (Circles Team, 2005). Before the principles were written there had been many changes within the setting, for instance children had access to the outside throughout the session, a café style system had been put in place, the routine had evolved and these changes had resulted in practitioners developing their understanding of an appropriate learning environment for children. By the time we wrote our principles the team was beginning to be aware that they were learners alongside the children. The ethos of a learning community was gradually gaining momentum.

After articulating our principles the team reflected on our practice and whether it was in line with our principles. Another of our principles was 'we recognize and cater for the needs of individuals, valuing their experience and promoting their personal development' (Circles Team, 2005). In order to gain an insight into the children's experiences and interests, so we could plan for the next steps in their learning, we needed to ensure that we actively listened to them and that our documentation systems provided opportunities for children to be heard. At this point we regularly wrote short observations, analysed these to find repeated patterns (schemas) in the children's actions/play and used this information to plan children's next steps. This practice was inconsistent and not rigorous. Therefore I embarked on a piece of action research to facilitate change and development of this practice. I wanted to explore how an 'in-house' workshop on 'Documenting Children's Learning' affected practitioners' understanding and use of documentation within the setting.

Action research introduces change

Change: Both as a way of dealing with practical problems and as a means of discovering more about phenomena, change is regarded as an integral part of research.

(Denscombe, 2007, p123)

This aspect of action research may give it an optimistic appeal. Practitioners can critically reflect on their practice and work out ways of implementing changes and it is possible for managers, academics and researchers to support this kind of professional engagement (Schön, 1983). As in the previous section, there may be concerns about whether the chosen change of practice masks other, more necessary, changes or highlights the need for structural changes which are beyond the practitioner's responsibility or influence.

Additionally, a constant demand for change may take attention away from good practice that needs to be protected and continued.

Before introducing changes in practice it is useful to engage with accounts of the historical development of structures and practice and to work out how similar challenges have been addressed elsewhere, perhaps in other countries. It would be a waste of practitioners' time and energy, to 'reinvent' practice which has already been developed by others and which can serve as a good starting point. A good understanding of why current practice has taken a particular form and how it is based on particular explanations and insights can help to ensure that change is more effective. A careful approach can also help to avoid the temptation to embark on arbitrary experiments. Professional commitment to the well-being of children, the need to 'get things right the first time' and a broadly ethical approach all caution against experiments in which practitioners are not reasonably confident that changes are likely to produce better outcomes.

Karen's research: more changes in practice and attitudes

During the in-house workshop on 'Documenting Children's Learning' (2006) practitioners shared that they had noticed that the children's behaviour had improved since we had started to do short observations, record repeated patterns (schema) in the children's play and use these for planning the next steps in their learning. Therefore they could see the benefits of developing the documentation systems. The content of the workshop included an introduction to the analytical framework of 'levels of involvement' (Laevers et al., 1997), practice in writing narrative observations and exploring other approaches to documenting children's learning. These included Learning Stories from New Zealand (Carr, 2001), documentation from Reggio Emilia (Giudici and Rinaldi, 2001) and children's profiles from Pen Green (for example Whalley and the Pen Green team, 2001).

After the workshop there was much enthusiasm and excitement about our new learning. In order to maintain the enthusiasm and excitement certain systems and strategies were put in place by the leadership team. Resources were provided – digital cameras, camcorders, a computer and printer and practitioners were also timetabled for non contact time each week and had a pedagogic support session with me every half term. During the pedagogic sessions there were opportunities to discuss the learning stories and consider individual children's possible learning. When appropriate I would also introduce other theories to them such as levels of well being (Laevers et al., 1997), Maslow's (1970) Hierarchy of Needs and, the principles of free flow play (Bruce, 1991) and learning dispositions (Katz, 1995).

The impact of the workshop was evident during each pedagogic support session. I observed:

- More learning stories were used to document the children's learning – practitioners were more confident when sharing their documentation with me during their pedagogic support sessions. The learning stories were used as a starting point to discuss a child's learning. At the same time I would introduce theory which would link with the practitioner's interests.

- Practitioners were more likely to document learning when a child was highly involved during an activity. This resulted in them providing an increasingly challenging learning environment for the children, in which children were more likely to become highly involved in their play.

- Practitioners were more confident to discuss a child's learning with their parents/carers.

- Practitioners were more confident and enjoyed documenting children's learning and then planning next steps.

As practitioners became more confident at observing children during high levels of involvement and using the learning story framework I interviewed them and asked them about their changing understanding and attitudes to documentation. These are a few of the comments that I recorded:

Karen H. said she had 'used a more "tick box" approach to observation in the past, identifying whether children have acquired certain skills and knowledge. But now I realise they provided a limited snapshot of a child and didn't provide any insight into a child's thinking.'

Rachel explained that she no longer uses observations to tick boxes. 'In the past observations I would have been used to ticking developmental milestones, for example I used to look to make sure they could cut with a pair of scissors. After the workshop I understand that observations and documentation can be used to inform the planning, building on children's interests or schema'.

Fiona told me that she 'used to think observations were used so we could see where the child was in their ability so we could help them to extend their abilities. My understanding now has changed. I now understand that they can be used to find out their interests and patterns of learning.'

Action research is cyclical

Cyclical process: Research involves a feedback loop in which initial findings generate possibilities for change which are then implemented and evaluated as a prelude to further investigation.

(Denscombe, 2007, p123)

Researching one's practice, introducing change, reflecting and sharing this information can be rewarding although it does cost time and energy and sometimes these costs mean that practitioners are only able to go through one cycle. Also, when the motivation to embark on action research arises from an assignment task for college or university it may be difficult to continue an enquiry. However, the full benefits of action research come from repeated revisiting of research questions. Forward planning can include identifying strategies to pass on insights to colleagues and to create opportunities for further cycles. Practitioner networks can form a good supporting system that allow members to pool insights and develop new research questions in collaboration, sometimes leading to spirals on spirals, as illustrated by McNiff and Whitehead, (2006). An approach allowing for evolving research spirals also highlights the creative messiness of action research. On the one hand this can make it difficult to justify research projects but on the other hand it does allow emerging questions to be followed up.

These research spirals and possible networks can also help to develop sustainable practice. To illustrate this point we can refer to the multitude of television series in which an expert (on child-rearing, cooking or fashion) advises practitioners (from parents to restaurant proprietors) on good practice but leaves after one cycle. When the expert returns after a few weeks or a year it often turns out that people have returned to their old ways.

Although at times action research may look like the individual exercise of reflective practice (think – do – think), the difference lies in a greater emphasis on theory which fuels the progression of the cyclical process once the research question has been developed. For example, Denscombe (2007) builds into his representation of the action research cycle the element 'Research: systematic and rigorous inquiry' before practitioners are invited to start their action. Most books on action research include a chapter on literature review. Another difference compared with reflective practice is the demand to disseminate findings to other practitioners and interested academics and researchers, ideally generating further questions and further cycles of action research projects.

Karen's research: the next part of the journey – entering the second cycle

The changes in practice and practitioners' attitudes and understanding meant we had completed the first cycle. When this new learning and practice became embedded within the practices of the setting we entered the second cycle of the action research.

Not only were the practitioners increasingly skilled and confident at documenting children's learning, analysing the documentation and then planning the next steps for the children but they were also becoming familiar with past and current theorists and their theories. All of us were gaining a deeper insight into our children as learners. We were excited about our new learning community. During pedagogic sessions practitioners and I would document our own learning and this helped us to gain a deeper understanding of both the children and ourselves as learners. However, during several discussions with the practitioners I sensed there was a need to further develop the documentation systems. It was agreed by the team that there should be a consistent framework when analysing the documentation.

Another INSET day was planned for the following academic year, 2007/2008. During the day the team considered what was important to them and which theorists had influenced our practice. Again other systems and frameworks

> such as Learning Stories were looked at and discussed. These discussions led to the team identifying the headings and concepts which they wanted to use and develop when analysing the documentation. Inspired by Margaret Carr's (2001) work the first heading was 'Taking an Interest'. The next came from Laevers et al. (1997), 'Well-being'. As a team we were very aware that children needed to be feeling good about themselves and the world in order for them to learn and reach their full potential, so we wanted to make sure that the children's well-being was at the forefront of our minds. 'Challenge' was the third heading. As a team we were unsure what challenge would look like in a learner led learning environment, so this was an area for further investigation which could develop into a third cycle. Finally, as our principles focus on the importance of valuing and recognising the links between the home, setting and community the last heading was 'Relationships'. This would recognise the many relationships that a child has within the setting and beyond.

Action research requires participation

Participation: Practitioners are the crucial people in the research process. Their participation is active, not passive.

(Denscombe, 2007, p123)

Action research makes two demands on the practitioner: first, he or she is an active researcher and second, the focus is on his or her own practice. If only the first demand is met, this kind of research is called practitioner research and can be research on any issue, for example the practice of others, but undertaken by the practitioner. However, what is actually meant by 'the practitioner as researcher' is not always quite clear. Often the researcher role includes collaboration with non-practitioner researchers, students or academics and of course, fellow practitioners (Kemmis and McTaggart, 1988). One condition of successful action research is that the involved people are clear on and agree on who is doing what. It seems to work well if there is recognition and acceptance of different roles and skills, for example, an academic researcher can be used as a 'reader', an 'interpreter' of academic knowledge and summariser of research reports (Nind, 2003).

However, it is not always clear how the democratic expectations concerning participation are played out. Participation may be constrained by the setting (Wilkie, 2006; Edwards, 2004; Burgess-Macey and Rose, 1997; Elliott, 1991), colleagues may be less willing to participate, or may feel threatened by the research questions and a head teacher may be reluctant to support research. Here diplomatic skills of researchers and willing practitioners are important. These challenges highlight the fact that action research is not by default emancipatory and that expectations about collaboration can hinder the research trajectory of individual practitioners and prevent research on controversial issues (Burgess-Macey and Rose, 1997).

It is often not clear whether everyone is expected to participate on the same level. For example, when action research is conducted in a nursery do practitioners, the manager, parents and children have the same responsibilities for working out the research question, changes in practice, data collection, reflection and initiation of the next cycle? Contemplating possible scenarios arising from this question shows how challenging the demand for participation is and highlights the potential for conflict. An emphasis on collaboration may mean that areas of potential conflict are not addressed, only topics where there is already agreement, leaving more sensitive areas untouched, even though these might benefit most from exploration and change.

Obtaining informed consent is a necessary precondition for ensuring that action research is ethical. Löfman et al. (2004) show the difficulties potential participants may experience in giving consent because part of the nature of action research is that it is not always clear where the project will lead. Employees in a setting may also feel they have limited choice in whether or not they participate in a programme of action research when managers are clearly keen to promote it. When children and/or vulnerable adults are also involved, which is quite likely in projects suitable for action research, ethical considerations require much care and attention.

Karen's research: Reflections on participation in action research

When embarking on my role as teacher within the setting I had the vision of establishing an environment where all participants were learners, children and adults alike. For all of us the initial cycle of action research had scaffolded the development of our documentation practices. Although I initiated the first cycle of the action research the relationships and my role in the team (teacher/researcher) enabled me to reflect on existing practice and sense the next area of development. My inside knowledge and understanding of the team and our practices ensured I was able to identify an aspect of practice to research which would make sense to others and enable them to be participants in the research. For instance during the first cycle of the action research the team realised the benefits of using short observations to inform the planning of activities for the children, so they were willing to develop the documentation systems. However the second cycle was initiated by the team. Many members of the team realised that we needed to develop our own framework of analysis for documentation, so the second INSET day was planned and carried out. Throughout this day practitioners were able to dialogue about the issues, theories and practices they believed were relevant and important to themselves, children and families.

My studies gave me opportunities to deepen my understanding of some theorists and theories and to learn about new theories and research. Not only was I modelling to the team that I was learning but I was also able to share my new understanding about children's learning during pedagogic support sessions. When sharing the learning stories each practitioner had the opportunity to consider what the stories revealed about the child's learning but we were also able to link this to theory. For instance, a practitioner had documented a child playing in the sand tray. To begin with she thought this child was involved, but when we analysed the learning story we realised the play was at a routine level. We referred to other observations of the child and to levels of well-being. We

---

> decided this child seemed to have low levels of well-being so we planned for the practitioner to spend more time with this child in her role as key person.
>
> Linking theory with practice helped us to plan for children's learning but it also provided common frameworks and vocabulary which enabled practitioners to share their own theories and ideas. For instance, when deciding on the themes for our learning story analytical framework they were able to enter into dialogue with each other. Their new learning and vocabulary enabled them to participate as practice was being developed. They also owned the systems that we developed, making our practice more sustainable. Linking theory with practice enabled practitioners to make sense of statutory and non-statutory expectations and guidelines from the DCSF and to engage critically with these in order to implement requirements in ways which would suit this setting's children, families and practitioners.

For most of the chapter we have concentrated on action research which aims to change practice at the micro level. However, there are hints of links to macro issues, for example the way national policies regulate and influence early childhood services. It is useful to remember that action research has its roots in social movements (Kemmis, 1993). The term action research implies dynamic and exciting activities with greater personal engagement by the researcher than is normally attached to traditional approaches which use established methods like observing children, interviewing parents and surveying practitioners. It is associated with the invigorating feeling of rolling up sleeves, balancing concerns about objectivity with passionate commitment to a cause and putting one's research skills at the disposal of people who may need them. This approach is exemplified by research on childminding in the 1970s by Jackson and Jackson (1979). Their work was political, aiming to improve the situation of children and childminders and they combined research with action.

From the beginning of the project we have tried to provoke action by others (issuing an Action Register, calling national conferences, making television programmes, urging blueprints from the research, ourselves (The Children's Centre in Huddersfield, The drop in Centre in Manchester, courses for childminders)). This has the virtue of getting something done, instead of having impotently to wait for years for possible government action; and action breeds action.

(Jackson and Jackson, 1979, p14)

Their research activities included the dawn watch (researchers spending time on English streets in the early morning hours, observing children being taken to childminders), interviews, observations and organising play and safety equipment for childminders and it led to the founding of the National Childminding Association. Many of their action research activities provided blueprints for services to support childminders. For example, the encouragement of childminder networks, toy libraries and start up packs which are still in place in many local authorities. Even more pressing needs for social change were identified by a study which found authoritarian forms of behaviour management in post-war Guatemalan parenting (Schrader McMillan, 2007) and several cycles of action research aimed to develop sustainable ways of reducing the child abuse associated with this.

Conclusion

In this chapter we have highlighted some of the characteristics, benefits and challenges of action research. This form of inquiry has promoted a number of qualitative methods raising the status of small scale research on day-to-day practice. However, action research does not exclude quantitative methods but, like any well organised research, it requires researchers to identify the approaches which are most appropriate to the questions asked. There are a number of people who criticise small scale action research projects and accuse them of being unscientific and lacking in rigour. They argue that research should avoid political issues and that researchers should remain neutral. We, however, see in action research a useful opportunity for practice to be explored from perspectives which are not easily accessible to the more remote, visiting researcher.

When practitioners combine their daily work with the role of researcher it can lead to development in two areas. Firstly, they improve their own practice by making better use of theory and, secondly, they contribute to new knowledge which, in turn, can help the wider community of early years practitioners, children and their families. Additionally, dissemination of findings from action research means that academics can receive insights into a world they could not access by themselves. A benevolent cooperation between academics and early years practitioners leads to theory and practice informing each other, removing unhelpful barriers. In practice it could mean that early years practitioners gain confidence in talking about and sharing their practice and learning. The emerging dialogue may shift hierarchical structures towards a more democratic way of relating to each other. For instance, taking reflective practice and engagement seriously will change relationships between managers, teachers and early years advisors. The participatory approaches developed during action research can influence policies and wider structures from the bottom up. In the political tradition of action research, practitioners and researchers can become effective advocates for children.

ACTIVITY *1*

Action research in the nursery

Katrina is a new member of staff in a nursery. In the resources room she finds a large set of giant wooden building blocks, which were purchased by the previous head of the nursery. It emerges that some of her colleagues value the opportunities these building blocks offer to children but others worry about health and safety issues, space and noise levels and question whether plain wooden building blocks are stimulating enough. At a meeting the staff agree that it would be a shame to leave these expensive resources in the cupboard and they start to plan how they can be introduced, beginning a cycle of action research.

The following questions may help you to consider how such a project might demonstrate the four characteristics of action research: being practical; introducing change; being cyclical and encouraging participation:

- *What could be the different stages of this giant wooden building blocks action research?*

continued

---

*ACTIVITY **1** continued*

- *What can be done to develop and maintain everyone's participation?*

- *What outside experts could be useful and what should be the focus of negotiations around their involvement?*

- *What kind of research cycles could you see emerging?*

- *How can insights and findings feed back into practice?*

- *What are the advantages and disadvantages of insider knowledge in the project?*

- *What ethical matters have to be taken into consideration?*

---

*ACTIVITY **2***

Action research at university

Think about the seminars and group work meetings you have attended. Are there any practices that puzzle, amaze or annoy you? What could you do to explore how these could be changed? How can you ensure that your inquiry is practical, introduces change, is cyclical and participatory? Adapt the questions listed above to consider how this student action research project might be conducted.

Mac Naughton, G and Hughes, P (2009) *Doing Action Research in Early Childhood Studies: A step by step guide*, Maidenhead: Open University Press and McGraw-Hill Education.

The book contains a wealth of practical advice and theories about the different approaches to action research. Examples are projects in early years, often conducted by students. The book addresses many concerns of potential researchers and offers useful suggestions about how to approach the challenges in this form of inquiry.

Chapter 8 in **Denscombe, M** (2007) *The Good Research Guide for small-scale social research projects* (3rd edn). Maidenhead and Philadelphia: Open University Press.

Here you will find a good overview of action research and links to other research approaches. Denscombe highlights ethical issues, advantages and disadvantages and provides a checklist which is useful when developing an action research project.

The journal *Educational Action Research*, published by Routledge, offers accounts of action research and related studies, reviews of literature on action research and a forum for dialogue on methodological and epistemological issues.

References

Abbott, L and Langston, A (2005) *Birth to Three Matters Supporting the Framework of Effective Practice*. Maidenhead: Oxford University Press.

Abbott, L and Nutbrown, C (2001) *Experiencing Reggio Emilia: Implications for Pre-school Provision*. Maidenhead: Open University Press.

Abbott, L and Pugh, G (eds) (1998) *Training to Work in the Early Years*. Buckingham: Open University Press.

Acredolo, L, Goodwyn, S and Abrams, D (2002) *Baby Signs: How to Talk with your Baby Before your Baby can Talk*. New York: McGraw Hill.

Ahnert, L (2005) Entwicklungspsychologische Erfordernisse bei der Gestaltung von Betreuungs- und Bildungsangeboten im Kleinkind- und Vorschulalter, in Sachverständigenkommission Zwölfter Kinder- und Jugendbericht (ed) *Bildung, Betreuung und Erziehung von Kindern unter sechs*. Jahren München: Deutsches Jugendinstitut.

Ainscow, M (1995) Education for all: Making it Happen, *Support for Learning*, 10: 4: 147–154.

Alcock, C, Payne, S and Sullivan, M (2004) *Introducing Social Policy*. Harlow: Pearson Education.

Alcock, P (2004) Social Policy and Professional Practice in Becker S and Bryman A (ed) *Understanding Research for Social Policy and Practice: Themes, Methods and Approaches*. Bristol: Policy Press.

Alcock, P, Erskine, A and May, M (eds) (2002) *The Blackwell Dictionary of Social Policy*. Oxford: Blackwell.

Alexander, R (ed) (2010) *Children, their World, their Education: Final Report and Recommendations of the Cambridge Primary Review*, Oxford: Routledge.

Altrichter, H, Feldman, A, Posch, P and Somekh, B (2006) *Teachers Investigating Their Work: An Introduction to Action Research Across the Professions*. London: Routledge.

Ancona, D, Malone, T, Orlikowski, W and Senge, P (2007) In Praise of the Incomplete Leader, *Harvard Business Review*, 92–102.

Anderson, T (1987) The Reflecting Team: Dialogue and Meta-dialogue. *Clinical Work Family Process*, 26, 415–428.

Anning, A and Edwards, A (2006) *Promoting Children's Learning from Birth To Five: Developing the New Early Years Professional* (2nd edn). Maidenhead: Open University Press.

Anning, A, Cottrell, D, Frost, N, Green, J and Robinson, M (2006) *Developing Multi-Professional Teamwork for Integrated Children's Services: Research, Policy and Practice*. Maidenhead: Open University Press.

Anning, A, Cullen, J and Fleer, M, (2009) *Early Childhood Education: Society and Culture*. London: Sage.

Armstrong, D (1986) The Invention Of Infant Mortality, *Sociology of Health and Illness*, 8 (211), 32.

Armstrong, D (1995) The Rise Of Surveillance Medicine, *Sociology of Health and Illness*, 17 (3), 393–404.

Arnot, M, Gray, J, James, M and Rudduck, J (1998) *Recent Research on Gender and Educational Performance*. London: HMSO.

Atkinson, M, Doherty, P, and Kinder, K (2005) Multi-agency Working: Models, Challenges and Key Factors for Success, *Journal of Early Childhood Research*, 3 (1): 7–17.

Atkinson, M, Wilkin, A, Stott, A, Doherty, P and Kinder, K (2002) *Multi-agency Working: A Detailed Study*. Slough: National Foundation for Educational Research.

Attard, K (2008) Uncertainty for the Reflective Practitioner: A Blessing in Disguise, *Reflective Practice*, 9 (3) 307–317.

Aubrey, C (2007) *Leading and Managing in the Early Years*, London: Sage.

Audit Commission (2003a) *Corporate Governance: Improvement and Trust in Local Public Services.* London: HMSO.

Audit Commission (2003b) *Services for Disabled Children: A Review of Services for Disabled Children and their Families.* London: HMSO.

Autorengruppe Bildungsberichterstattung (2008) Bildung in Deutschland 2008: *Ein indikatorengestützter Bericht mit einer Analyse zu Übergängen im Anschluss an den Sekundarbereich I.* Bielefeld: Bertelsmann.

Avolio, B and Gardner, W (2005) Authentic Leadership Development: Getting To The Roots of Positive Forms Of Leadership. *The Leadership Quarterly*, 16, 315–338.

Axford, N, Little, M and Morpeth, L (2003) Children's Service in the UK 1997–2003: Problems, Developments and Challenges for the Future. *Children and Society Special Issue: New Labour Policy and its Outcomes for Children*, 17 (3), 205–14.

Ball, S (2008) *The Education Debate: Policy and Politics in the Twentieth First Century*. Bristol: Policy Press.

Banton, M (1987) *Racial Theories*. Cambridge: Cambridge University Press.

Barker, R (2009) *Making Sense of Every Child Matters: Multi-professional Practice Guidance*. Bristol: Policy Press.

Barnes, J (2001) Using Observations to Evaluate Paid Child Care Settings, in: Petrogiannis, K and Melhuish, E (eds) *The Pre-School Period: Care-Education-Development: Findings from International Research*. Athens: Kastaiotis.

Bass, B (1985) *Leadership and Performance Beyond Expectation*. New York: Free Press.

Bax, M (2001) Endeavours of Parents, Editorial in *Developmental Medicine and Child Neurology*, 43:291.

Begley, P (2001) In Pursuit of Authentic School Leadership Practices, *International Journal Leadership in Education*. 4(4) 353–365.

Beher, K, Hoffman, H and Rauschenbach, T (1999) *Das Berufsbild Der Erzieherinnen: Vom Fächerorientierten Zum Tätigkeitsorientierten Ausbildungskonzept, Neuwied*. Berlin: Luchterhand.

Bekoff, M. and Byers, J. (1998) *Animal Play*. Cambridge: Cambridge University Press.

Bell, A and La Valle, I (2005). *Early Stages of the Neighbourhood Nursery Initiative: Parents' Experiences, Sure Start Unit Research Report 006*. London: DfES.

Bell, J (1999) *Doing your Research Project: a guide for first-time researchers in education and social science*. 3rd edn. Buckingham: Open University Press.

Bertram, A and Pascal, C (1999) *The OECD Thematic Review of Early Childhood Education and Care: Background Report for the United Kingdom*. Worcester: Centre for Research in Early Childhood.

Bertram, H (ed) (2008) *Mittelmaß für Kinder: Der UNICEF-Bericht zur Lage der Kinder in Deutschland.* München: C. H. Beck.

Biddulph, S (2006) *Raising Babies: Should Under 3s go to Nursery?* London: Harper Thorsons.

Billington, T (2006) *Working with Children.* London: Sage.

Bilton, H (2002) *Outdoor Play in the Early Years Management and Innovation,* 2nd edn. London: David Fulton Publishers.

Bitew, G (2008) Using "Plasma TV" Broadcasts in Ethiopian Secondary Schools: A brief survey. *Australasian Journal of Educational Technology,* 24 (2) 150–167.

Blake, R and Moulton, J (1964) *The Managerial Grid.* London: Bloomsbury.

Blakemore, K and Griggs, E (2007) *Social Policy: an Introduction*, 3rd edn. Buckingham: Open University Press.

Blakemore, S, Wolpert, D and Frith C (2000) Why Can't You Tickle Yourself? *NeuroReport* 11:11.

Blakeslee, S and Blakeslee, M (2007) *The Body Has a Mind of its Own: How Body Maps in Your Brain Help You to do (almost) Everything Better.* New York: Random House.

Blunkett, D (2002) Integration with Diversity: Globalisation and the Renewal of Democracy and Civil Society, in Griffith, P and Leonard, M (eds) *Reclaiming Britishness.* London: The Foreign Policy Centre.

BMFSFJ Bundesministerium für Familie Senioren Frauen und Jugend (ed) (1998) *Zehnter Kinder- und Jugendbericht: Bericht über die Lebenssituation von Kindern und die Leistungen der Kinderhilfen in Deutschland, (13/11368).* Bonn: Bundestagsdrucksache.

BMFSFJ Bundesministerium für Familie Senioren Frauen und Jugend (ed) (2002) *Bericht über die Lebenssituation junger Menschen und die Leistung der Kinder- und Jugendhilfe in Deutschland – elfter Kinder- und Jugendbericht, (13/11368).* Bonn: Bundestagsdrucksache.

BMFSFJ Bundesministerium für Familie Senioren Frauen und Jugend (ed) (2005) *Zwölfter Kinder- und Jugendbericht: Bericht über die Bildung, Betreuung und Erziehung vor und neben der Schule.* Berlin: Bundestagsdrucksache.

Bodrova, E and Leong, D (2001) *Tools of the Mind: A Case Study of Implementing the Vygotskian Approach in American Early Childhood and Primary Classrooms. Innodata Monographs 7.* Geneva: UNESCO. Available at: www.ibe. unesco.org/publications/innodata/inno07.pdf

Bodrova, E and Leong, D (2006) *Tools of the Mind: The Vygotskian Approach to Early Childhood Education.* 2nd edn. Columbus, OH: Merrill/Prentice Hall.

Bottery, M (1992) *The Ethics of Education Management,* London: Cassell Educational.

Boud D, Keogh R and Walker D (1985) *Reflections: Turning Experience into Learning.* London: Routledge.

Bourner T, O'Hara S and Barlow J (2002) Only Connect: Facilitating Reflective Learning with Statements of Relevance. *Innovations in Education and Teaching International,* 37(1).

Bowlby, J (1953) *Childcare and the Growth of Love.* Harmondsworth: Penguin.

Bowlby, J (1969) *Attachment and Loss: Vol. 1 Attachment.* New York: Basic.

Bradbury, B and Jantti, M (1999) Child Poverty across Industrialised Nations. *Innocenti Occasional Papers EPS 1971.* Florence: UNICEF.

Bransby, E (1946) The Diets of Families with Children, *British Medical Journal*, 1/6/46, 832–5.

Brechin, A (2000) The Challenge of Caring Relationships in Brchin, A, Brown, H and Eby, M *Critical Practice in Health and Social Care*. Oxford: Oxford University Press.

Brewer, M, Clark, T and Wakefield, M (2002) *Social Security Under New Labour: what did the Third Way mean for Welfare Reform.* London: Institute of Fiscal Studies.

Bridgeman, B (1992) 'On the Evolution of Consciousness and Language', *Psycoloquy* 3(15) http://www.cogsci.ecs. soton.ac.uk/cgi/psyc/newpsy?3.15

Bronfenbrenner, B (1979) *The Ecology of Human Development*. Cambridge, MA: Harvard University Press.

Broadhead, P (2006) Developing an Understanding of Young Children's Learning through Play: the place of observation, interaction and reflection. *British Educational Journal*, 32(2), pp. 191–207.

Brooker, L (2005) Learning to be a Child: Cultural Diversity and Early Years Ideology, in Yelland, N (ed) *Critical Issues in Early Childhood Education*. Maidenhead: Open University Press.

Broström, S (1997) Children's Play: Tools and Symbols in Frame Play, *Early Years,* 17, 2, 16–21.

Brown, B (1998) *Unlearning Discrimination in the Early Years*. Stoke on Trent: Trentham.

Brown, K and Rutter, L (2008) *Critical Thinking for Social Work*, 2nd edn. Exeter: Learning Matters.

Bruce, T (1991) *Time to Play in Early Childhood Education*. London: Hodder & Stoughton.

Bruce, T (1996) *Helping Young Children to Learn through Play*. London: Hodder and Stoughton

Bruce, T and Meggitt, C (2006) *Child Care and Education,* 4th edn. London: Hodder Education.

Bruner, J (1966) *Toward a Theory of Instruction.* Cambridge, MA: Harvard University Press.

Bruner, J, Goodnow, J and Austin, J (1956) *A Study of Thinking.* New York: John Wiley and Sons.

Bryman, A (2004) *Social Research Methods*. Oxford: Oxford University Press.

Buber, M (2004) *I and thou*. London: Continuum.

Burchardt, T, Tsang, T and Vizard, P (2009) *Specialist Consultation on the List of Central and Valuable Capabilities for Children.* Manchester: Equality and Human Rights Commission.

Burgess-Macey, C and Rose, J (1997) Breaking Through the Barriers: Professional Development, Action Research and the Early Years, *Educational Action Research*, 5: 1: 55–70.

Burke, C and Grosvenor, I (2003) *The School I'd Like – Children and Young People's Reflections on an Education for the 21st Century*. London: RoutledgeFalmer.

Burman, E (1994) *Deconstructing Developmental Psychology*. London: Routledge.

Burns, J (1978) *Leadership*. New York: Harper and Row.

Cabinet Office (2005) *Improving the Life Chances of Disabled People*. London: Strategy Unit.

CACE, Central Advisory Council for Education (1967) *Children and their Primary Schools*. London: HMSO.

Cadwell, L (2003) *The Reggio Approach to Early Childhood Education: Bringing Learning to Live*. New York: Teachers College Press.

Caims, K (2002) *Attachment, Trauma and Resilience: Therapeutic Caring for Children*. London: BAAF.

Callendar, C (2000) *The Barriers to Childcare Provision, Research Report RR231*. London, Department for Education and Employment.

Cambridge Primary Review (2009) The Final Report: Cambridge Primary Review briefing, October 2009, www.primaryreview.org.uk/Downloads/Finalreport/CWE-briefing.pdf.

Cameron, C and Boddy, J (2006) Knowledge and Education for Care Workers: What do they Need to Know?, in Boddy, J. Cameron, C. and Moss, P (eds) *Care Work: Present and Future*. London and New York: Routledge.

Camfield, L and Cafere, Y (2009) 'No, Living Well does not mean being Rich': Diverse Understandings of Well-being among 11–13-Year-Old Children in Three Ethiopian Communities, *Journal of Children and Poverty*, 15: 2, 119–138.

Campbell, A, McNamara, O and Gilroy, P (2004) *Practitioner Research and Professional Development in Education*. London: Paul Chapman Publishing.

Campbell-Barr, V (2009a) Contextual Issues in Assessing Value for Money in Early Years Education, *National Institutes Economic Review*, 207, January 2009.

Campbell-Barr, V (2009b) Care and Business Orientations In The Delivery of Childcare: an exploratory study, *Journal of Early Childhood Research*, 7: 76–93.

Carr, M (2001) *Assessment in Early Childhood Settings Learning Stories*. London: Paul Chapman Publishing.

Carter, R (2009) *The Brain Book*, London: Dorling Kindersley.

Casas, F (2000) *Quality of life and the life experience of children*. Ghent: International Interdisciplinary Course on Children's Rights.

Chaiklin, S. (2003) The Zone of Proximal Development in Vygotsky's Theory of Learning and School Instruction. In A. Kozulin, B. Gindis, V.S. Ageyev, & S.M Miller (eds.), *Vygotsky's Educational Theory in Cultural Context*. Cambridge: Cambridge University Press.

Chambers P, Clarke B, Colombo M and Askland L (2003) Significant Learning Incidents and Critical Conversations in an International Context: Promoting Reflexivity with Inservice Students, *Journal of In-Service Education*, 29(1).

Champy, J (2009) Authentic Leadership, *Leader to Leader*, 2009:54.

Child to Child www.child-to-child.org/about/approach.html

CIA, Central Intelligence Agency (2009) *The World Factbook*. CIA. https://www.cia.gov/library/publications/the-world-factbook/geos/it.html

Circles Team (2005) *Setting's Principles*. Document produced following team inset day July 2005

Claire, H, Maybin, J and Swann, J (eds) (1993) *Equality Matters: Case Studies from the Primary School.* Clevedon PA, Adelaide: Multilingual Matters.

Clark, A (2001) *Mindware: An Introduction to the Philosophy of Cognitive Science*. Oxford: Oxford University Press.

Clarke, A and Clarke, A (2003) *Human Resilience: A Fifty Year Quest*. London: Jessica Kingsley Publishers.

Claxton, G (1994) *Noises from the Dark Room: The Science and Mystery of the Mind*. London: Aquarian/Harper Collins.

Clemens, S, Ullman, A, and Kinnaird, R (2006) *Childcare and Early Years Providers Survey 2005: Overview Report*. Department for Education and Skills Research Report 764. London: DfES.

Cockburn, T (1998) Children and Citizenship in Britain. *Childhood*, 5 (1), 99–117.

Cohen, D (2002) *How the Child's Mind Develops*. London: Routledge.

Cohen, L, Manion, L and Morrison, K (2007) *Research Methods in Education,* 6th edn. London and New York: RoutledgeFalmer.

Cohen, S (1972) *Folk Devils and Moral Panics: The Creation of the Mods and Rockers*, London: MacGibbon and Kee.

Cohn, J and Tronick, E (1987) Mother–infant Face-to-face Interaction; the Sequence of Dyadic States at 3, 6, and 9 Months. *Developmental Psychology,* 23 (1): 68–77.

Cole, M & Wertsch, J (1996) Beyond the Individual-Social Antinomy in Discussions of Piaget and Vygotksy. *Human Development*, 39, 250–256 www.massey.ac.nz/~alock/virtual/colevyg.htm

Coleman, M and Campbell-Stephens, R (2010) Perceptions of Career Progress: The Experience of Black and Minority Ethnic School Leaders, *School Leadership and Management*, 30 (1), 35–49.

Coles, A and McGrath, J (2010) *Your Education Research Project Handbook*. Harlow: Pearson Education.

Comenius, J (1657/1923) *The Great Didactic* (trans. Keatinge, M). London: A&C Black.

Cooley, C (1902) *Human Nature and the Social Order*. New York: Scribner.

Cotterill, R (1998) *Enchanted Looms: Conscious Networks in Brains and Computers.* Cambridge: Cambridge University Press.

Csikszentmihalyi, M (1992) *Flow: the Psychology of Happiness.* London: Rider Books.

Cummins, J (1984) *Bilingualism and Special Education: Issues in Assessment and Pedagogy*. Clevedon: Multilingual Matters.

Cummins, J (2000) *Language, Power and Pedagogy: Bilingual Children in the Crossfire.* Bristol: Multilingual Matters.

Cunningham, H (1991) *The Children of the Poor: Representations of Childhood since the Seventeenth Century*. Oxford: Blackwell.

Cunningham, H (2006) *The Invention of Childhood*. London: BBC.

Curtis, L and Burton, D (2009) Naïve Change Agent or Canny Political Collaborator? The Change in Leadership Role from Nursery School to Children's Centre. *Education*, 3, 287–299.

CWDC, Children's Workforce Development Council (2006) *Early Years Professional Status*. London: HMSO.

CWDC, Children's Workforce Development Council (2007) *Prospectus: Early Years Professional Status*. Leeds: CWDC.

Dahlberg, G, Moss, P and Pence, A (1999) *Beyond Quality in Early Childhood Education and Care: Postmodern Perspective.* London: RoutledgeFalmer.

Daniel, B, Wassel, S and Gilligan, R (1999) *Child Development for Child Care and Protection Workers*. London: Jessica Kingsley.

Daniel, H (2005) *An Introduction to Vygotsky*. Hove: Routledge.

Daniel, P and Ivatts, J (1998) *Children and Social Policy*. Hampshire: Macmillan Press.

Dasgupta, P and Weale, M (1992) On Measuring the Quality of Life, *World Development*, 20 (1) 119–31.

Davidoff, L, Doolittle, M, Fink, J and Holden, K (1999) *The Family Story – Blood, Contract and Intimacy, 1830–1960*. London: Longman.

Davin, A (1990) When is a Child Not a Child, in Corr, H and Jamieson, L. (eds) *Politics of Everyday Life – Continuity and Change in Work and the Family*. London: Macmillan.

DCLG, Department for Communities and Local Government (2001) *Learning to Listen: Core Principles for the Involvement of Children & Young People.* London: HMSO.

DCSF, Department for Children, Schools and Families (2007a) *Principles into Practice Cards for the Early Years Foundation Stage*. Nottingham: DCSF.

DCSF, Department for Children, Schools and Families (2007b) *The Children's Plan: Building Brighter Futures.* Norwich: The Stationery Office/DCSF.

DCSF, Department for Children, Schools and Families (2008a) *Statutory Framework for the Early Years Foundation Stage: Setting the Standards for Learning, Development, and Care for Children from Birth to Five.* Nottingham: DCSF.

DCSF, Department for Children, Schools and Families (2008b) *Practice Guidance for the Early Years Foundation Stage*. Nottingham: DCSF.

DCSF, Department for Children, Schools and Families (2008c) *The Early Years Foundation Stage: Setting the Standards for Learning, Development and Care for Children from Birth to Five.* (CD Rom) Nottingham: DCSF.

DCSF, Department for Children, Schools and Families (2008d) *Bullying Involving Children with Special Educational Needs and Disabilities. Safe to Learn: Embedding Anti-Bullying Work in Schools.* Nottingham: DCSF.

DCSF, Department for Children, Schools and Families (2008e) *Children's Trusts: Statutory Guidance on Inter-Agency Cooperation to Improve Well-Being of Children, Young People and their Families.* Nottingham: DCSF.

DCSF, Department for Children, Schools and Families (2008f) *Statutory Guidance: The Roles and Responsibilities of the Lead Member for Children's Services and the Director of Children's Services.* Nottingham: DCSF.

DCSF, Department for Children, Schools and Families (2008g) *Social and Emotional Aspects of Development: Guidance for Practitioners Working in EYFS.* Nottingham: DCSF.

DCSF, Department for Children, Schools and Families (2008h) *2020 Children and Young People's Workforce Strategy*. Nottingham: DCSF.

DCSF, Department for Children, Schools and Families (2009a) *Special Educational Needs (SEN) – A Guide for Parents and Carers.* Nottingham: DCSF.

DCSF, Department for Children, Schools and Families (2009b) *Common Assessment Framework: Managers' and Practitioners' Guides*. Nottingham: DCSF.

DCSF, Department for Children, Schools and Families (2009c) *Implementing the Single Funding Formula*: *Practice Guidance*. London: DCSF.

DCSF, Department for Children, Schools and Families (2009d) *Children's Minister Dawn Primarolo Written Ministerial Statement*. www.dcsf.gov.uk/pns/DisplayPN.cgi?pn_id=2009_0245

DCSF, Department for Children, Schools and Families (2009e) *Social Work Task Force* www.dcsf.gov.uk/swtf/

Dean, H (2005) *Social Policy: Short introductions.* Cambridge: Polity Press.

DEC, Disasters Emergency Committee (2010) *Disasters Emergency Committee*. www.dec.org.uk/

Dempsey, M, Halton, C and Murphy, M (2001) Reflective Learning in Social Work Education: Scaffolding the Process. *Social Work Education* Volume 20(6) Carfax

Denscombe, M (2007) *The Good Research Guide for Small-Scale Social Research Projects*, 3rd edn. Maidenhead PA: Open University Press.

Derman-Sparks, L (1989) *Anti-bias Curriculum: Tools for Empowering Young Children*. Washington DC: NAEYC.

Desforges, C and Abouchaar, A (2003) *The Impact of Parental Involvement, Parent Support and Family Education on Pupil Achievement and Adjustment: A Literature Review. Research Report 433*. London: DfES Publications.

Devereux, J and Miller, L (2003) *Working with Children in the Early Years*. London: David Fulton.

Devereux, J (2003) Observing Children in Devereux, J and Miller, L (eds) *Working with Children in the Early Years*. London: David Fulton, pp181–92.

Dewey, J (1933) *How We Think*. Boston: D C Heath and Co.

Dewey, J (1938) *Experience and Education*. New York: The Macmillan Company.

DfEE, Department for Education and Employment (1998a) *Meeting the Childcare Challenge: A Consultation Document*. London: HMSO.

DfEE, Department for Education and Employment (1998b) *National Childcare Strategy*. London: HMSO.

DfEE, Department for Education and Employment (2001) *Early Excellence Centre Pilot Programme Annual Evaluation Report 2000*. London: HMSO.

DfES, Department for Education and Skills (2002) *Birth to Three Matters: a Framework to Support Children in their Earliest Years*. London: DfES.

DfES, Department for Education and Skills (2003) *Every Child Matters* (Green Paper). London: HMSO.

DfES, Department for Education and Skills (2004a) *Every Child Matters: Next Steps*. Nottingham: DfES.

DfES, Department for Education and Skills (2004b) *Removing Barriers to Achievement: The Government's Strategy for SEN*. London: DfES.

DfES, Department for Education and Skills (2004c) *Every Child Matters: Change for Children*. London: HMSO.

DfES, Department for Education and Skills (2004d) *Five Year Strategy for Children and Learners: Putting People at the Heart of Public Services*. Norwich: TSO

DfES, Department for Education and Skills (2005) *Common Core of Skills and Knowledge for the Children's Workforce*. London: HMSO.

DfES, Department for Education and Skills (2006a) *Learning Outside the Classroom Manifesto*. Nottingham: DfES.

DfES, Department for Education and Skills (2006b) *Implementing the Disability Discrimination Act (DDA) in Schools and Early Years Settings*. London: DfES.

DfES, Department for Education and Skills (2006c) *Children's Workforce Strategy: Building an Integrated Qualifications Framework*. Nottingham: DfES Publications.

Department for Education and Skills (2007) *National Standards for Leaders of SureStart Children's Centres*. London: HMSO.

DfID, Department for International Development (1999) *Introduction to the Sustainable Livelihoods Approach*. Sussex: Institute of Development Studies ELDIS Document Store http://www.eldis.org/vfile/upload/1/document/0901/section1.pdf

Diamond, KE (2002) Social Competence in Children with Disabilities, in Smith, PK and Hart, CH (eds) *Blackwell Handbook of Children Social Development*. Oxford: Blackwell.

Diller, A and Rauschenbach, T (eds). (2006) *Reform oder Ende der Erzieherinnenausbildung? Beiträge zu einer Kontroversen Fachdebatte*. München: DJI Verlag Deutsches Jugendinstitut.

Dinham, A (2007) Raising Expectations or Dashing Hopes? Well-being and Participation in Disadvantaged Areas. *Community Development Journal*, 42: 181–93.

DoH, Department of Health (2000) *Framework for the Assessment of Children in Need and their Families*. Norwich: The Stationery Office.

DoH, Department of Health (2002) *National Standards for the Provision of Children's Advocacy Services*, London: Department of Health Publications.

DoH, Department of Health (2004) *National Service Framework for Children, Young People and Maternity Services*. London: HMSO.

DoH, Department of Health (2008) *Healthy Weight, Healthy Lives: A Cross-Government Strategy for England*. London: Department of Health Publications.

DoH, Department of Health (2009) *Healthy Lives, Brighter Futures: The Strategy for Children and Young People's Health*. www.dh.gov.uk/en/Publicationsandstatistics/Publications/PublicationsPolicyAndGuidance/DH_094400

Doherty, J and Hughes, M (2009) *Child Development; Theory and Practice 0–11*. Harlow: Pearson Education.

Doherty-Sneddon, G (2003) *Children's Unspoken Language*. London: Jessica Kingsley Publishers.

Doherty-Sneddon, G (2004) Don't look now… I'm trying to think. *The Psychologist*, 17 (2), February 82–5.

Donald, M (1991) *Origins of the Modern Mind: Three Stages in the Evolution of Culture and Cognition*. Cambridge MA: Harvard University Press.

Donaldson, M (1978) *Children's Minds*. London: Fontana.

Dreyer, R and Hildebrandt, H (2009) *Frühpädagogik Studieren! Suche nach Studiengängen*. www.fruehpaedagogik-studieren.de/suche

Drummond, M & Jenkinson, S (2009) *Meeting the Child: Approaches to Observation and Assessment in Steiner Kindergartens*. Plymouth: University of Plymouth.

Duffy, B and Marshall, J (2007) *Leadership in Multi-agency Work* in Siraj-Blatchford I, Clarke, K and Needham M (2007) *The Team Around the Child: Multi-Agency Working in the Early Years*. Stoke-on-Trent: Trentham Books.

Dunbar, R (1998) *Grooming, Gossip and the Evolution of Language*. Cambridge MA: Harvard University Press.

Duncan, A (2003) *Mother, Care and Employment: Value Theories*. Bradford: Cava.

Dunhill, A, Elliott, B & Shaw, A (eds) (2009) *Effective Communication and Engagement with Children and Young People, their Families and Carers*. Exeter: Learning Matters.

Dwork, D (1987) *War is Good for Babies and other Young Children: A History of the Child Welfare Movement in England*, 1898–1918. London: Tavistock.

DWP, Department of Work and Pensions (2008) *In Work Better Off: Next step to full employment*, Norwich: The Stationery Office.

Earley, P and Weindling D (2004) *Understanding School Leadership.* London: Sage.

Edgington, M (2004) *The Nursery Teacher in Action Teaching 3, 4 and 5 years-olds* (3rd ed), London: Paul Chapman Publishing.

Edwards, A (1999) Research and Practice: is There a Dialogue? in Penn H. (ed) *Theory, Policy and Practice in Early Childhood Services.* Buckingham: Open University Press.

Edwards, A (2004) Understanding Context, Understanding Practice in Early Education, *European Early Childhood Education*, 16: 1: 85–101.

Edwards, C, Gandini, L and Foreman, G (1998) (eds) *The Hundred Languages of Children* (2nd edn). Norwood NJ: Ablex.

EGGE, European Commission's Expert Group on Gender and Employment Issues (2009) *The Provision of Childcare Services: A Comparative Review of 30 European Countries.* Luxembourg: European Commission.

EHRC, Equality and Human Rights Commission (2008) *Response of the EHRC to the Consultation on a National Framework for Assessing Children and Young People's Continuing Care. Department of Health.* London: EHRC.

Elias, N (1969) Sociology and Psychiatry in S. H. Foulkes and G. Steward Prince (eds) *Psychiatry in a Changing Society.* London: Tavistock.

Elias, N (1978) *What is Sociology?* London: Hutchinson.

Elias, N (1985) *The Loneliness of the Dying.* Oxford: Blackwell.

Elias, N (1987) *Involvement and Detachment.* Oxford: Blackwell.

Elias, N (1991) *The Society of Individuals.* Oxford: Blackwell.

Elias, N (1998) The Civilizing of Parents, in Goudsblom, J and Mennell, S (eds) *The Norbert Elias Reader.* London: Blackwell.

Elias, N (2000) *The Civilizing Process.* London: Blackwell.

Elias, N (2006) *The Court Society.* Dublin: University College Dublin Press.

Elliott, J (1991) *Action Research for Educational Change.* Buckingham: Open University Press.

Ellis, D and Fisher, B (1994) *Small Group Decision-making: Communication and the Group Process.* Singapore: McGraw-Hill.

Eraut, M (1994) *Developing Professional Knowledge and Competence.* London; Falmer.

FAO, Food and Agriculture Organisation of the United Nations (2009) *The State of Food Insecurity in the World.* Food and Agriculture Organisation of the United Nations. www.fao.org/hunger/en.

Farmer, G (2002) Dolls with Stories to Tell, in C. Nutbrown (ed) *Research studies in Early Childhood Education.* Stoke-on-Trent: Trentham.

Farrell, P (2001) Special Education in the last 20 Years: Have Things Really Got Better? *British Journal of Special Education*, 28: 1: 3–9.

Fiedler, F (1978) Situational Control and a Dynamic Theory of Leadership, in Pugh, D (ed) *Organisational Theory: Selected Readings.* Harmondsworth: Penguin Business.

Fiedler, F and Chemers, M (1974) *Leadership and Effective Management.* Glenview IL: Scott Foresman & Co.

Field, T (2005) Prenatal Depression Effects on the Foetus and Neonate. In J. Nadel and D. Muir (eds.) *Emotional Development.* Oxford: Oxford University Press.

Fisher, J (ed) (2002) *The Foundations of Learning.* Buckingham: Open University Press.

Fisher, J (2008) *Starting from the Child,* 3rd edn. Maidenhead: OUP.

Fisher, P and Goodley, D (2007) The Linear Medical Model of Disability: Mothers of Disabled Babies Resist with Counter Narratives, *Sociology of Health and Illness*, 29 (1), 66–81.

Fitzgerald, D (2004) *Parent Partnership in the Early Years.* London; Continuum.

Fleer, M (2003) Early Childhood Education as an Evolving 'Community of Practice' or as Lived 'Social Reproduction': Researching the 'Taken-For-Granted', *Contemporary Issues in Early Childhood*, 4 (1), 64–79.

Fletcher, S and Welton, J (eds) (1912) *Froebel's Chief Writings on Education.* London: Edward Arnold & Co.

Fogel, A (1997) *Developing through Relationships: Origins of Communication, Self and Culture*, Chicago: University of Chicago Press.

Fook, J (1997) *The Reflective Researcher.* London: Allen and Unwin.

Ford, B (ed) (1982) *From Blake to Byron, Vol. 5 of the New Pelican Guide to English Literature*. Harmondsworth: Penguin.

Forman, F and Baldwin, N (2007) *Mastering British Politics*, 5th edn. Basingstoke: Macmillan Press.

Foster, W (1989) Towards a Critical Practice of Leadership in Smyth J (ed) *Critical Perspectives of Educational Leadership*. London: Falmer Press.

Fowler, K and Robins, A (2006) Being Reflective: Encouraging and Teaching Reflective Practice, in Robins, A (ed) *Mentoring in the Early Years*. London: Sage.

Francis, B and Skelton, C (2005) *Reassessing Gender and Achievement: Questioning Contemporary Key Debates.* London: Routledge.

Frier, J (2007) *Epidemiological Information on Children's and Young People's Mental Health Problems in Plymouth.* Plymouth: Public Health Development Unit, PCT.

Fröhlich-Gildhoff, K (2006) *Studiengang Bachelor of Arts (BA) "Pädagogik der Frühen Kindheit" an der Evangelischen Fachhochschule Freiburg – erste Erfahrungen.* www.kindergartenpaedagogik.de/1241.html

Gaine, C (1995) *Still no Problem Here.* Stoke-on-Trent: Trentham Books.

Gaine, C (2005) *We're All White Thanks: The Persisting Myth About 'White' Schools.* Stoke-on-Trent: Trentham Books.

Garcia, J (2002) *Sign with your Baby: How to Communicate with Infants Before they can Speak.* Seattle: Northlight Communications.

Gardner, H, Torff, B and Hatch, T (1996) The Age of Innocence Reconsidered: Preserving the Best of the Progressive Traditions in Psychology and Education, in Olsen, D and Torrance, N (eds) *The Handbook of Education and Human Development*. Oxford: Blackwell.

Gauvain, M (2001) *The Social Context of Cognitive Development*. New York: Basic Books.

Geertz, C (1973) *The Interpretation of Cultures*. New York: Basic Books.

Gelder, U (2003) Carving out a Niche? The Work of Tagesmütter in the New Germany, in Mooney, A and Statham, J (eds) *Family Day Care: International Perspectives on Policy, Practice and Quality*. London: Jessica Kingsley Publishers.

Gendercide (2010) *Case Study: The Srebrenica Massacre, July 1995*. www.gendercide.org/case_srebrenica.html

Gerhardt, S (2004) *Why Love Matters: How Affection Shapes a Baby's Brain*. Hove: Brunner Routledge.

Gerstenberger, G, Wagner, A and von Behr, A (2008) *Frühpädagogik Studieren: Ein Orientierungsrahmen für Hochschulen*. Stuttgart: Robert Bosch Stiftung.

GEW, Gewerkschaft Erziehung und Wissenschaft (2005) *Erzieherinnen Ausbildung an die Hochschule: Der Anfang ist Gemacht*. Frankfurt am Main: GEW.

Ghaye, A and Ghaye, K (1998) *Teaching and Learning through Critical Reflective Practice*. London: David Fulton.

Gibbs, G (1988) *Learning by Doing: A Guide to Teaching and learning Methods*. London: Further Education Unit.

Gittins, D (1998) *The Child in Question*. London: Macmillan.

Giudici, C and Rinaldi, C (eds) (2001) *Making Learning Visible: Children as Individual and Group Learners*. Reggio Emilia: Reggio Children.

Glass, N (1999) Sure Start: The Development of an Early Intervention Programme for Young Children in the United Kingdom. *Children & Society*, 13: 4: 257–264.

Goldschmied, E and Hughes, A (1986) *Infants at Work: Babies of 6–9 Months Exploring Everyday Objects* (videocassette). London: NCB Books.

Goleman, D (1996) *Emotional Intelligence*. London: Bloomsbury.

Goleman, D (1998) *Working with Emotional Intelligence*. London: Bloomsbury.

Goleman, D, Boyatzis, R and McKee, A (2002) *The New Leaders*. London: Little Brown.

Gopnik, A, Meltzoff, A and Kuhl, P (1999) *How Babies Think*. London: Weidenfield & Nicholson.

Gorst, J (1906) *The Children of the Nation: How their Health and Vigour should be Promoted by the State*. London: Methuen.

Goswami, U and Bryant, P (2007) *Children's Cognitive Development and Learning (Primary Review Research Survey 2/1a)*. Cambridge: University of Cambridge.

Gottlieb, A (2004) *The Afterlife is Where we Come From: The Culture of Infancy in West Africa*. Chicago: University of Chicago Press.

Gould N and Taylor I (1996) *Reflective Learning For Social Work: Research Theory and Practice*. Bodmin: Arena.

Graham, H (1991) The Concept of Caring in Feminist Research: The Case of Domestic Services, *Sociology*, 25: 1: 61–78.

Grameen Bank (2010) *Banking for the Poor: Grameen Bank*. www.grameen-info.org/index.php?option=com_frontpage&Itemid=68

Graue, ME and Walsh, DJ (1998) *Studying in Context: Theories, Methods and Ethics*. Thousand Oaks: Sage.

Gronn, P (2002) Distributed Leadership as a Unit of Analysis, the Leadership Quarterly, vol.13(4), pp423–451.

GTC, General Teaching Council for England (2003) *Researching Effective Pedagogy in the Early Years*. London: General Teaching Council for England.

Gutek, G (2004) *The Montessori Method: the Origins of an Educational Innovation*. Lanham MD: Rowman & Littlefield.

Hakim, C (2000), *Work-Lifestyle Choices in the 21st Century: Preference Theory*. Oxford: Oxford University Press.

Hankin, L (2009) Global Citizenship and Comparative Education, in Sharp, J, Ward, S and Hankin, L (eds) (2009) *Education Studies: An Issues Based Approach* (2nd edn). Exeter: Learning Matters.

Harris, A and Allen, T (2009) Ensuring Every Child Matters: Issues and Implications for School Leadership, *School Leadership and Management*. 29(4), pp337–352.

Harris, A (2007) Distributed Leadership: Conceptual Confusion and Empirical Reticence, *International Journal Leadership in Education*, 10 (3) 315–325.

Harris, B (1995) *The Health of the Schoolchild – A History of the School Medical Service in England and Wales*. Buckingham: Open University Press.

Harris, P (1989) *Children and Emotion*. Oxford: Blackwell.

Hart, R (1997) *Children's Participation: The Theory and Practice of Involving Young Citizens in Community Development and Environmental Care*. London: Earthscan.

Hart, T (2003) *The Secret Spiritual World of Children*. Makawao HI: Inner Ocean Publishing.

Hartley, D (2007) The Emergence of Distributed Leadership in Education: Why Now? *British Journal of Educational Studies*. 55(2) 202–214.

Hatten, W, Vinter, L and Williams, R (2003) *Dads on Dads: Needs and Expectations at Home and at Work*. London: MORI.

Hay, D & Nye, R (2006) *The Spirit of the Child*. London: Jessica Kingsley Publishers.

Head, J (1999) *Understanding the Boys*. London: Falmer.

Hendrick, H (1994) *Child welfare: 1870–1989*. London: Routledge.

Hendrick, H (1997) *Children, Childhood and English Society, 1880–1890*. Cambridge: Cambridge University Press.

Hendrick, H (2003) *Child Welfare – Historical Dimensions, Contemporary Debate*. Bristol: Policy Press.

Hepper, P (2003) Prenatal Psychological and Behavioral Development in Valsiner J and Connolly KJ (eds) *Handbook of Developmental Psychology*. London: Sage.

Hersey, P and Blanchad, K (1977) Management of Organisational Behaviour: Utilising Human Resources. Englewood Cliff: Prentice Hall.

Heywood, C. (2001) *A History of Childhood – Children and Childhood in the West from Medieval to Modern Times*. Cambridge: Polity.

HM Treasury (2004) *Choice for Parents, the Best Start for Children: A Ten Year Strategy for Childcare.* London: HMSO.

Hobbs, T (1992) *Experiential Training: Practice Guidelines*. Chatham: Tavistock/Routledge.

Hobson, P (2002) *The Cradle of Thought: Exploring the Origins of Thinking*. London: Macmillan.

Hochschild, A (1983) The Managed Heart: Commercialisation of Human Feeling. Berkeley, CA: University of California Press.

Hoggart, L, Campbell-Barr, V, Ray, K and Vegeris, S (2006) *Staying in Work and Moving Up: Evidence from the UK Employment Retention and Advancement (ERA) Demonstration.* Sheffield. DWP.

Hornby, G (2000) *Improving Parental Involvement.* London: Cassell.

Horwath, J and Thurlow, C (2004) Preparing Students for Evidence Based Child and Family Social Work: An Experiential Learning Approach. *Social Work Education*, 23(1) Carfax.

Houlton, D (1986) *Cultural Diversity in the Primary School*. London: B.T. Batsford.

HPA (2008) *Measles figures soar*. [Online]. Available at: www.hpa.org.uk/webw/HPAweb&HPAwebStandard/HPAweb_C/1227774034336?p=1204186170287

Hughes, S (2009) Leadership, Management and Sculpture: How Arts Based Activities can Transform Learning and Deepen Understanding. *Reflective Practice*, 10(1) 77–90.

Hurley, S and Chater, N (2005) *Perspectives on Imitation: From Neuroscience to Social Science* (Vols. 1 & 2). Cambridge MA: MIT Press.

Hyde, B (2008) *Children and Spirituality: Searching for Meaning and Connectedness.* London: Jessica Kingsley Publishers.

Hyder, T and Kenway, P (1995) *An Equal Future: a Guide to Anti-Sexist Practice in the Early Years*. London: the National Early Years Network in partnership with Save the Children / Equality Learning Centre.

Isaacs, S (1932) *The Nursery Years* (2nd edn). London: Routledge and Kegan Paul.

Iwaniuk, A, Nelson, J and Pellis, S (2001) Do Big-brained Animals Play More? *Journal of Comparative Psychology*, 115, 29–41.

Jackson, B and Jackson, S (1979) *Childminder: A Study in Action Research.* London: Routledge and Kegan Paul.

James, A and James, AL (2004) *Constructing Childhood – Theory, Policy and Social Practice*. Basingstoke: Palgrave Macmillan.

James, A and Prout, A (1997) *Constructing and Reconstructing Childhood* (2nd edn). London: Falmer.

James, A, Jenks, C, and Prout, A (1998) *Theorising Childhood*. Cambridge: Polity.

Janeway, J (1830) *A Token for Children.* London: Religious Tract Society.

Jaspars, S and O'Callaghan, S (2008) *Challenging Choices: Protection and Livelihoods in Darfur.* London: Overseas Development Institute.

Jaszus, R, Büchin-Wilhelm, I, Mäder-Berg, M and Gutmann, W (2008) *Sozialpädagogische Lernfelder für Erzieherinnen.* Stuttgart: Holland + Josenhans Verlag.

John, M (1996) *A Child's Right to a Fair Hearing.* London: Jessica Kingsley Publishers.

John, M (2003) *Children's Rights and Power; Gearing Up for a New Century*. London: Jessica Kingsley Publishers.

Jones, C and Pound, L (2008) *Leadership and Management in the Early Years: From Principles to Practice*. Maidenhead: Open University Press.

Jordanova, L (1989) Children in History: concepts of Nature and Society, in Scarre, G (ed.) *Children, Parents and Politics*. Cambridge: Cambridge University Press.

Katz, L (1995) Talks with Teachers of Young Children: A Collection. Norwood, NJ: Ablex.

Keenan, T (2002) *An Introduction to Child Development.* London: Sage Publications.

Kemmis, S (1993) *Action Research and Social Movements: A Challenge for Policy Research.* Education Policy Analysis Archives, Vol 1(1).

Kemmis, S and McTaggart, R (1988) *The Action Research Planner* (3rd edn). Geelong Vic: Deakin University Press.

Koch, T and Kralik, D (2006) *Participatory Action Research in Health Care.* Oxford: Blackwell.

Kolb, D (1984) *Experiential Learning: Experience as the Source of Learning and Development*. Englewood Cliffs NJ: Prentice Hall.

Koshy, V (2010) *Action Research for Improving Educational Practice: A Step-by-Step Guide.* London, Thousand Oaks; New Delhi: Sage.

Kostelny, K (2006) Helping War-affected Children, in Boothby, N, Strang, A and Wessel, M (eds) *A World Turned Upside Down: Sociological Ecological Approaches to Children in War Zones*. Bloomfield CT: Kumarian Press.

Kozulin, A (2001) *Psychological Tools: A Sociocultural Approach to Education*. Cambridge MA: Harvard University Press.

Kugiumutzakis, G, Kokkinaki, T, Makrodimitraki, M amd Vitalaki, E (2005) Emotions in Early Mimesis, in Nadel, J and Muir, D (eds) *Emotional Development.* Oxford: Oxford University Press.

Kuhn, TS (1970) *The Structure of Scientific Revolutions*, 2nd edn. Chicago: University of Chicago Press.

Kurtz, Z (2003) Outcomes for Children's Health and Wellbeing, *Children and Society Special Issue: New Labour Policy and its Outcomes for Children*, 17 (3) 173–83.

Laevers, F, Vandenbussche, E, Kog, M and Depondt, L (1997) *A Process-oriented Child Monitoring System for Young Children*. Leuven, Belgium: Centre for Experiential Education.

Lam, C, Wong, H and Leung, T (2007) An Unfinished Reflexive Journey: Social Work Students' Reflection on their Placement Experiences; *British Journal of Social Work*, 37(1) 91–105(15).

Lamb, B (2009) *Lamb Inquiry: Special Educational Needs and Parental Confidence*. London: Deparment for Children, Schools and Families.

Laming, H (2009) *The Protection of Children in England: A Progress Report*. London: The Stationery Office.

Laming, H (2003) *The Victoria Climbié Inquiry: report of an inquiry by Lord Laming*. London: HMSO.

Lancaster, P (2002) *Listening to Young Children*. London: National Children's Bureau.

Land, H and Lewis, J (1998) Gender, Care and the Changing Role of the State in the UK in Lewis J. (ed) *Social Care and Welfare State Reconstructing in Europe.* Aldershot: Ashgate.

Lansdown, G (2010) The Realisation of Children's Participation Rights: Critical Reflections. In Percy-Smith, B and Thomas, N (eds) *A Handbook of Children and Young People's Participation*. Oxford: Routledge.

Lave, J and Wenger, E (1991) *Situated Learning: Legitimate Peripheral Participation.* Cambridge: University of Cambridge Press.

Lawler, J and Bilson, A (2010) *Social Work Management and Leadership.* London, Routledge.

Lawrence, C (1994) *Medicine in the Making of Modern Britain 1700–1920.* London: Routledge.

Layard, R and Dunn, J (2009) *A Good Childhood: Searching for Values in a Competitive Age.* London: Penguin.

Leeson, C (2006) *My Life in Care; Experiences of Non-Participation in Decision Making Processes.* Child and Family Social Work. 12(3): 268–277.

Leeson, C (2009) *The Involvement of Looked After Children in Making Decisions about their Present and Future Care Needs.* Unpublished PhD Thesis, University of Plymouth.

Leiba, T (2003) Mental Health Policies and Interprofessional Working, in Weinstein, J, Whittington, C and Leiba, T (2003) *Collaboration in Social Work Practice.* London: Jessica Kingsley Publishers.

Leu, H (2005) Kindertagesbetreuung – ein Feld in Bewegung, in Riedel, B. Gadow, T. van Santen, E. Fuchs, K. Schilling, M and Leu, H (eds) *Zahlenspiegel 2005: Kindertagesbetreuung im Spiegel der Statistik.* Berlin: Internetredaktion des Bundesministerium Familie, Senioren, Frauen und Jugend.

Lewin, K (1946) Action Research and Minority Problems. *Journal of Social Issues,* 2(4): 34–46.

Lewis, K and Barton, R (2004) Playing for Keeps: Evolutionary Relationships between Social Play and the Cerebellum. *Human Nature* 15:1 5–21.

Liddiard, M (1928) *The Mothercraft Manual.* London: Churchill.

Likert, R (1967) *The Human Organisation: its Management and Value.* New York: McGraw Hill.

Lindon, J (2006) *Equality in Early Childhood: Linking Theory and Practice.* London: Hodder Arnold.

Lindon, J and Lindon, L (2000) *Mastering Counselling Skills.* Basingstoke: MacMillan.

Lloyd, E (2008) The Interface between Childcare, Family Support and Child Poverty Strategies under New Labour: Tensions and Contradictions, *Social Policy and Society,* 7 (4): 479–494.

Locke, J (1824) *The Works of John Locke in Nine Volumes,* 12th edn. London: Rivington. http://oll.libertyfund.org/title/761/80711/1923121

Löfman, P, Pelkonen, M and Pietilä, A–M (2004) Ethical Issues in Participatory Action Research, *Scandinavian Journal of Caring Science,* 18: 3: 333–340.

London Borough of Brent (1985) *A Child in Trust: The Report Of The Panel of Inquiry Into The Circumstances Surrounding The Death Of Jasmine Beckford;* London Borough of Brent.

Lorek, A, Sheridan, M, Ehntholt, K, Nesbitt, A, Wey, E, Githinji, C, Rossor, E and Wickramasinghe, R (2009) The Mental and Physical Health Difficulties of Children Held within a British Immigration Detention Centre: A Pilot Study. *Child Abuse and Neglect,* 33: 9 573–585.

LSCB, Local Safeguarding Children Board (2009) *Serious Case Review: Baby Peter.* Haringey: Haringey.

Lucas, J, Jitta, J, Jones, G and Wilczynska-Ketende, K (2008) Community-Based Approaches that Work in Eastern and Southern Africa, in Garcia, M, Pence, A, and Evans, J (eds.) (2008) *Africa's Future, Africa's Challenge: Early Childhood Care and Education in Sub-Saharan Africa*. Washington: The World Bank.

Luff, P (2007) Written Observations or Walks in the Park? Documenting Children's Experiences. In Moyles, J (ed) *Early Years Foundations Meeting The Challenge*. Maidenhead: Open University Press.

Lumby, J (2007) Parent Voice: Knowledge, Values and Viewpoint, *Improving Schools*. 10(3), pp220–232.

Lumsden, F (2005) Joined Up Thinking in Practice: An Exploration of Professional Collaboration in Wuller, T (ed) *An Introduction to Early Childhood: a Multidisciplinary Approach*. London: Paul Chapman Publishing.

MacLure, M (2006) *Entertaining Doubts: On Frivolity as Resistance*, in Satterthwaite, J, Martin, W and Roberts, L (eds) *Discourse, Resistance and Identity Formation*. London: Trentham.

Mac Naughton, G and Hughes, P (2009) *Doing Action Research in Early Childhood Studies: A Step By Step Guide*. Maidenhead: Open University Press and McGraw-Hill Education.

Magee, H (1944) War and the Nutritional State. *Monthly Bulletin of the Ministry of Health and the Emergency Public Health Laboratory Service*, 30/3/46, 475–82.

Make Poverty History (2005) *Make Poverty History*. www.makepovertyhistory.org/

Malaguzzi, L (1998) History, Ideas and Basic Philosophy: An Interview with Lella Gandini. In Edwards, C, Gandini, L and Foreman, G (eds) *The Hundred Languages of Children: The Reggio Emilia Approach – Advanced Reflections* (2nd edition). London: Ablex.

Malik, H (2009) *A Practical Guide to Equal Opportunities* (3rd edn). Cheltenham: Nelson Thornes.

Manning-Morton, J (2006) The Personal is Professional: Professionalism and the Birth to Threes Practitioner. *Contemporary Issues in Early Childhood*. 7:1 42–52.

Martin, V and Henderson, E (2001) *Managing in Health and Social Care*. Padstow: Routledge.

Martini, M and Kirkpatrick, J (1981) Early Interactions in Marquesas Islands in Field, T, Sostek, A. Vietze, P and Leiderman, P (eds) *Culture and Early Interactions*. Hillsdale NJ: Erlbaum.

Maslow, A (1970) *Motivation and Personality*, 2nd edn. New York: Harper and Row.

Mason J (2002) *Researching Your Own Practice: the Discipline of Noticing*. London: RoutledgeFalmer.

May, T (2001) *Social Research: Issues, Methods and Process*, 3rd edn. Buckingham: Open University Press.

McBride, P and Maitland, S (2001) *Putting Emotional Intelligence into Practice*. London: McGraw-Hill.

McBrien, B (2007) Learning from Practice – Reflections on a Critical Incident. *Accident and Emergency Nursing*. 15(3) 128–133.

McClelland, D (1987) *Human Motivation*. Cambridge: Cambridge University Press.

McDowell, L, Ward, K, Faga, C, Perrons, D and Ray, K (2006) Connecting Time and Space: The Significance of Transformations in Women's Work in the City. *International Journal of Urban and Regional Research* 30 (1): 141–58.

McDrury, J and Alterio, M (2000) Achieving Reflective Learning Using Storytelling Pathways. *Innovations in Education and Teaching International*, 38(1).

McGilchrist, I (2009) *The Master and His Emissary: The Divided Brain and the Making of the Western World*. New Haven CT/London: Yale University Press.

McGillivray, G (2008) Nannies, Nursery Nurses and Early Years Professionals: Constructions of Professional Identity in the Early Years Workforce in England, *European Early Childhood Education Research Journal*, 16 (2): 242–254.

McKimm, J and Phillips, K (eds) (2009) *Leadership and Management in Integrated Services*. Exeter: Learning Matters.

McLaughlin, J (2005) Exploring Diagnostic Processes: Social Science Perspectives, *Archives of Diseases in Childhood*, March, 90, 284–7.

McNiff, J and Whitehead, J (2006) *All You Need to Know about Action Research.* London: Sage.

Mead, GH (1934) *Mind, Self and Society*, Chicago: University of Chicago Press.

Melhuish, E (2004) *A Literature Review of the Impact of Early Years Education on Young Children, With Emphasis Given to Children From Disadvantaged Backgrounds.* London: National Audit Office.

Meltzoff, A and Moore, M (1977) Imitation of Facial and Manual Gestures by Human Neonates. *Science*, 198, 75–78. (also in Slater, A and Muir, D (eds) (1999) The *Blackwell Reader in Developmental Psychology*. Oxford: Blackwell)

Mezirow, J (1981) A Critical Theory of Adult Learning and Education. *Adult Education*, 32(1).

Miell, D and Dallos, R (1996) *Social Interaction and Personal Relationships*. Buckingham: Open University Press.

Miller, A (1987) *Thou Shalt Not be Aware: Society's Betrayal of the Child*. London: Pluto.

Miller, L (2008) Developing Professionalism within a Regulatory Framework in England: Challenges and Possibilities. *European Early Childhood Education Research Journal*, 16 (2): 255–268.

Miller, L, Rustin, M and Shuttleworth, J (eds) (1989) *Closely Observed Infants*. London: Duckworth.

Milner, D (1983) *Children and Race - Ten Years On.* London: Ward Lock Education.

Ministry of Education (1996) *Te Whāriki: He Whāriki Matauranga mōngā Mokopuna o Aotearoa: Early Childhood Curriculum.* Wellington, NZ: Learning Media.

Montessori, M (1948/1967) *The Discovery of the Child* (6th edn tr Costelloe, M). New York: Random House.

Mook, D (2004) *Classic Experiments in Psychology*. Westpoint, CT: Greenwood Press.

Moss, P (2000) The Parameters of Training, in Penn, H (ed) *Early Childhood Services: Theory, Policy and Practice.* Buckingham: Open University Press.

Moss, P and Petrie, P (2002) *From Children's Services to Children's Spaces: Public Policy, Children and Childhood.* London: Routledge.

Motluk, A (2001) Read my Mind. *New Scientist*, 169, 2275.

Moyles, J (2005) *The Excellence of Play* (2nd ed). Maidenhead: Open University Press.

Moyles, J (2006) *Effective Leadership and Management in the Early Years.* Maidenhead: Open University Press.

Mukherji, P and Albon, D (2010) *Research Methods in Early Childhood: An Introductory Guide*. London: Sage.

Murray, L and Cooper, P (eds) (1997) *Postpartum Depression and Child Development.* New York: Guilford Press.

Murray, L and Trevarthen, C (1985) Emotional Regulation of Interactions between Two-Month-Olds and Their Mothers, in Field, T and Fox, N (Eds.) *Social Perception in Infants.* Norwood NJ: Ablex.

National College (2009) DCS Leadership Programme www.nationalcollege.org.uk/index/professional-development/dcsleadershipprogramme.htm.

NCSL, National College for School Leadership (2004) *National Professional Qualification in Integrated Centre Leadership.* Nottingham: NCSL.

NDNA, National Day Nurseries Association (2006) *The Early Years Entitlement – The Future.* Huddersfield: National Day Nurseries Association.

Neale, B (2002) Dialogues with Children: Children, Divorce and Citizenship. *Childhood,* 9(4) 455–75.

Newburn, T (2007) *Criminology.* Cullompton: Willan Publishing.

Newson, J and Newson, E (1974) Cultural Aspects of Childrearing in the English-speaking World, in Richards, M (ed) *The Integration of a Child into a Social World.* Cambridge: Cambridge University Press.

Newton, J (2004) Learning to Reflect: a Journey. *Reflective Practice,* 5(2), 155–166.

Nias, J, Southworth, G and Yeomans, R (1989) *Staff Relationships in the Primary School.* London: Cassell Educational.

Nind, M (2003) Enhancing the Communication Learning Environment of an Early Years Unit through Action Research. *Educational Action Research,* 11: 3: 347–364.

Noddings, N (1991) Stories in Dialogue: Caring and Interpersonal Reasoning, in Witherell, C and Noddings, N (eds) *Stories Lives Tell: Narrative and Dialogue in Education.* New York: Teachers College Press.

Noddings, N (1993) Caring: A Feminist Perspective, in Strike, K and Ternasky, P (eds) *Ethics for Professionals in Education: Perspectives for Preparation and Practice.* New York and London: Teachers College Press Columbia University.

Noë, A (2004) *Action in Perception.* Cambridge, MA: MIT Press.

Northouse, P (2009) *Leadership: Theory and Practice,* 5th edn. London, Sage.

Nutbrown, C (2006) *Threads of Thinking: Young Children Learning and the Role of Early Education,* 3rd edn. London: Sage.

Oates, J, Wood, C and Grayson, A (2005) *Psychological Development and Early Childhood.* Milton Keynes: The Open University.

Oberhuemer, P, Schreyer, I and Neuman, M (2009) *Professionals in Early Childhood Education and Care Systems: European Profiles and Perspectives.* Opladen & Farmington Hills, MI: Barbara Budrich.

OECD, Organisation for Economic Co-operation and Development (1998) *Human Capital Investment: An International Comparison.* London: OECD.

OECD, Organisation for Economic Co-operation and Development (2000) *OECD Country Note: Early Childhood Education and Care Policy in the United Kingdom.* London: OECD.

OECD, Organisation for Economic Co-operation and Development (2006a) *Education at a Glance: OECD Briefing Notes for Germany.* http://www.oecd.org/dataoecd/51/24/37392789.pdf

OECD, Organisation for Economic Co-operation and Development (2006b) *Starting Strong II: Early Childhood Education and Care.* Paris: OECD.

Oliver, C (2003) The Care Of the Illegitimate Child: The Coram Experience 1900–1945, in Brannen, J and Moss, P (eds) *Rethinking Children's Care*. Buckingham: Open University Press.

ONS, Office for National Statistics (2009a) *Gender Pay Gap: Gender Pay Gap Narrows*. www.statistics.gov.uk/cci/nugget.asp?id=167

ONS, Office for National Statistics (2009b) *Early Years Education*. www.statistics.gov.uk/cci/nugget.asp?id=1766.

OPM, Office for Public Management (2008) *Reviewing Childcare Sufficiency Assessments: Report for the Department of Children Schools and Families*. London: OPM.

Osborn, A and Millbank, J (1987). *The Effects of Early Education: A Report from the Child Health and Education Study*. Oxford: Clarendon Press.

Osgood, J (2006) Deconstructing Professionalism in Early Childhood Education: Resisting the Regulatory Gaze. *Contemporary Issues in Early Childhood*, 7(1) 5–15.

Ouvry, M (2003) *Exercising Muscles and Minds: Outdoor Play and the Early Years Curriculum*. London: National Children's Bureau.

Owen, H (2000) *In Search of Leaders*. Chichester: Wiley & Sons.

Paige-Smith, A and Craft, A (eds) (2008) *Developing Reflective Practice in the Early Years*. Maidenhead: Open University Press.

Parker-Rees, R (1999) Protecting Playfulness, in Abbott, L and Moylett, H (eds) *Early Education Transformed*. London: Falmer.

Parker-Rees, R (2007a) Liking to be Liked: Imitation, Familiarity and Pedagogy in the First Years of Life. *Early Years*, 27,1, 3–17.

Parker-Rees, R (2007b) Primary Communication – What Can Adults Learn From Babies?' In Moyles, J (ed) *Early Years Foundations: Meeting the Challenge*. Maidenhead: Open University/McGraw Hill.

Parker-Rees, R (2010) Hunting and Gathering: How Play Helps us to Let in, as well as Get in, Information about our Environment. In Moyles, J (ed) *The Excellence of Play*, 3rd edn. Maidenhead: Open University.

Pasternack, P and Schildberg, A (2005) 'Die Finanzielle Auswirkung einer Akademisierung der ErzieherInnen-Ausbildung', in S. Z. K.-u. Jugendbericht (ed) *Entwicklungspotenziale institutioneller Angebote im Elementarbereich: Materialien zum Zwölften Kinder- und Jugendbericht, Band 2*. München: Deutsches Jugendinstitut.

Pearce, C (2009) *From Closed Books to Open: West Africa's Literacy Challenge*. http://www.oxfam.org.uk/resources/policy/education/downloads/closed%20books%20_west_africa_literacy.pdf.

Pemberton, S (2006) *Quietly Far Reaching: The Influence of the Mentor during the First Year of the NPQICL Rollout 2005/2006* (unpublished).

Penn, H (1997) *Comparing Nurseries: Staff and Children in Italy, Spain and the UK*. London: Paul Chapman Publishing.

Penn, H (2000) Is Working with Young Children a Good Job? In Penn, H (Eed), *Early Childhood Services: Theory, Policy and Practice*. Buckingham: Open University Press.

Penn, H (2005) *Unequal Childhoods: Young Children's Lives in Poor Countries*. London and New York: Routledge.

Penn, H (2008) *Understanding Early Childhood: Issues and Controversies*, 2nd edn. Maidenhead: Open University Press.

Penn, H (2010a) Does it Matter what Country You are in? in Smidt, S (ed) *Key Issues in Early Years Education*. London: Routledge.

Penn, H (2010b) Shaping the future: how human capital arguments about investment in early childhood are being misused in poor countries. In N. Yelland (Ed) (2010) *Contemporary Perspectives on Early Childhood Education*. Maidenhead: McGraw HIll/Open University Press.

Perner, J (1991) *Understanding the Representational Mind*. Cambridge MA: MIT Press.

Petrie, P (2003) Social Pedagogy: An Historical Account of Care and Education as Social Control, in Brannen, J and Moss, P (eds) *Rethinking Children's Care*. Buckingham: Open University Press.

Pfeifer, R and Bongard, J (2007) *How the Body Shapes The Way We Think: A New View of Intelligence*. Cambridge MA: Bradford Books/MIT Press.

Phillips, A (1998) *The Beast in the Nursery*. London: Faber and Faber.

Phillips, A (2006) *Going Sane*. London: Penguin.

Phillips, K (2009) Leading in Complex Environments in McKimm, J and Phillips, K (eds) *Leadership and Management in Integrated Services*. Exeter: Learning Matters. pp57–72.

Piaget, J (1952) *The Origins of Intelligence in Children*. New York: Norton.

Piaget, J (1954) *The Construction of Reality in the Child*. New York: Basic Books.

Piaget, J (1962) *Play, Dreams and Imitation in Childhood*. New York: Norton.

Piaget, J (1970) *Genetic Epistemology*. New York: W.W. Norton and Company.

Piaget, J (1977) Development and Learning, in Gauvain, M and Cole, M (eds) *Readings on the Development of Children*. New York: W H Freeman and Company.

Pickles, T (2003) *Experiential Learning on the Web*.
http://reviewing.co.uk/research/experiential.learning.htm

Piper, C (2008) *Investing in Children: Policy, Law and Practice in Context*. Cullompton: Willan Publishing.

Plotz, J (2001) *Romanticism and the Vocation of Childhood*. New York: Palgrave.

Pollard, A (2002) *Reflective Teaching: Effective and Evidence-Informed Professional Practice*. London: Continuum.

Practical Action (2010) *Bicycle Ambulances in Nepal*.
http://practicalaction.org/?id=bicycle_ambulances

Pre-school Learning Alliance (2001) *Equal Chances: Eliminating Discrimination and Ensuring Equality in Pre-school settings*. London: Pre-school Learning Alliance.

PriceWaterhouseCoopers (2006) *DfES Children's Services: The Childcare Market*. London: DfES.

Prott, R (2006) 30 Jahre Ausbildungsreform – Kritische Anmerkungen eines Insiders, in Diller, A and Rauschenbach, T (eds) *Reform oder Ende der Erzieherinnenausbildung? Beiträge zu einer kontroversen Fachdebatte*. München: DJI Verlag Deutsches Jugendinstitut.

Pugh, G (2005) Policies in the UK to Promote the Well-being of Children, in Scott, J and Ward, H (eds) *Safeguarding and Promoting the Well-Being of Children, Families and Communities*. London: Jessica Kingsley Publishers.

Punch, K (2009) *Introduction to Research Methods in Education*. London: Thousand Oaks / New Delhi: Sage.

Purcell, M (2009) *Leadership Development Programme for Current and Aspirant Directors of Children's Services*. Nottingham: National College.

QCA/DfES, Qualifications and Curriculum Authority/Department for Education and Employment (2000) Curriculum Evidence for the Foundation Stage. London: QCA.

QCA, Qualifications and Curriculum Authority (2003a) *The Foundation Stage Profile Handbook*. London: QCA.

QCA, Qualifications and Curriculum Authority (2003b) *Creatively: Find it, Promote it*. www.ncaction.org.uk/creativity/

Rabe-Kleberg, U (2006) Mütterlichkeit und Profession – oder: Mütterlichkeit, eine Achillesferse der Fachlichkeit?, in Diller, A and Rauschenbach, T (eds) *Reform oder Ende der Erzieherinnenausbildung? Beiträge zu einer Kontroversen Fachdebatte*. München: DJI Verlag Deutsches Jugendinstitut.

Randall, V (2000) *The Politics of Child Daycare in Britain*. Oxford: Oxford University Press.

Rauschenbach, T (2006) Ende oder Wende', in Diller, A and Rauschenbach, T (eds) *Reform oder Ende der Erzieherinnenausbildung? Beiträge zu einer kontroversen Fachdebatte*. München: DJI Verlag Deutsches Jugendinstitut.

Rauschenbach, T, Beher, K and Knauer, D (1995) *Die Erzieherin: Ausbildung und Arbeitsmarkt*, Weinheim: Beltz.

Reason, P and Bradbury, H (eds) (2001) *The Handbook of Action Research: Participative Inquiry and Practice* London: Sage.

Reason, P and McArdle, K (2004) The Theory and Practice of Action Research, in Becker, S and Bryman, B (eds) *Understanding Research for Social Policy and Practice*. Bristol: The Policy Press.

Reddy, V and Trevarthen, C (2004) What We Learn About Babies From Engaging with their Emotions, *Zero to Three*, 24(3), 9–15.

Ribble, M (1943) *The Rights of Infants*. New York: Columbia University Press.

Richardson, K and Sheldon, S (1988) *Cognitive Development to Adolescence*. Mahwah, NJ: Lawrence Erlbaum.

Riedel, B (2005) Ausgewählte Daten zum Personal in Tageseinrichtungen für Kinder', in Riedel, B, Gadow, T, van Santen, E, Fuchs, K. Schilling, M and Leu, H (eds) *Zahlenspiegel 2005: Kindertagesbetreuung im Spiegel der Statistik* Berlin: Internetredaktion des Bundesministerium Familie, Senioren, Frauen und Jugend.

Riley, D (1983) *War in the Nursery – Theories of the Child and Mother*. London: Virago.

Rizzolatti, G, Fadiga, L, Gallese, V and Fogassi, L (1996) Premotor Cortex and the Recognition of Motor Actions. *Cognitive Brain Research*, 3(1996) 131–141.

Robert Bosch Stiftung (2006) *PiK – Profis in Kitas: Der Reformkatalog*. Stuttgart: Robert Bosch Stiftung GmbH.

Roberts-Holmes, G (2005) *Doing Your Early Years Research Project: A Step by Step Guide*. London: Sage.

Robinson, C and Kellett, M (2004) Power, in Fraser, S (ed) *Doing Research with Children and Young People*. Sage: London.

Rochat, P (2004) Emerging Co-Awareness, in Bremner, G and Slater, A (eds) *Theories of Infant Development*. Oxford: Blackwell.

Roche, J (2001) Quality of Life for Children, in Foley, P, Roche, J and Tucker, S (eds) *Children in Society*. Basingstoke: Palgrave.

Rodd, J (1994) *Leadership in Early Childhood (1st edn)*. Buckingham: Open University Press.

Rodd, J (1998) *Leadership in Early Childhood (2nd edn)*. Buckingham: Open University Press.

Rodd, J (2005) *Leadership in Early Childhood (3rd edn)*. Buckingham: Open University Press.

Rogoff, B (1990) *Apprenticeship in Thinking: Cognitive Development in Social Context*. Oxford: Oxford University Press.

Rogoff, B (2003) *The Cultural Nature of Human Development*. Oxford: Oxford University Press.

Rohrmann, T (2009) *Gender in Kindertageseinrichtungen: Ein Überblick über den Forschungsstand.* München: DJI.

Rose, N (1990) *Governing the Soul*. London: Routledge.

Rousseau, J (1762/1911) Émile (trans. Foxley, B) London: Dent.

Rovee-Collier, C and Hayne, H (1987) Reactivation of Infant Memory: Implications for Cognitive Development in Reese, H (ed) *Advances in Child Development and Behavior*. New York: Academic Press.

Ruch, G (2002) From Triangle to Spiral: Reflective Practice in Social Work Education, Practice and Research. *Social Work Education*, 21(2).

Ruch, G (2003) *Reflective Practice in Contemporary Child Care Social Work*. www.hants.gov.uk/TC/sspm/pi4.html

Saltiel, D (2003) Teaching Research and Practice on a Post Qualifing Child Care Programme. *Social Work Education*, 22(1).

Samuel, M (2007) Parents Jailed for 'Sustained Cruelty' to Disabled Daughter; *Community Care*, www.communitycare.co.uk/Articles/2007/02/09/103300/Parents-jailed-for-39sustained-cruelty39-to-disabled.htm

Saunders, K (2000) *Happy Ever Afters: A Storybook Guide to Teaching Children about Disability*. Stoke-on-Trent: Trentham.

Sawyer, R (2001) *Creating Conversations: Improvisation in Everyday Discourse.* Cresskill NJ: Hampton Press.

Scheiwe, K and Willenkens, H (eds) (2009) *Child Care and Preschool Development in Europe: Institutional Perspectives.* Basingstoke: Palgrave Macmillan.

Schön, D (1983) *The Reflective Practitioner. How Professionals Think in Action.* London: Temple Smith.

Schrader McMillan, A (2007) Learning at the Edges: Action Research and Child-Maltreatment in Post-War Guatemala. *Bulletin of Latin American Research*. 26: 4: 516–532.

Schweinhart, L, Barnes, H and Weikhart, D (eds) (1993) *Significant Benefits: the High/Scope Perry Pre-school Study through age 27.* Ypsilanti MI: High/Scope Press.

SCIE, Social Care Institute for Excellence (2003) *Learning and Teaching in Social Work Education.* Southampton: Policy Press.

Scourfield, J and Welsh, I (2003) Risk, Reflexivity and Social Control in Child Protection: New Times or Same Old Story? *Critical Social Policy*. 23 (3).

Self, A and Zealey, L (2007) *Social Trends, No. 37*, Basingstoke: Office for National Statistics / Palgrave Macmillan.

Sevenhuijsen, S (1998) *Citizenship and the Ethics of Care: Feminist Considerations on Justice, Morality and Politics.* London and New York: Routledge.

Singer, P (2006) *Children at War.* Berkeley and Los Angeles: University of California Press.

Siraj-Blatchford, I (2010) Diversity, Inclusion and Learning in the Early Years, in Pugh, G and Duffy, B (eds) *Contemporary Issues in the Early Years* (5th edn). London, Thousand Oaks / New Delhi and Singapore: Sage.

Siraj-Blatchford, I and Manni, L (2006) Effective Leadership in the Early Years Sector (ELEYS) study. London: Institute of Education, University of London.

Siraj-Blatchford, I and Sylva, K (2004) Researching pedagogy in English Pre-Schools. *British Educational Research Journal.* 30 (5), 713–30.

Skelton, C and Hall, E (2001) *The Development of Gender Roles in Young Children: a Review of Policy and Literature.* Manchester: Research and Resources Unit, Equal Opportunities Commission.

Smart, C, Neale, B and Wade, A (2001) *The Changing Experiences of Childhood – Families and Divorce.* Cambridge: Polity.

Smidt, S (2006) *The Developing Child in the 21st Century: A Global Perspective on Child Development.* Abingdon: Routledge.

Smidt, S (2008) *Supporting Multilingual Learners in the Early Years: Many Languages – Many Children.* Abingdon: Routledge.

Smith, P (2010) *Children and play.* Chichester: Wiley-Blackwell.

Smith, P, Cowie, H and Blades, M (2003) *Understanding Children's Development,* 4th edn. Oxford: Blackwell Publishing.

Smith, S and Morris, T (2005) Child Health, in Waller, T (ed) *An Introduction to Early Childhood – A Multidisciplinary Approach.* London: Sage.

Somekh, B (2003) Theory and Passion in Action Research. *Educational Action Research.* 11: 2: 247–264.

SOS Children's Villages (2009) *Child Soldiers.* http://www.child-soldier.org/

Southworth, G (1998) *Leading Improving Primary Schools; The Work of Headteachers and Deputies.* London: Falmer Press.

Speth, C (2010) *Akademisierung der Erzieherinnenausbildung? Beziehung zur Wissenschaft.* Wiesbaden: VS Verlag für Sozialwissenschaften.

Spock, B (1946) *Baby and Child Care.* New York: Duell, Sloan and Pearce.

Stacey, M (2009) *Teamwork and Collaboration in Early Years Settings.* Exeter: Learning Matters.

Stainton Rogers, R (2004) The Making and Moulding of Modern Youth: A Short History in Roche, J, Tucker, S, Thomson, R and Flynn, R (eds), *Youth in Society: Contemporary Theory in Policy and Practice* (2nd edn). London: Sage.

Stainton Rogers, R and Stainton Rogers, W (1992) *Stories of Childhood – Shifting Agendas of Adult Concern.* Hemel Hempstead: Harvester Wheatsheaf.

Statham, J and Mooney, A (2003) *Around the Clock: Childcare services at Atypical Times.* London: Joseph Rowntree Foundation.

Statistisches Bundesamt (2009a) 2009: Jedes fünfte Kind unter drei Jahren in Kindertagesbetreuung: Pressemitteilung 427 vom 11. 11. 2009. Wiesbaden: Statistisches Bundesamt.

Statistisches Bundesamt (2009b) Statistisches Jahrbuch für die Bundesrepublik Deutschland. Wiesbaden: Statistisches Bundesamt.

Steedman, C (1995) *Strange Dislocations: Childhood and the Idea of Human Interiority, 1780–1930.* Cambridge, MA: Harvard University Press.

Stefani, L, Clarke, J and Littlejohn, A (2000) Developing a Student-Centred Approach to Reflective Learning. *Innovations in Education and Teaching International,* Vol. 37(2).

Stenhouse, L (1975) *An Introduction to Curriculum Research and Development.* London: Heinemann.

Stokes, L and Wilkinson, D (2007) *Value for Money Comparison of Public and Voluntary Sector Provision of Pre-school Childcare and Education: Literature Review.* London: Office for National Statistics and National Institute of Economic and Social Research.

Stone, R (2008) *Avoiding Cases like Baby P and Victoria Climbié. Community Care* 18/11/08.

Sutherland, P (1992) *Cognitive Development Today: Piaget and his Critics.* London: Paul Chapman Publishing.

SWSF, Steiner Waldorf Schools Fellowship (2008) *The Kindergarten Day.* www.steinerwaldorf.org/downloads/earlyyears/More_details_about_Steiner_EY.pdf

Sylva, K, Melhuish, E, Sammons, P, Siraj-Blatchford, I and Taggart, B (2004) *The Effective Provision of Pre-School Education (EPPE) Project. Technical Paper 12 – The Final Report: Effective Pre-School Education.* London, DfES/Institute of Education.

Sylva K, Melhuish E, Sammons P, Siraj-Blatchford I and Taggart B (2006) *The Effective Provision of Pre-School Education (EPPE) Project.* London: DfES and Institute of Education, University of London.

Sylva, K, Melhuish, E, Sammons, P, Siraj-Blatchford, I, Taggart, B and Elliott, K (2003) The Effective Provision of Pre-School Education (EPPE) Project: Findings from the Pre-School Period. *Research Brief No RBX 15-03.* London: Department for Education and Skills.

Sylva, K and Pugh, G (2005) Transforming the Early Year in England, *Oxford Review of Education,* 31 (1) 11–27.

Tan, C (2006) Philosophical Reflections from the Silver Screen: Using Film to Promote Reflection in Pre-service Teachers. *Reflective Practice,* 7(4), 483–497.

Tannenbaum, R and Schmidt, W (1973) How to Choose a Leadership Pattern: *Harvard Business Review.* May Issue.

Tarr, P (2004) Consider the Walls in *Beyond the Journal: Young Children on the Web.* www.naeyc.org/files/yc/file/200405/ConsidertheWalls.pdf

Taxpayers Alliance (2009) www.taxpayersalliance.com

Taylor, C, Wilkie, M and Baser, J (eds) (2006) *Doing Action Research: A Guide for School Support Staff.* London: Paul Chapman Publishing.

Telford, H (1996) *Transforming Schools Through Collaborative Leadership.* London: Falmer Press.

Thelen, E and Smith, L (1994) *A Dynamic Systems Approach to the Development of Cognition and Action.* Cambridge MA: MIT Press.

Thole, W and Cloose, P (2006) Akademisierung des Personals für das Handlungsfeld Pädagogik der Kindheit, in Diller, A and Rauschenbach, T (eds) *Reform oder Ende der Erzieherinnenausbildung? Beiträge zu einer Kontroversen Fachdebatte.* München: DJI Verlag Deutsches Jugendinstitut.

Thompson, N (2006) *Anti-Discriminatory Practice: Challenging Discrimination and Oppression*, 4th edn. Basingstoke: Palgrave MacMillan.

Thurston, C and Church, J (2001) Involving Children and Families in Decision Making about Health Ed, in Foley, P, Roche, J anf Tucker, S (eds) *Children in Society, Contemporary Theory, Policy and Practice.* Basingstoke: Open University.

Titmuss, R (1950) *Problems of Social Policy*. London: HMSO.

Tobin, J (2005) Quality in Early Childhood Education: An Anthropologist's Perspective, *Early Education & Development*, 16 (4) 421–434.

Trevarthen, C (1979) Communication and Cooperation in Early Infancy: a Description of Primary Intersubjectivity, in Bullowa, M (ed) *Before Speech: The Beginning of Interpersonal Communication.* New York: Cambridge University Press.

Trevarthen, C (2003) Making Sense of Infants Making Sense, *Intellectica (Revue de l'Association pour la Recherche Cognitive)*, 2002/1, 34: 161–188. Paris, France. www.psy.ed.ac.uk/Staff/staff/colwynt/papers/Intellectica%202003.htm

Trevarthen, C (2004) Learning about Ourselves, from Children: Why a Growing Human Brain Needs Interesting Companions *Perception in Action*, November 2004 http://www.perception-in-action.ed.ac.uk/PDFs/Colwyn2004.pdf

Trevarthen, C and Hubley, P (1978) Secondary Intersubjectivity: Confidence, Confiding and Acts of Meaning in the First Year, in Lock, A (ed) *Action, Gesture and Symbol: The Emergence of Language.* London: Academic Press.

Tronto, J (1993) *Moral Boundaries: A Political Argument for the Ethics of Care.* New York and London: Routledge.

Truby King, F (1937) *Feeding and Care of Baby* (revd edn). London: Oxford University Press.

Tsang, N (2007) Reflection as Dialogue, *British Journal of Social Work*, 37(4), 681–694.

Tylor, E (1871/1924) *Primitive Culture*. 2 vols (7th ed). New York: Brentano's.

UK Government (2009) *Sure Start Children's Centres*. www.direct.gov.uk/en/parents/preschooldevelopmentandlearning/nurseriesplaygroupsreceptionclasses/dg_173054

UN, United Nations (1989) *UN Convention on the Rights of the Child.* http://www.unesco.org/education/pdf/CHILD_E.PDF.

UN, United Nations (2008) *The Millennium Development Goals Report.* New York: United Nations. http://mdgs.un.org/unsd/mdg/Resources/Static/Products/Progress2008/MDG_Report_2008_En.pdf#page=44

UNDP, United Nations Development Programme (2010) *Millennium Development Goals.* www.undp.org/mdg/

UNICEF, United Nations Children's Fund (2004) *Botswana Statistics.* http://www.unicef.org/infobycountry/botswana_statistics.html#55

UNICEF, United Nations Children's Fund (2006a) *The State of the World's Children.* www.unicef.org/sowc06/

UNICEF, United Nations Children's Fund (2006b) *Child Protection Information Sheets.* New York: UNICEF.

UNICEF, United Nations Children's Fund (2007a) *Child Poverty in Perspective: An Overview of Child Well-Being in Rich Countries (Report Card 7)*, Florence: Innocenti Research Centre.

UNICEF, United Nations Children's Fund (2007b) Progress for Children: A World Fit for Children, *Statistical Review Number 6,* December 2007. New York: UNICEF.

UNICEF, United Nations Children's Fund (2008) *UNICEF Emphasises Child Health Benefits of Breast Feeding.* UNICEF. www.unicef.org.uk/press/news_detail.asp?news_id=1359

Urban, M (2008) Dealing with Uncertainty: Challenges and Possibilities for the Early Childhood Profession, *European Early Childhood Education Research Journal.* 16 (2) 135–152.

Van Maurik, J (2001) *Writers on Leadership.* London: Penguin.

Vygotsky, L (1966) Development of Higher Mental Functions in Leontyev in A, Luria, A and Smirnov, A (eds) *Psychological Research in the USSR.* Moscow: Progress Publishers.

Vygotsky, L (1968) *Thought and Language* (tr Hanfmann, E and Vakar, G). Cambridge MA: MIT Press.

Vygostky, L (1978) *Mind in Society: The Development of Higher Psychological Processes.* Cambridge MA: Harvard University Press.

Wall, K (2003) *Special Needs and Early Years: a Practitioner's Guide.* London: Sage.

Wall, K (2006) *Special Needs and Early Years: a Practitioner's Guide,* 2nd edn. London: Sage.

Watson, J (1924) *Behaviourism.* New York: Norton.

Wesley, J (1872) *Works.* London: Wesleyan Conference Office.

West-Burnham, J, Farrar, M and Otero, G (2007) *Schools and Communities: Working Together to Transform Children's Lives,* London: Network Continuum.

Whalley, M (2001) *Involving Parents in their Children's Learning.* London: Paul Chapman Publishing.

Whalley, M (2006a) *Sustaining Leaders and Learners.* Conference Papers. Pen Green.

Whalley, M (2006b) Children's Centres: The New Frontier for the Welfare State and the Education System? *Early Interventions for Infants and Small Children in Families at Risk.* Oslo: National College for Leadership of Schools and Children's Services.

Whalley, M (2008) *Leading Practice in Early Years Settings.* Exeter: Learning Matters.

Whalley, M and the Pen Green team (2001) *Involving Parents in their Children's Learning.* London: Paul Chapman Publishing.

White, M (2001) Taking Children Seriously, *The Guardian* and Save the Children supplementary publication for the UN Special Session (September 2001) withheld and issued May 2002.

WHO, World Health Organisation (2007) *50 facts: global health situation and trends* 1955–2025. www.who.int/whr/1998/mediacentre/50facts/en/

WHO, World Health Organisation (2009) *Media Centre Fact Sheet: Measles.* www.who.int/mediacentre/factsheets/fs286/en/

Wickett, K (2006) *How does the Workshop 'Documenting Children's Learning' Impact on Practitioners Understanding and Practice of Documentation within the Setting?* Plymouth: University of Plymouth, Faculty of Education.

Wicks, P, Reason, P and Bradbury, H (2008) Living Inquiry: Personal, Political and Philosophical Groundings for Action Research Practice, in Reason, P and Bradbury, H (eds) *The Sage Handbook of Action Research,* 2nd edn. London: Sage.

Wilkie, M (2006) Benefiting from Action Research, in Taylor, C, Wilkie, M and Baser, J. (eds) *Doing Action Research: A Guide for School Support Staff.* London: Paul Chapman Publishing.

Williams, F (2004) *Rethinking Families.* London: Calouste Gulbenkian Foundation.

Wirtz, L, Franks, M, Johnson, F and Nandy, L (2009) *Hidden Children – Separated Children at Risk.* London: The Children's Society.

Wood, D, Burner, J and Ross, G (1976) The Role of Tutoring in Problem Solving. *Journal of Child Psychology and Psychiatry,* 17 89–100.

Woods, M (1998) Early Childhood Education in Preschool Settings, in Taylor, J and Woods, M (eds) *Early Childhood Studies: An Holistic Introduction.* London, New York, New Delhi: Arnold.

Wordsworth, W (1888) *The Complete Poetical Works.* London: Macmillan and Co.

World Bank (2008) *World Bank Updates Poverty Estimates for the Developing World.* http://econ.worldbank.org/ WBSITE/EXTERNAL/EXTDEC/EXTRESEARCH/0,,contentMDK:21882162~pagePK:64165401~piPK:64165026~theSit ePK:469382,00.html

Wouters, C (2007) *Informalization: Manners and Emotions since 1890.* London: Sage.

Young, M and Willmott, P (1957) *Family and Kinship in East London.* Harmondsworth: Penguin.

Zelizer, V (1985) *Pricing the Priceless Child: The Changing Social Value of Children.* New York: Basic Books.

UK Government Acts can be obtained from the Office of Public Sector Information: www.opsi.gov.uk

Index

Added to a page number 'f' denotes a figure.